A NEW SPIRITUAL TAPESTRY

Woven from the frayed threads of traditional Christianity

A NEW SPIRITUAL TAPESTRY

A NEW SPIRITUAL TAPESTRY

Woven from the frayed threads of traditional Christianity

Glennis Johnston

Published by Fire-Light Books

Email: Firelightpublishing@gmail.com

© 2018 Glennis I. Johnston

All rights reserved.
No part of this publication may be reproduced
in any manner without prior written permission
of the publisher.

ISBN   9780994639813

Key topics include: Process theology, emerging Christianity, progressive spirituality, the New Story, biblical storytelling, eco-spirituality, bioregionalism, abundance, social justice, the shadow self, creative transformation

Cover Design by Joanna Holden
Printed in Australia by Ingramspark

ACKNOWLEDGEMENTS

I am grateful for the continued encouragement from my husband Craig and the unwavering support of my friend Lesley Bryant throughout the writing process. I owe my faithful companions, Chester and Pyp, many backyard games for their patience during months of boredom while I was engrossed in writing.

I am especially indebted to the gifted Alison Green for her invaluable editing assistance.

CONTENTS

1. A New Starting Point — 15
- Prioritising Values — 17
- Is it Biblical? — 21
- Holiness — 24
- The Implications of Believing in a Traditional God — 27
- Christians Trapped by Church Doctrine — 33
- An Alternative Vision of God — 37
- Is Worship Real? — 41
- Moving Towards a New Story — 49

2. Paradise Lost?
Can Something That Never Existed Be Restored? — 57
- The 'Garden of Eden' Origin Myth — 59
- The 'Garden of Eden' Theology and Human Evolution — 63
- The 'Garden of Eden' in the Matrix of the Fertile Crescent — 71
- Use of 'The Fall' in Christian Theology — 76
- An Alternative View of Humanity — 82

3. Non-Violence and Peacemaking   86

    Ancient Tribal Traditions   87

    The Sacrifice of Jesus   91

    A Violent God   95

    The Mythology of Violence in the Old Testament   98

    The Mythology of Violence in the New Testament   103

    Two Competing Spiritual Visions   106

    Peace-building in the Old Testament   110

    Peace-building in the New Testament   120

    Non-Violence, Peacemaking and Us   125

4. Abundance, Scarcity or Enough?   129

    A Story of Abundance   132

    The First Principle of the New Story – Fair Distribution   136

    The Second Principle of the New Story – Take Time Out   140

    Social Justice in the New Story – The Sabbatical Year, Gleaning and the Jubilee   144

    Summarising the Economic Vision of Abundance   150

    Jesus and New Economic Vision   152

    The Spirituality of Economics and Christianity   157

5. Trees, Rivers, Geese, Humans, Soil, Stars – The New Story of Us   164

    Welcoming the Input of Scientific Discovery   165

    Eco-Spirituality   170

    Place-Centred Commitment to Nature and Community   177

    Interconnectedness and Faith   188

6. Dismantling the Barriers That Separate Us   196

    Jesus and the Woman   205

    Breaking Barriers of Gender, Ethnicity and Religion   208

    Separating the Sacred from the Secular   214

    The Early Church was Forced to Rethink its Beliefs   217

    When Theology Conflicts with Our Experience of God   221

    Breaking Barriers of Custom and Culture   223

7. Our Beautiful, Messy Lives   229

    Sin, Judgement and Shame   230

    Who is Really Blind?   236

    The Shadow Self and the False Self   239

    Our Imperfect, Messy Lives   244

    Morality   249

    Creative Transformation   254

8. Let Me Tell You A Story — **263**

   1. The God Who Attempted to Destroy Evil — 266

   2. How Should We Judge? — 274

   3. Holding the Abuse of Power to Account — 284

   4. Assumptions of Entitlement — 293

   5. The Healing Touch — 300

   6. Every Little Thing Matters — 307

   7. Step Out In Faith — 313

9. Hopes and Dreams of a Better Future — **321**

   Jesus' Comprehensive Vision For His Time — 323

   A More Beautiful World — 326

   The Kingdom of God is Among You — 332

Recommended Reading — **337**

PREFACE

We live in a world of competing 'stories' that attempt to give meaning to: the relationship between human beings and the planet, the purpose of community, the way status is ascribed to individuals, the idea of a divine presence, the complexity of our lives, what has enduring value and how power should be exercised.

Along with the rest of society, people of faith participate in this debate over competing visions of life. However, religious institutions have offered their members little help in navigating the vast scope of these issues. Beyond affirming basic values of equality and compassion, the religious approach has shown itself to be inflexible in addressing the deeper questions of our day. Churches have been hindered by belief systems that were adopted within an ancient worldview and elevated to the status of truth for all time.

At times, conflict arises between contemporary values and traditional beliefs. Modern Christians attempt to hold together incompatible concepts because they fear being unfaithful if they question traditional doctrines. As a result, well-intentioned, earnest people of faith lack credibility in the eyes of outsiders who see the inconsistencies that the church cannot admit. Consequently, many thoughtful people raised in religious communities have either drifted away from their church or remain uneasily connected with increasing uncertainty around what to believe. I have written this book in response to questions from these faithful Christians. Although I have always found rich meaning in the symbolism of the Christian tradition, I believe we must radically revise the inherited teachings. Twenty-first century Western culture needs a coherent New Story and a nurturing spirituality.

Although still a minority within the church, progressive Christians are part of a growing movement of speakers and authors who care deeply about the future we are shaping for the next generation. The theological debates of the last few decades were argued largely within the church. I see little value in in-house discussion of such important matters. I prefer to engage with prophetic thinkers from many disciplines including economics, science and cultural history so that our shared insights can enrich each other. I have been inspired by a variety of authors whose input will be reflected in the following pages. People of faith should take heart that amidst divisive social attitudes, a readiness for aggression and war-mongering in public life and ruthless self-interest in business, there is a groundswell of voices calling for a 'New Story', a new life-enhancing vision of humanity.

Even when not acknowledged as such, philosophy and pervasive social values have always influenced the interpretation of scripture. There is no such thing as pure exegesis. We all bring ourselves to the text, as did the ancient church authorities who compiled and authorised the creeds in a pre-scientific world. It is not a question of whether our philosophy and values will influence the religious agenda, but which ones we will allow to have such influence. The perspective of a relational universe, as described by process philosophy, resonates with my own experience and thinking. Rather than an uncritical allegiance to the traditional image of a coercive and judgemental God, we might consider how a relational God of unwavering love and beauty interacts with a relational world. Process thought is consistent with the critique of our society coming from a range of cultural critics. It is time for Christians to identify and prioritise the values that determine their spiritual lives.

Participating in the global discussion of values does not mean we should ignore our spiritual heritage. In the process of re-examining and discarding some of the central tenets of the church's foundational beliefs, we can also identify those aspects of traditional faith that are worthy of preservation. Beginning with the premise that values rather than doctrinal beliefs should guide the process, I have set out to gather together some threads of wisdom from the Christian tradition that can enrich our lives. Drawing on select biblical stories and the insights of contemporary knowledge, I have attempted to weave these threads into a cohesive whole — a new spiritual tapestry.

Glennis Johnston
Dorrigo 2018

CHAPTER ONE

A New Starting Point

> *The Old Story that the world*
> *is built on is falling apart.*
> *By acting from a different Story*
> *we disrupt the psychic sub-structure of*
> *our mythology and offer an alternative.*
>
> Charles Eisenstein

Unlike Dante's gates of hell, the entrance to this book might read, "Abandon certainty and fear all ye who enter here." But we will not abandon hope. For those who have a religious background, going back to basics in a conversation on the spiritual life requires the courage, faith and determination of a pilgrim.

The very first starting point is to put away fear. We have nothing to fear from the truth and we certainly do not need to protect or defend God from the truth. Therefore, no question should be off limits. No niggling concerns over belief, values or destiny should be off the table. It is not possible to go on this pilgrimage without surrendering the comforts of inherited certainties. Sifting through the old Christian tradition in search of a more satisfying faith perspective will only appeal to those with a healthy sense of curiosity and a deep desire for what is real.

The new spirituality that is now emerging from the frayed threads of the Christian tradition is vastly different from the old. Large numbers of church members and former church attendees have become dissatisfied with the doctrines with which they were raised, and the institutional ways of the church itself. For them, the Old Story of religion is no longer credible. Yet many of these people of faith are not willing to give up on the essence of the spiritual life. Experiences of belonging, acceptance, care for neighbours and especially the mysterious 'Other' have been too precious to let go lightly. Hence the widespread search for a new spirituality that preserves the best of the old tradition without being dictated to by its doctrines and forms. This book is written as an aid to those who have begun searching.

It is still too early for this new faith perspective to have just one name. There is a spectrum of views and emphases within the conversation that defies containment by one title. Progressive Christianity, the Emerging Church, Process Theology, Eco-spirituality, the New Story, and the Great Economy all contribute to its diverse developments. It is important to find some starting points so that we can discern what to discard and what to preserve from the old Christian tradition. What follows in this chapter is generally held by many progressive or emerging scholars, authors and leaders. However, not presuming to speak for everyone engaged in this quest, it first and foremost expresses my own convictions.[1]

Prioritising Values

If asked where their values came from, most Christians would answer, their belief in God, the Bible and perhaps their family. Christians tend to make an unexamined assumption that values like compassion, honesty, the equality of all people, care for the environment and non-violence derive from their faith in God according to the Bible. It is true that one hears these values expounded in sermons in mainstream churches today. And yes, apart from environmental protection, one can find biblical texts to support most of these values. However, they have not grown directly out of Christian beliefs. These values are shared at least as much within secular society as in the church. In some cases, for example the equality of women, the church's values have followed only slowly behind the rest of the community. Our modern values have

---

[1] My own convictions have been informed and nurtured by various scholars, spiritual directors and experiences in ministry. I have shared these more extensively in my first book, *Turning Points of the Spirit: A journey from institutional religion to authentic spirituality* (Firelight, 2016).

developed independently from the church across the breadth of Western culture during the last fifty years.

The prominent convictions of any society are affected by its level of education in science and the humanities, the means of wealth-creation, its rules of governance, the authority structures of its religious organisations, its level of cross-cultural awareness, its grasp of psychological development and by the power structures within its families. The church's teaching has both assumed and served these dominant social values ever since it established itself as an institution of power in the Roman Empire.[2]

As people embedded in a specific place and time, Christians have been able to make use of the Bible to teach whatever they value. It has always been so, whatever those values happened to be. The Bible is easily manipulated. Prominent social values are read back into the church's teaching, broadly through theological reflection and locally through sermons. Christian faith, like all other religions, is strongly influenced by the culture in which it is practised. In turn, it contributes to the discussion of values within that culture. But prophetic Christians who challenge the values of the dominant society have always been a very small minority. The worldviews of society and the church are in a two-way relationship, but heavily skewed on the side of society influencing the church.

---

[2] It is generally accepted that the church transitioned from being a marginal group in the ancient world to an institution of power following the conversion of the emperor Constantine in 312CE.

A New Starting Point

There was a time when the church: proclaimed the wickedness of the Jews as 'Christ-killers'; expounded the ungodliness of non-Christians and the righteousness of fighting in the Crusades; gruesomely tortured and killed its own members whom it called 'heretics' for disagreeing with authorised Christian doctrine[3]; excommunicated, tortured or killed its members for suggesting that the earth was not the centre of the universe; taught the superiority of whites over all others; insisted that women were inferior to and less intelligent than men; hammered the need for sinners to repent lest they burn in hell for eternity; taught that famines, earthquakes, plagues, floods, the unexpected death of children and AIDS were God's punishment for sin. Throughout the eras of changing social values, the church's teaching has been based upon the same Bible, the same creeds and represented the same God as many Christians believe in today.

Even in our own lifetime, we have seen a change in the values expressed by the church concerning the equality

---

[3] Reading the history of torture by the church, or by the state as the arm of the church, is enough to turn the stomach of the strongest. According to the early church Father, Augustine, coercing someone to adopt the truth with "great violence" was justified. Burning alive, impaling, skinning alive, cutting off body parts, killing children in front of their parents, tearing off flesh until one died from loss of blood, slaughter on a battlefield, burying upside down, drowning and crucifying were all used as methods to rid the church of anyone who thought differently from authorised doctrines. From 4th until the 19th century, many, many thousands of men, women and children were killed by order of the church for heresy. The last Christian executed in Europe for heresy was a schoolmaster who was hanged in Spain in 1826 for substituting the words 'Praise be to God' in place of 'Ave Maria' in school prayers.

of women, people of other cultures, ethnic origins and faiths, sexual orientation, marriage and divorce, environmentalism, poverty, overseas missions and social justice. In comparison with fifty years ago, the Bible is now used to support different values within mainstream churches. Education levels, research in psychology, scientific discovery, social justice activism and greater diversity in communities have all contributed to these changes in the church.

Human beings always bring their own assumptions to the reading of their sacred texts. The study of this dynamic is what the scholars call 'hermeneutics'. Quite naturally, Christians see their values reflected in the Bible and the life of Jesus. Because of changed social values, some passages that were used in preaching even until a hundred years ago are now ignored. The ecumenical creeds from the third and fourth centuries now take a lesser place, although still used in baptisms, as required by the church. The Old Testament prophets are still read because of their social justice focus while the horrific stories of the warrior God of Israel are rarely mentioned. Most popular with preachers these days are the parables and Gospel stories of Jesus, rather than the exclusive texts of John's doctrinal assertions or the theologising of Paul.

Let's acknowledge, then, that a whole range of values can be, and have been, supported by reference to the Bible. The books that make up the Christian scriptures contain diverse and sometimes diametrically opposed values and even ideas of what God is like. Accordingly, the

Christian community has always been selective about which parts of the Bible are read in public. Progressives have been criticised for choosing the parts of the Bible that suit them, when in fact traditionalists have always done the same — one only needs look at the official lectionary for preaching to see how that operates.

All Christians pick and choose the elements of Christian faith that they like and respect. It is confusing then, even non-sensical, for anyone to say that they hold 'biblical values'. Which of the many, disparate values in the Bible would they be? As it has been throughout the centuries, 'biblical values', for many people, are simply their own values that they find in, or read into, the scriptures. It is the premise of this book that we do in fact need to be judicial in how we draw upon biblical material to inspire and support our spirituality. Because our values will inevitably guide this process, we need to examine critically the values that will shape us.

Is it Biblical?

We need to dismantle unhelpful religious doctrines, while developing an alternative spiritual vision at the same time. To do this requires a careful approach to the Bible. Scholars have demonstrated for well over a century that a literal reading of scripture is inappropriate. But the resurgence in fundamentalism over recent decades has worked against Christians learning to read the Bible with greater discernment.

There are tomes published on how to distinguish what may have been original to Jesus in the New Testament and what has been constructed by a later generation of his followers. Similarly with the Old Testament, numerous scholars have explained its repeated editing process. We know that at least four layers of original writing and editing over a few centuries were combined into its final form. Once we understand that the biblical documents were edited and re-edited, we realise that human authors interpreted and re-interpreted the events being described for their own generation and community. These interpretations originated in the faith experience and beliefs of the authors in their own time. That is quite distinct from the idea that they originated in God.

A literal reading of the Bible requires people to leave their intellect at the door of the church. The Uniting Church was wise in its *Basis of Union* in referring to the Old and New Testaments as "unique prophetic and apostolic testimony, in which it *hears* the Word of God…" This was an attempt, fifty years ago, to counsel its members not to take all scripture literally and not to regard every text as 'the word of God'. Scriptural documents were written by human beings and reflect the convictions of the communities within which they emerged. Some texts are inspiring to this day, while others express motives and beliefs that we would not associate with God.

A New Starting Point

Communities of faith have reflected on their experiences of life, belonging, prosperity, hardship, slavery, freedom, social ethics, as well as military victories and defeats in the light of what they believed about God. Like others in the ancient, pre-scientific world, almost everything, good and bad, was attributed to an external, powerful and largely unapproachable deity. With this assumption, they wrote and rewrote the stories that later were included in the scriptures. The Bible should be treated with respect as an amazing written witness of these societies and their belief systems. It is a unique foundational document of the institution of the church and, as such, has historical significance.

But in our search for a new spiritual perspective, it is important not to twist ourselves in knots with worries about what is and is not 'biblical'. Remember that we are seeking what is real, true and good. If we are called to be faithful, it is not to a book, but to our glimpse of the divine. If our lives are dictated by what is in this book from an ancient world — a book that has been used to justify a whole range of conflicting values — we will be left confused and in turmoil. Chosen carefully, there are, nonetheless, many provocative, prophetic, and surprising biblical stories that are worth preserving. Read wisely, they can enrich our spirituality.[4] Evocative stories — historically based,

---

[4] Chapter 8 of this book looks closely at some of the helpful stories within the Bible that are worth preserving for future generations. They need careful interpretation so that the wisdom of the narrative is not lost in literalism.

fictional and parabolic — have the power to speak to us over and over again, often with different levels of meaning, in various situations. Demonstrating this very point, in almost every chapter that follows I have drawn heavily upon biblical stories for inspiration and wisdom.

Holiness

A new spiritual tradition needs a new concept of holiness. Old ideas of the holy have had damaging effects on the human personality and the world. There is a passage in Matthew's Gospel where Jesus says that the holiness of his followers must be greater than that of the Pharisees.[5] For Jesus, the intention of the heart was of greater importance than religious observance. Unfortunately, instead of stressing integrity and the holiness of compassion and love, the church became moralistic, demanding an unreal notion of perfection of its members. Even today, people raised within the church describe how they have had to deal with the layers of guilt that their religion placed upon them.

The concept of holiness has been based upon a dualistic opposition of flesh and spirit. The spirit was imagined in opposition to the material world. Nature itself and natural relationships associated with the flesh were regarded as profane. On the other hand, ordination means a 'setting apart' from normal life and the behavioural

---

[5] Matthew 5: 20

expectations of the ordained clergy were strangely associated with a higher level of psychological 'purity' than that of the ordinary person. For many centuries, clergy and religious men and women were expected to be celibate. Those who chose to have families lived according to a lower scale of holiness. The church has not yet adequately dealt with this legacy — it has not developed a coherent teaching on imperfection and holiness. Only in our own day are the tragic consequences of this value system being revealed — clergy sexual abuse of the vulnerable. Later, I will explore the issues of perfection / imperfection and what they might mean for our spiritual perspective.[6]

Because the Christian religion devalued the natural world, it looked elsewhere for the sacred — things and places that point to God. These came to be associated with the church itself — icons, ceremonies, buildings and hierarchical office. God resided within religion rather than the world. This resulted in a utilitarian attitude to the natural world — valued only for what it can do for us. The material elements of the earth were said to be provided expressly for human exploitation and animals were valued according to their usefulness. Again, in our own day, we are reaping the destructive consequences of this dualistic philosophy.

In the broader community, many thinkers are suggesting we need a different Story — a new meta-narrative that gives meaning to our communal and cosmic

---

[6] See chapter seven, *Our Beautiful Messy Lives*

experience. Rather than devaluing the natural world and separating humanity from it, we are beginning to see everything as interconnected — spirit and flesh. Quantum physics suggests that all things impinge upon each other in ways that we had not realised. Perhaps we are not totally separate beings in this world after all. In this philosophical transition, we are recovering an awareness of the dignity of the material world. Increasingly, the distinction between the profane and the holy is revealed to be artificial. Those who grasp this changing perspective are at the forefront of shaping a new and more nourishing spirituality.

The same can be said of the idea of *God*. This will sound strange to some ears. It is common to use the term 'God' as though everyone knows who or what that means. Generally, we don't ask someone what they think God is like. We ask them if they believe in God. The assumption behind that question is that there is only one God that you either believe in or not. We need to acknowledge that, as the old advertisement says, "oils ain't oils." There may be only one God, but there are many ideas of God. This matters because what we think God is like influences how we live and interact with the world.

It is time to engage our sense of curiosity as we ask some very basic questions about the nature of God. Let's explore two alternative visions of God and see where they lead.

The Implications of Believing in a Traditional God

Consider God as a separate, transcendent being who created the universe and rules over all that happens on earth and in heaven. 'Ruling' means that nothing happens in this world without God's intention or permission. This God loves humanity but judges us according to an abstract ideal of perfection and demands punishment for failings and deliberate 'sin'. He (this kind of God is usually spoken of as male) is able to forgive human beings only because blood has been sacrificed to pay the penalty for sin.[7] This traditional image of God is consistent with the moralistic and authoritarian attitudes that the institutional church has exhibited for the best part of two thousand years.

When we worship that kind of God, subconsciously we are worshipping a form of power, coercive power — power that is exercised over the universe and over humanity. Although this God loves humanity and the world, the arbitrary choice to punish human faults with death is a choice that is central to God's nature. One of the traditional names for this God is 'the Almighty' — a title of power. Psychologically, if we worship that kind of power — the power of judgement, punishment and victory over all others — then we are subtly given permission to act similarly ourselves. We absorb into our own attitudes the

---

[7] Chapter two, *Paradise Lost?* explores where the idea of death being the punishment for sin originated and chapter three, *A Violent Tradition*, looks more closely at the mythology surrounding death.

values of the God we believe in. Although this is not a conscious process, it is very real.

Mirroring God, the church assumed for itself the authority to dictate who should be judged and for what. (Perhaps it should be noted here that Christianity is not the only religion that believes in this kind of God. But as this conversation is taking place within the Christian tradition, it is our primary focus.) Christian clergy were given the right to pronounce God's punishment or forgiveness upon the people. This privilege of priesthood is held on to strongly in the Roman Catholic Church, but also features in Protestantism. During protestant worship services a prayer of confession is often followed by the minister proclaiming, "Your sins are forgiven. Thanks be to God." Being forgiven meant being saved from punishment, not because there was no punishment but because that punishment had been applied to Jesus. Subtly and not so subtly, all Christian worship traditions reinforce the notion of a powerful God who demands punishment for sin.

If I worship a God who judges, punishes and acts arbitrarily to show mercy only on a select portion of humanity, it can influence the kind of person I become. Worshipping a judgemental God leads me in the direction, at least subconsciously, of becoming judgemental myself. Worshipping a God of coercive power subtly legitimises my own use of power over others. If God punishes the sinful through violence, eternal torture in hell or even natural calamities, it legitimises violence by those who serve God.

A New Starting Point

If our God fights for us against ungodly people, we can justify going to war in the name of God.

Christians would not say that God has a sexual identity in the same way as human beings. And we know that the concept of gender is derived directly from the body — sex organs, hormones and general physique. Logically therefore, God cannot be male as humans understand maleness. Nevertheless, most Christians treasure their male-gendered images for God. Traditionally, God is Father, and definitely not mother. The male human is usually more powerful than the female, so a powerful God is naturally male. We model ourselves on our God. Because the male God governs over everyone, in the family unit the male is head of the household. Worshipping God, as traditionally imagined, has reinforced male power over women wherever Christianity has flourished throughout the centuries. Women have had to struggle for recognition as equals in the Christian community as much as anywhere else. In the West today, most churches lag behind secular society both is accepting and implementing gender equality.

There are some cultures today where the rates of domestic violence are particularly high. In the well-known example of the Pacific Island nations, church attendance is also very high. Worship of a male-gendered, powerful God in these conservative Christian communities may help to explain, at least in part, why the Christian faith has done nothing to reduce this social problem. Researchers have also shown that women were esteemed more highly in these same traditional cultures before European missionaries brought Christianity.[8]

If I presume that God's 'Kingdom' has no room for people with gender identity struggles or different spiritual beliefs, then the society I shape will reflect those same rigid boundaries. Inevitably, definitions of who we believe is acceptable or unacceptable to God creates social boundaries of exclusion. Whoever God rejects, I, likewise, will feel justified in rejecting. A conservative Christian rhetoric currently supports the rise in exclusive nationalism in the West. For example, in 2016-18 the evangelical Christian lobby in the USA supported a far-right government's push to stop Muslim immigration, the exclusion of homosexual people from sections of the workforce and an anti-female rhetoric by the President. A conservative Christian faith that alienates all who do not belong to 'God's people' is founded on an image of an exclusionary God.

This God is totally pure and cannot coexist with imperfection. Only that which is pure or purified can approach God. Therefore, purity rituals are performed in many religious communities who have this image of God. The worshipper is purified through confession and acceptance of Jesus' sacrifice. In many Christian churches special garments are worn to symbolise purity — the baptismal robe of the child or adult and the vestments of

---

[8] Vanessa Griffen, *Gender Relations in Pacific cultures and their impact on the growth and development of children*, a paper prepared for a seminar on "Children's Rights and Culture in the Pacific", 2006.

A New Starting Point

the priest or minister. All of this imagery is based on the idea that human imperfection separates us from a perfect God. Without any logical questioning of the concept of perfection itself,[9] human frailty has been associated with sinfulness.

Following on from this vision of God, people of faith long to hear that God has forgiven them. Yes, I deserve to be punished, but Jesus died 'in my place', so that I am forgiven and my place in heaven is secured. This is why I worship Jesus. Being reassured of forgiveness and my place in God's Kingdom here and especially in the hereafter, I emerge from a worship service feeling accepted, loved and special to God. And isn't this just what so many look for in an age when fragile people are coping with broken relationships and an insecure social environment? However, underlying this comforting feeling is the knowledge that God would not forgive me unless blood had been shed. Perhaps Christians don't want to ask the question, but they need to. What does all this say about the nature of God?

Consequently, the most loving thing believers can do for others is to convert them, so that they also can be saved from God's punishment. The focus of the work and message of the church has been to convert as many individual souls as possible. Traditionally, Christians have cared about the community and the world, but primarily as

---

[9] Chapter seven, *Our Beautiful Messy Lives*, examines the ideas of perfection and imperfection more closely.

the arena in which people are drawn to God. Making the world a safer, happier place is considered good. But if pushed, traditional Christians understand that this happens mostly as a by-product of individuals being converted and then being used by God to encourage godly behaviour. Because the world is material and will one day fall away, the ultimate purpose of Christian action is saving souls for heaven.

In the service of this mission, the church of the past became almost obsessed with convincing people of their sin so that they might repent. The success of this message lay in its ability to deal with feelings of guilt. Even people of good conscience feel at some point in their lives that they have failed their friends or disappointed themselves. A sermon about sinfulness only serves to underscore a person's self-blame. Almost everyone hopes at some point that they will be forgiven, either by someone they have hurt or by God. The church's proclamation of the forgiveness of sin provides one way to feel at peace concerning unwise choices in our lives, which is the pastoral appeal of Christianity.

However, although the feeling of being forgiven is important psychologically, the traditional proclamation of forgiveness assumes, in the first instance, a God of judgement and punishment. A healthy spirituality will need to disentangle one from the other. The new spiritual tapestry takes healthy psychological growth seriously as well as the need for moral development and personal transformation, without a judgmental God.

Christians Trapped by Church Doctrine

With its message of sin, and itself holding the only key to forgiveness, the Christian church wielded enormous power over people's lives. It evolved through the centuries into a moralistic institution placing spiritual and psychological burdens on millions of ordinary people. As a judgemental religion, the church exhibited the exact opposite of the values of the historical Jesus. Social power in Europe was strongly in the church's hands during medieval times when its literate elite had almost exclusive access to written documents. But that institutional power was bound to crumble with the dawn of the Renaissance, the invention of the printing press and the emergence of the modern era.

Broad-based education robbed the church of some of its mystique and credibility. Discoveries in astronomy demonstrated that the church's insistent views on the cosmos were dramatically wrong. Research into psychological development and biology have shown that what the church taught were sins of the flesh were in most cases simply a natural expression of human existence. An awareness of the psychological importance of a positive self-image came up against the traditional message of inherent sinfulness. Identifying the systemic causes of injustice stretched our understanding of sin. Tackling the excesses of global poverty revealed the narrowness of a religion concerned primarily with the after-life. And exploring the complexity of modern ethics led to a dissatisfaction with a dualistic, out-dated religion.

Consequently, in the modern era millions of people walked away from the church, unimpressed with its authoritarian, moralistic ideas and its God. For decades, the mainstream denominations have assumed that this decline in attendance was due to old-fashioned music or styles of worship. The fundamentalist churches, with commercially-produced modern music, comfort those who enjoy the certainties of simple, straightforward answers to unsettling, complex questions. Mainstream churches, to their credit, have been unwilling to return to the dualism of days gone by. Unfortunately, they have not responded adequately to the deeper dissatisfaction of a better educated and scientifically aware generation. Post-modern seekers of spiritual experience look for a more informed vision of themselves and the cosmos. They walk away from the whole Christian scene because, in their eyes, the church's teaching has lost credibility.

Remarkably, many mainstream Christians have privately altered their perception of God while retaining the traditional belief system of the ancient church. Intellectually, they still agree with the doctrine that a holy God must condemn and punish sin, while their language indicates a personal preference for a God of unconditional love. They fail to see the discrepancy in their own belief system. The Jesus of former centuries was seated at the 'right hand of God' up in the sky somewhere, waiting to

A New Starting Point

come "to judge the living and the dead".[10] But in today's popular Christian culture, Jesus is "my friend". Punishment in hell for those who do not believe in the saving death of Jesus is a little awkward and rarely mentioned. Many Christians skirt around it saying, "I leave that up to God who is loving and just. It is not my place to judge others." This may be an understandable interim answer for Christians whose view of God is out of step with what they were taught. But it is not an adequate answer in the long term. More thinking is required.

The formal doctrines of all churches are still based upon the centrality of judgement and the offer of pardon from punishment, conditional upon belief. The Christian creeds have not changed since the fourth century. Some ministers do play with writing new creeds for use in worship. But clergy and congregations cannot change the church's belief system from the bottom up. Formal change of central doctrines can only happen through a deliberate movement to do so by the hierarchy and councils of the church, in most cases altering the constitution of the denomination itself. That would entail a world-altering, radical step for any church. But without it, the church is locked into an ancient belief system that many of its own clergy wish to leave behind. Without a formal doctrinal change, ordinary, local church members will continue to be confused by the contradictory images in prayers, creeds, songs and sermons. There is no consistency, except perhaps

---

[10] According to the Apostles Creed.

in those rare progressive congregations that exist precariously on the fringe of the church.

People of faith tend to respond to this transition time in the church in one of two ways. Some 'dig in their heels', recite the creeds with more gusto and decry the compromised faith of the liberals. They sing their commitment to the 'Almighty' and to the traditional worldview even more loudly. Clergy and lay members alike put their heads in the sand and don't even acknowledge that other thinkers, scholars, spiritual directors and authors are asking different questions and finding new answers. Alternatively, some people of faith reject the old worldview and drift away, no longer feeling sure of what is real.

This book affirms that there is a third option. I join my own voice to the inspiring minority who are calling for a new social narrative. A 'New Story' of the world, God and the spirit is being articulated for those who share our longings. The search for a more satisfying spiritual life might appropriately begin with our image of God.

We are touching on the ultimate mystery when we speak of God. Therefore, with humility, an alternative spiritual worldview depends upon recognising how much we do not know. Although many have responded to the confusion and inconsistencies of traditional Christianity described above by rejecting all ideas of God, this book supports the groundswell of people of faith who sense that God, differently imagined, is inviting us to explore a new vision of life.

An Alternative Vision of God

> *He said, "Go out and stand on the mountain before the Lord, for the Lord is about to pass by." Now there was a great wind, so strong that it was splitting mountains and breaking rocks in pieces before the Lord, but the Lord was not in the wind; and after the wind an earthquake, but the Lord was not in the earthquake; and after the earthquake a fire, but the Lord was not in the fire; and after the fire a sound of sheer silence. When Elijah heard it, he wrapped his face in his mantle and went out and stood at the entrance of the cave. Then there came a voice to him that said, "What are you doing here, Elijah?"*
>
> 1 Kings 19: 11-13

A larger-than-life prophet, a cave, a tornado, an earthquake, a firestorm and an eerie silence — this is the stuff of legends. The stories of Elijah are set almost three thousand years ago and yet this poetic description of the elusive presence of God could have been penned yesterday. Since time immemorial, human beings have wrestled with how to connect with that ultimate 'Other' whose presence is both longed for and feared. No-one has adequately plumbed the depths of beauty and mystery that we call God. Our theology can only ever be a humble attempt to describe the qualities that we sense belong to the One from whom we derive hope and love. Therefore, with this constant awareness of the inadequacy of words, let's explore an alternative vision of God.

Try to imagine a God without coercive power. What if the divine mystery at the heart of the universe does not have the kind of power we always assumed goes with the territory of 'God'? Suppose that God was not a distant being separated from the material world. Could there be a divine presence whose very nature is relational and who delights in the creative process *with* human beings and the rest of the cosmos? What if the power of this God is the power of invitation? Consider the idea of a God who is experienced by all living things as the lure towards whatever is good, true, loving, just and beautiful in every moment of existence.

Process theologians[11] have introduced the faith community to this radically revised concept of the divine. Based on the understanding of reality put forward by the philosopher Alfred North Whitehead,[12] process theologians reject the idea of coercive divine power. Although some, following Whitehead, prefer to speak of the 'initial aim of life', it is not true that this reduces God to an impersonal force. Rather, the view of God as the constant presence, who invites us all towards the good, corresponds with an

---

[11] For an introduction to Process Theology, visit the *Process and Faith* website at processandfaith.org

[12] Alfred North Whitehead (1861 – 1947) was an English mathematician and philosopher who founded the school of process philosophy. Perhaps the most prominent academic in this school of thought today is Dr John Cobb.

A New Starting Point

image of God as Love. Love, by definition, is relational and cannot be impersonal. According to this vision, even as the 'creator', God is and has always been in relationship with the cosmos through the power of invitation. Marjorie Suchocki[13] describes it this way.

> *God is by all means Creator, calling the world into existence in every moment. But God creates <u>with</u> the world, not independently of the world. The world enters into something like a creative dance with God, emerging anew in every moment as it takes its past and God's future into its becoming self.*

In other words, the universe itself can be thought of as relational, where all lifeforms are interconnected with the whole cosmos. This stretches our imagination, as it should. If it doesn't, we are simply projecting our limited human thought patterns and needs onto a God of our own creation. We end up doing exactly what the ancient people did in describing the deity that they worshipped — we want to feel powerful, so we imagine a God with coercive power. We want to feel that our own community is safe and superior, so we imagine a God who is on our side and who fights for us against our enemies. We want those who harm us to be punished, so we imagine a God who will take

---

[13] Marjorie Hewitt Suchocki, is Professor Emerita, Claremont School of Theology, and a co-director of the Center for Process Studies and its related program, Process & Faith. Her publications include *The End of Evil*; *God-Christ-Church: A Practical Guide to Process Theology*; *Divinity and Diversity*; and *The Fall to Violence*.

vengeance on our behalf. We want judgement of the wicked, but we also want to be forgiven ourselves. So, we imagine a judging God who punishes sinners but forgives us because we are special. The special, forgiven ones are the ones who believe what we do. But can we pause to wonder what reality might look like if God were *not* like us?

Perhaps religious concepts of judgement and punishment derive from our own limited assumptions about life. It is possible that the desire for punishment is alien to God. That is not to suggest that God is powerless in the face of evil. But God's power does not need to be that of forceful intervention, aimed at defeating, killing and tormenting the ones who perform evil acts. Rather, God's powerful response to evil may be the power of transformation. Imagine a God who has no desire to inflict pain and suffering on anything, not even on those who seem to 'deserve it'. According to this *relational* view of divinity and the cosmos, God *feels* the world and is *changed by* the world. Everything wondrous and beautiful is experienced, delighted in, absorbed into and treasured within the 'heart of God' forever. And all that is evil is painfully experienced, taken in, judged, transformed and integrated also within God's being. The creative transformation that God works for the world within God's own being is one way of understanding forgiveness, reconciliation and resurrection.

The new spirituality is founded upon this vision of God. The invitational power of Love may be the ultimate alternative to the human-like God who we were taught 'ruled' the world. Could it be that the universe is far more expansive than we previously imagined? Could it be that the creative power that sustains it is of a different order entirely to that assumed by religious doctrines? In the chapters that follow, as various threads of the spiritual tapestry are teased out, this vision of God will surface as integral to much of the discussion. Rather than 'doing away with' God, this new spiritual perspective invites us to consider a more thoroughly encompassing and irrepressibly life-giving image of God.

Is Worship Real?

If God's intention for the world is not punishment but transformation and healing, we will need to reset many of the doctrines on which the church is founded. We will need new, evocative language for worship and new patterns of communal life to replace the faded ceremonies of the old Christian tradition. Throughout the world, many progressive clergy and congregations are already experimenting with new forms of gathering as a response to new concepts of God and faith.

However, before exploring the new spirituality further, it is important to articulate some very basic yet complex questions on this point. If we rethink our image of God, does that invalidate our worship experience of the past? If our theology has been founded on concepts we now wish to reject, what does that imply about our earlier relationship with God? If we embrace new ideas of God, while our friends still hold to traditional Christian doctrines, is their experience of worship somehow 'less than' ours?

Although Christians believe that they can worship anywhere privately and that their acts of obedience to God are also a form of worship, these questions primarily concern communal worship within the church. At the risk of categorising people too simplistically, consider the following two descriptions of the worship experience. The first collection of experiences is found within the traditional church, while the second describes the variety of experiences that flow from this new spirituality.

1. Generalising somewhat, the first group of worshippers attend a church service to honour God, to be strengthened in their daily challenges and to encourage one another in faith. They participate in a prayer of confession because they believe that they need forgiveness. They sing songs of praise to the 'Almighty' because they believe in God's ultimate power over all. Their act of praise expresses the deeply held conviction that it is appropriate to humble themselves before a perfect and loving God. Their worship is an act of faith and obedience, expressing their belief that only God is worthy of worship. They listen to the public reading of the scriptures that confirms their understanding of the world and encourages them to maintain their hope in God for the future. Through the sermon, they may receive spiritual encouragement to keep going through difficult times. Their attendance at worship

may not alter their view of society or how the world works, but it does inspire them to live 'good' lives.

These believers usually leave a service feeling uplifted. Because they have fellowshipped with like-minded friends and taken time out to contemplate the things of God, their experience is refreshing and even therapeutic. Any suggestion that their worship has not been real would be offensive, and rightly so. Their participation in the act of worship can vary from largely dutiful and intellectual to open and emotional, depending on their own personality and needs. For them, worship according to the doctrines of the church is the 'right thing to do' even when their own faith does not feel strong. Belonging to the community of faith reaffirms their identity as 'God's people' and meets that basic need for belonging, even if they do not like everyone in the community.

Within this group, those who maintain an analytical attitude to the content of worship will not feel so much refreshed by the service as affirmed in their identity and beliefs. For them, the worship service is primarily one of maintaining a sense of security — a reassurance that no matter what chaos threatens outside, their own worldview is sound, and life makes sense. On the other hand, those who are more freely emotional are likely to emerge buoyed by the experience of being loved, forgiven, perhaps even healed. Their hope for the future is strengthened, knowing that their own relationship with God is on a firm footing. The church is the place where they are accepted and comforted because they believe in 'the gospel' and their lives matter.

All of us who were raised within the church can identify with some dimension of this experience. Is this worship real? *Yes.* Was it real for all of us when we simply accepted the traditional view of God? *Yes.* Does it move us towards the creative transformation of our lives and the life of the world? *Sometimes.* It should be clear that precisely what happens within the spirit of a person attending worship depends on a variety of factors, including the theological content communicated through the service and the psychological disposition of the worshipper. A person overwhelmed by guilt or low-self-esteem might experience real healing in traditional worship. Their experience should never be belittled by those who embrace a progressive faith. Someone attending worship with an open spirit, desiring to enter the divine presence will do so, because God is always present to us no matter what our background, theology, education, or life experience. In summary, despite the negative implications of the power-oriented God, traditional worship can be up-lifting, refreshing, strengthening and even healing. So why, "sometimes"? Why is traditional worship not *always* transformational?

We all have a capacity for self-delusion and a tendency towards self-protection. Therefore, unless we realise the benefit of being confronted with disturbing and challenging truths, we can shield ourselves too well from anything unsettling, including a raw and honest encounter

A New Starting Point

with the divine presence. Although God is the one who draws us towards loving and beautiful possibilities for ourselves and the world, sometimes those possibilities require us to rethink and let go of our self-protecting beliefs. There is a saying that good worship comforts the disturbed and disturbs the comfortable. That is very true. Healthy spiritual development is not always experienced as comfortable.

Because our participation in a church service presumes that we already agree with the doctrines of the church, it is reasonably easy to enjoy worship and go home with all our prejudices, arrogance or preoccupations intact. Unless we hear the prophetic word that upsets our sense of comfort, entitlement and privilege we will not hear the invitation to be transformed. Simply being reaffirmed as God's people is not enough to help us embrace change. In many cases it does the opposite — confirms our judgement that it is others who need to change. When we approach worship with this inner disposition, even moving experiences of God's love do not change us but are channelled into strengthening our mindset. Our use and abuse of power, modelled on God's coercive power, can be reinforced by the traditional images that we are exposed to in worship. No new insights are born because we keep those at bay. Outwardly, we are worshipping God, but inwardly, our spirits are not wholeheartedly open to the real presence of the divine. We miss out on those unexpected, unguarded moments when God invites us into unexplored possibilities.

2. The second broadly defined worship experience can be described as *attending, centering* and *connection*. According to the new image of God, we worship when we consciously 'attend to' the presence of the divine. Because God is always present, offering us life-supporting possibilities, worship simply means stilling ourselves to become aware of this reality, to appreciate it, be thankful for it and celebrate it. We don't *enter* the presence of God when we attend worship, we simply *attend* to the God who is always present in every moment. An unhurried, unforced, unguarded attending in this way may well lead us to an experience of confession. A raw honesty, about what needs to change within us, does not come from a need to be 'saved' but from a liberating self-awareness that is welcome, even when it is confronting. Letting all pretensions fall away and operating from the 'true self' is the path to our own transformation. Sometimes this 'being real' is called 'centering'. It is as though, like Elijah, we have learned that God is not found in the loud, intrusive, demanding events of life but in the 'still small voice' within.

Attending to the Real by focussing on the simple things around us and within us is a spiritual practice that we can do anywhere, anytime. The result of attending and centering is the experience of *connection* — an awareness of our direct relationship with God, each other and the rest of the world. More than connecting as separate entities, it is a realisation that together we are part of a larger whole, part of one another. Even with God, this dynamic inter-relationship is experienced like a flowing back and forth,

A New Starting Point

each participating in the other. The intriguing thing is that the beauty of the divine can surprise us when we open our hearts to others for whom God is also present. This can happen over morning coffee, at the theatre, observing nature or playing with our children — anywhere. And of course, it can happen in a worship service. When we gather together to celebrate this dynamic inter-relationship with each other, our experience of God is heightened.

Of course, this also applies to those who worship in the traditional church. Hence, the answers to the above questions about 'real worship' are complex. But although we may genuinely experience the divine presence in traditional services, worshippers are often diverted into serving a different agenda — the agenda of the church. That doctrinal framework directs the thoughts of worshippers into a worldview in which humans are intrinsically separated from God and the rest of the world. Unhelpful images of sin, salvation and belief, imposed upon the worship experience, do not free people to 'centre' themselves. The gentle, persuasive prompting of the divine impulse can be smothered by too much else that demands the attention of worshippers — doctrinally formed prayers, songs, preaching, and especially narrow expectations of what members should be thinking and feeling.

Fortunately, in other churches with progressive leaders, the doctrinal framework of the church sits very lightly and allows worshippers greater freedom to simply be themselves and attend to the still small voice. In those situations, worshippers from all theological backgrounds can have transformational experiences of the divine. Much depends upon how rigidly the church agenda dictates the practice of worship. Space does not permit a comprehensive exploration of the worship phenomenon. Suffice to say, none of us can judge what takes place within the spirit of another. We should be careful about making assumptions concerning others' experience based solely on their identification as 'traditional' or 'progressive'.

Put another way, although I believe the doctrines that guide traditional Christian worship are in urgent need of revision, I respect the intentions of the heart and the authenticity of the worship experience of many traditional church members. Because our hearts and our heads can operate on different levels, a person's heart-connection with the force of Love can refresh their spirit, while in their head, their worldview remains limited by fourth century religious ideas. Traditionalists can leave a worship service up-lifted and encouraged but entrenched in their thinking. Not realising the flaws in the church's teaching, these Christians insist that worship in the traditional church is empowering and essential for them. When it is criticised, they feel their experience of God is under attack.

The same is also possible for progressives. However progressives, on the whole, are less attached to doctrine, and therefore more open to new thought patterns. My personal story is that, although for most of my life I worshipped in a traditional Christian setting, my experience of God then was as much an awareness of the invitational divine presence as it is now. I have embraced the relational image of God and the new perspective on our interconnected world because it articulates what I have always sensed as real. My understanding of faith has developed and changed enormously over the years. And yet, my inner experience of what I call 'the divine' has simply continued and deepened. My hope is that Christians will re-examine their thinking about God and faith, not because the old tradition has not 'worked' for many of them, but because the world is looking for a more credible Story.

Moving Towards a New Story

The New Story of the world affirms the discoveries of science, the unique worth of every person and living thing, and the goodness and Love that sustains it all. Charles Eisenstein[14] describes the Old Story of the world, the one that is falling apart, as built on the mythology of our separate selves. In the old worldview, all things happen because force is exerted upon them. The cause and effect of a Newtonian universe is predictable. Newton believed God created the universe with its laws of physics based on force, and now it ticks over like a machine.

However, quantum physics has now questioned the predictable nature of how the world works and has discovered a relationship between the observer and the

---

[14] Charles Eisenstein (1967 -) is a public speaker, gift economy advocate, and the author of several books including *The Ascent of Humanity*, *Sacred Economics*, and *The More Beautiful World Our Hearts Know Is Possible*.

observed. It appears that we are not all distinct, separate selves after all. In line with this relational reality, Eisenstein suggests that the New Story is not based upon force, but upon Love. Process theology expresses a similar thought. From different fields and backgrounds, thinkers and specialists are bringing their own language to express the same convictions. In the New Story, we will be more committed to engaging with others, inspired by a vision of hope and connectedness. Even small actions carry significance in an interconnected universe powered by Love.

The late Tom Harpur,[15] a prominent Canadian theologian, expressed concern that some progressive scholars had dismantled traditional Christianity without offering a sufficient alternative for the "care of souls".[16] It is the precise conviction of this book that a new, satisfying spirituality not only makes sense of lived reality, but also nurtures our souls through the constancy of the divine presence and the invitation to creatively shape the future. The motive for defining a new faith perspective is not simply that we must give people what they want. To do that

---

[15] Thomas William Harpur (1929 – 2017), was a Canadian author, broadcaster, ordained priest and theologian. He earned an Honours BA at the University of Toronto and later studied classics at Oxford as a Rhodes Scholar. After his theological studies in Canada, he returned to Oxford for post-graduate studies in Patristics. His books include *For Christ's Sake* (1986), *Life after Death* (1996), *The Pagan Christ* (2004), and *Born Again* (2011 and 2017).

[16] Tom Harpur, *New Creeds*, in *The Emerging Christian Way*, Michael Schwartzentruber (ed), CopperHouse, 2006, p.56.

would justify the old criticism by Karl Marx that religion is the opium of the people. Weaving together a meaningful spirituality is not an attempt to cater for a niche market. Rather, it gives shape and voice to that which resonates broadly with lived experience — that we all are connected with the Real. This is another way of describing what Tom Harpur called the *Christ Principle*. In 2006 he wrote,

> *After thinking, reading and reflecting on this matter ... for the past 30 years I am even more fully convinced than I was when I wrote "For Christ's Sake" in 1986 that Jesus' chief teaching was not about sin and certainly not about founding a new religion. It was about the kingdom of God, God's active presence everywhere. More specifically, it was about the kingdom as an inner reality — the divinity of every one of us. God in our midst; God within.*[17]

It would be a mistake to think that this is just another feel-good, soft option in place of a more demanding faith. Rather, it is to recognise that welcoming the inner divine impulse towards the good gives direction to all that we do. At times the good and compassionate option may not be popular and may lead us into conflict with those who rob others of their dignity or human rights. If the divine impulse is present to us all, then we must beware of erecting barriers between human communities.[18] The lure

---

[17] Ibid, p57.
[18] The issue of divisions between people is addressed in chapter six, *Dismantling the Barriers that Separate Us*.

of God is to create a community in which barriers that alienate people from one another are broken down. The new spiritual perspective will challenge smallness of mind, lead into social advocacy and require personal transformation. It is definitely not the soft option nor concerned only with the individual. At times it is not easy or even comfortable but is fulfilling and nurturing.

If the lure of God is present to every soul, it follows that every person should be treated with respect and dignity. It implies strong values of radical equality — no sexism, racism, or distinguishing between human beings whatever their culture, education, religious background or lack thereof. Injustice of any kind is contrary to the lure of God. Quite naturally then, advocacy, community building and social action all flow from attending to the divine impulse.[19] The interconnected nature of all things leads us to seek the wellbeing of those who might be disadvantaged, the health of our local ecology and ultimately the planet. This will affect how we farm, eat, shop and interact with our neighbours.

The invitation to the individual towards goodness, creativity and justice, is an invitation to shape the community according to these values. There is a seamless connection between the personal and the global because God is not individualistic. Rather than a limited concept of

---

[19] With reference to some texts from the scriptural tradition, chapter three, *Abundance, Scarcity or Enough?* explores the assumptions about the world on which social justice is founded.

A New Starting Point

God who is primarily 'for me and mine', in this perspective God longs for the creative happiness of the whole community. Therefore, it is inappropriate to set the needs of the individual over against the health of society or the world.

What are the convictions that people of faith in the future will want to share with the world? The old evangelical message about belief in Jesus the Christ for personal salvation no longer holds credibility or respect in a broadly educated population. Personal salvation itself is a concept that has been shown to lack relevance to the pressing issues of our communal life and the future of the planet. Can we gather together the values and issues that will inspire the future faith-filled community? I acknowledge that the spiritual convictions of the next generation are already strong and gathering momentum around the world. My concern is that the Christians, formed in the religious era, will be left behind for want of a pathway towards the New Story. This book aims to assist the Christian community in finding a way forward in the changing landscape of beliefs and values.

In summary form, the following suggested tasks for the Christian community all have an important part to play in this transition. Each will be explored in the following chapters.

* Because values inevitably shape actions, we must consciously choose which values we will prioritise in our lives. As a starting point, we can dialogue around issues of equality, compassion, generosity, social justice, creativity, inclusion, humility and beauty. We can then assess our beliefs by the values we hold most dear. According to these values, we need to reject those scriptural texts that are violent, distasteful or generally unhelpful, while preserving the stories that express an enduring wisdom. Re-reading the Garden of Eden origin myth, we should re-examine the idea that God's penalty for sin is death. Developing new perspectives on holiness, imperfection and personal integrity, we can find beauty in all the struggles and achievements of our lives. We need to attend deeply to the divine impulse in the world and re-envisage God's nature as Love rather than coercive power. We need to work towards forgiveness, change and reconciliation in personal and communal experience.

* Aligned with the historical Jesus, we must commit to non-violence in all social action. We can urge our society to exercise restraint on the accumulation of wealth, enabling all people to live with dignity. We can take time out from work and production to appreciate and develop the non-economic gifts of family and community.

* Redefining the 'sacred' to include the natural world, we can affirm the inherent value of the land and waters with all their natural life-forms, protecting them from thoughtless destruction. We can care for the soul through commitment to a specific place with its local, inclusive community. We can work to dismantle the artificial, destructive barriers between people. We should never allow the sadness and grief of the world to extinguish the impulse of hope and love.

A New Starting Point

This new spiritual perspective may sound like a fanciful utopia or a beauty quest entrant saying she wants to create "world peace". But this vision of God, and the community that aligns with it, has the possibility of shaping a life-supporting alternative to the harsh, self-protective society that is increasingly promoted in today's world. Everyone acts out what they value, and everyone contributes to the future, even those who do not think in such terms. Therefore, it is critical that more of us think through what exactly it is we believe and value, and what we want the future to look like. We cannot opt out of the process of creating the emerging world, either in partnership with God or in self-interest or apathy. Because we constantly make significant choices, the world will emerge better if we choose the direction of our lives thoughtfully. The inspiration of the New Story suggests possibilities for our shared future on this planet and our creative part in it.[20] Instead of the old traditional focus on a future judgement and heaven, the New Story imagines a more beautiful life now.

This all-encompassing perspective has been promoted by various scholars, activists and philosophers during the last half-century and many indigenous communities for centuries. Eco-theologian Thomas Berry, with his cosmic perspective, was one of the early authors in this field. Those who stress a local expression of

---

[20] Chapter nine, *Hopes and Dreams of a Different Future*, explores this in more detail.

interconnectedness include Sally McFague, Wendel Berry and Ched Myers. Some, like Catholic activist priest Daniel Berrigan and biblical scholar Ched Myers, have focussed on the human side of non-violence and social justice. Others like Vietnamese Buddhist monk, Thich Nhat Hanh, and Jesuit mystic and activist, Thomas Merton, have emphasised the connection between inner reflection, attentiveness and creating a peaceable society. Gift Economy advocate, Charles Eisenstein, describes the transition from the Old Story to the New Story in terms of disrupting the old mythology of our separateness. These are just a few of the many thinkers who contribute to a new satisfying spirituality for our times. There are vast, rich resources in books and pod-casts to draw upon. We have many friends on this journey. Transitioning from a traditional Christian background to this New Story requires a good deal of rethinking. These authors and speakers will stretch our minds and excite our spirits throughout our own journey.

Being co-creators with God of a more beautiful world whose future is not planned out in some 'heavenly drawing room', gives our present actions eternal significance. Without any guarantee of the institutional support of churches or other religious groups, we need to encourage one another in this task. Judiciously drawing upon the biblical tradition, in the following chapters I highlight those threads of wisdom that are critical for a new, cohesive, interwoven spirituality.

CHAPTER TWO

Paradise Lost:
Can Something that Never Existed be Restored?

> Whatever he was — that robot in the Garden of Eden, who existed without mind, without values, without labour, without love — he was not man.
>
> John Galt, character from *Atlas Shrugged*

Have we 'fallen' from some utopia or Paradise to which we can be restored? According to the metanarrative of Christendom, the answer is 'yes'. In this chapter I ask readers to revisit this age-old assumption, including the biblical story on which it is founded. If we arrive at a different answer, what does this mean for faith and spirituality?

The event referred to in Christian teaching as 'the Fall' describes how human beings originally lived in harmony with God but fell from this wonderful state by choosing to act in defiance of God's command. The expulsion of humanity from the Garden of Eden was the consequence. That expulsion meant struggle and death. According to the church throughout the centuries, death is our punishment from God for our original human sin of disobedience. Christian faith has always taught that the path back to union with God and life eternal is through faith in Jesus, whose death paid the price for humanity's disobedience.

Adam and Jesus are described as opposites in the Christian scriptures. Although the story of the Garden of Eden is not in the forefront of everyday thinking for most Christians, embedded in their consciousness is the belief that Adam's sin of disobedience resulted in death and alienation from God. This is true for Christians, even those who regard Adam as a representative human being and not an historical person. The Garden of Eden has represented, either literally or metaphorically, the time before it all went wrong. This is the essential backstory to the Christian proclamation.

It cannot be emphasised enough how central this teaching is to traditional Christian faith. The Fall is the Christian, metaphorical explanation of why human beings are estranged from God and why death is required to restore that relationship. If there was no Fall, there would be no need for a 'Saviour'. If there was no Fall, it would be possible to revise our theology of human nature, morality and our relationship with God. An alternative reading of the sin and disobedience tradition in Genesis would provide a pathway to a renewed understanding of ourselves. This is where we must begin if we are to construct a New Story of faith. The Fall is a tradition long overdue for review.

The 'Garden of Eden' Origin Myth

To re-examine the foundational doctrine of the Fall, we must revisit its source in Genesis. Notice that the story of the Fall is only found in the second creation account and not in the first. The second creation story by the Yahwist has a more human-focussed, folktale character to it than that of the Elohist, the author of Genesis 1.[21] Because this tradition is so critical to Christian faith, I have included extensive excerpts from Genesis 2-3.

> (From Genesis 2) *In the day that the Lord God made the earth and the heavens, when no plant of the field was yet in the earth and no herb of the field had yet sprung up — for the Lord God had not caused it to rain upon the earth, and there was no one to till the ground; but a stream would rise from the earth, and water the whole*

---

[21] Volumes have been written on the differences of style and language between the two authors. Just very briefly, The Yahwist uses the name Yahweh for God, Reuel for Moses' father-in-law, Sinai for the holy mountain, and Canaanites for the residents of Palestine. The Elohist uses the name Elohim for God, Jethro for Moses' father-in-law, Horeb for the holy mountain and Amorites for the Palestinians.

face of the ground — then the Lord God formed man from the dust of the ground, and breathed into his nostrils the breath of life; and the man became a living being. And the Lord God planted a garden in Eden, in the east; and there he put the man whom he had formed. Out of the ground the Lord God made to grow every tree that is pleasant to the sight and good for food, the tree of life also in the midst of the garden, and the tree of the knowledge of good and evil.

... The LORD God took the man and put him in the garden of Eden to till it and keep it. And the LORD God commanded the man, "You may freely eat of every tree of the garden; but of the tree of the knowledge of good and evil you shall not eat, for in the day that you eat of it you shall die." ... Therefore a man leaves his father and his mother and clings to his wife, and they become one flesh. And the man and his wife were both naked, and were not ashamed.

(Beginning of Genesis 3) *Now the serpent was more crafty than any other wild animal that the Lord God had made. He said to the woman, "Did God say, 'You shall not eat from any tree in the garden'?" The woman said to the serpent, "We may eat of the fruit of the trees in the garden; but God said, 'You shall not eat of the fruit of the tree that is in the middle of the garden, nor shall you touch it, or you shall die.'" But the serpent said to the woman, "You will not die; for God knows that when you eat of it your eyes will be opened, and you will be like God, knowing good and evil." So when the woman saw that the tree was good for food, and that it was a delight to the eyes, and that the tree was to be desired to make one wise, she took of its fruit and ate; and she also gave some to her husband, who was with her, and he ate. Then the eyes of both were opened, and they knew that they were naked; and they sewed fig leaves together and made loincloths for themselves ... [T]hey heard the sound of the LORD God walking in the garden at the time of the evening breeze, and the man and his wife hid themselves from the presence of the LORD God among the trees of the garden ... To the woman he said,*

"I will greatly increase your pangs in childbearing;
in pain you shall bring forth children,
yet your desire shall be for your husband,
and he shall rule over you."

And to the man he said,
"Because you have listened to the voice of your wife, and have eaten of the tree
about which I commanded you,
'You shall not eat of it,'
cursed is the ground because of you;
in toil you shall eat of it all the days of your life;
thorns and thistles it shall bring forth for you;
and you shall eat the plants of the field.
By the sweat of your face you shall eat bread

> *until you return to the ground,*
> *for out of it you were taken;*
> *you are dust, and to dust you shall return."*
>
> *The man named his wife Eve, because she was the mother of all living. And the LORD God made garments of skins for the man and for his wife and clothed them ... Then the LORD God said, "See, the man has become like one of us, knowing good and evil; and now, he might reach out his hand and take also from the tree of life, and eat, and live forever" —therefore the LORD God sent him forth from the garden of Eden, to till the ground from which he was taken. He drove out the man; and at the east of the garden of Eden he placed the cherubim, and a sword flaming and turning to guard the way to the tree of life.*
>
> (Excerpts from Genesis 2 and 3)

Readers familiar with cultural legends and ancient literature will recognise this story immediately as an 'origin myth'. All ancient cultures have some mythology explaining how the world, natural features, human society and cultural traditions came into being. Australians are familiar, for example, with the first Australians' Rainbow Serpent and other stories of the Dreamtime, dating back many thousands of years. Many origin myths from cultures around the globe have been studied by historians and sociologists. How did it all begin? We need to draw upon the findings of scientists and cultural historians for an informed reflection.

The 'Garden of Eden' Theology and Human Evolution

Consider the development of life on our planet. Until a certain point in evolution, all creatures lived according to instinct. As mammals evolved, so too did relationships, communication and communal groups. Some species developed sufficient intelligence for play, comfort, anger, happiness, embarrassment, even grief and love. Scientists observe these features of animal life today. For example, some mammals, like elephants, display compassion and care of the more vulnerable members of their group. By and large, leadership in communal groups of non-human species was, and still is, determined by physical prowess.

Then, approximately 250,000 — 300,000 years ago, a new species of mammal evolved.[22] Homo sapiens developed an intelligence that allowed for complex language and the ability to create new technologies. These humans, though not the strongest of all living creatures, were able to out-think and therefore dominate the others. Most importantly for our discussion, only humans were

---

[22] There is still much to learn from scientific and archaeological research, of course. Nevertheless, it is estimated that fossils found in Morocco, attributed to Homo sapiens, along with stone tools dated to approximately 300,000 years ago, are the earliest evidence of modern human beings. Also, according to a 2015 study, the hypothetical man Y-chromosomal Adam is estimated to have lived in East Africa about 250,000 years ago. He would be the most recent common ancestor from whom all male human Y chromosomes are descended. (Karmin, M; Saag, L; Vicente, M; et al, "A recent bottleneck of Y chromosome diversity coincides with a global change in culture", Genome Research, April 2015.)

able to use their intelligence to reflect upon their own actions, relationships, community, origins and choices. For human beings, instinct was no longer the only factor determining behaviour, as self-reflection and conscience were added to the mix. A whole new dimension had entered the behavioural choices of creatures on the earth — moral complexity.

Origin myths from all human cultures suggest that the "knowledge of good and evil" — the exercise of conscience — is integral to being human. The ability to reflect and weigh up the ethical complexity of decisions distinguished Homo sapiens from other species. As well as conscience, our own species was marked out as different from other mammals by our search for meaning or a perceived purpose in existence. Unlike other advanced animals, who seem content to simply live, form relationships and care for the family or tribe, *humans wanted to understand why.* As a species, we have always searched for an explanation of life's mysteries, seeking to imbue both our life and our death with meaning. Since the advent of writing, ancient literature attests to this intellectual and spiritual quest.

Given this development, do we really believe that there was once a time in the history of humanity when we always chose the morally 'good'? Putting the question in religious terms, do we believe the teaching that, once upon a time, human beings lived in perfect harmony with God in an undefiled "Paradise", never making unwise or unethical choices? The Christian and Jewish traditions have always taught that the answer is 'yes'. Even Christians who do not read the Garden of Eden story literally, accept the notion that there was a Fall — a time when we lost our previous union with God, and that we long to recover it. Most Christians believe that we are born into this state of estrangement from God. Others believe that the Fall happens still in every life — a time when we lose the innocence of the newborn and live estranged from God thereafter until it is recovered through our faith in Jesus.

Whichever way Christians imagine the Fall, the assumption is that there is a long-lost, perfect relationship with God that can be recovered for our spiritual health and happiness. Although a perfect restoration of our harmony with God is assumed to be complete only after our death, the life of the believer is cast in terms of becoming 'like Christ', moving towards that total restoration. The remnants of sin in the believer's life are forgiven because the penalty of our sin has been paid by Jesus. But the whole idea that the penalty for sin is death can be traced back to the Garden of Eden story. According to this reading, we humans lost our place in Paradise, were never allowed to eat from the Tree of Life and must return to the earth as 'dust to dust'.

The old tradition teaches that our human ancestors were thrown out of Paradise to a life of hardship, suffering and death. The Christian tradition teaches that Adam and Eve (or the humanity they represent) were disobedient and arrogant, desiring to become 'like God'. In the ancient mythology, independent moral choice, the understanding of good and evil, was only ever intended for the gods, not for humans. It follows that we all have inherited this arrogance, this sinful tendency, this desire to go our own way against God. We all bear the guilt of that independent streak and need to repent.

According to the old tradition, we need to be 'saved' because, "The wages of sin is death."[23] The apostle Paul used that phrase in relation to the consequences of Adam's sin.[24] In other words, the primary source of this teaching goes all the way back to the story of Adam and Eve's banishment from the Garden of Eden. Unable to eat from the mythical Tree of Life, Adam and Eve were denied access to immortality. Emerging through Paul's influence, the Christian idea was that death entered human existence because of that original sin, in which we all participate. It is upon this important foundation that a whole set of doctrines has been built. All this, despite the fact that the words "sin", "price" "wages" and "punishment" are never mentioned in the story itself.

In the context of human evolution, the story reflects the intellectual and spiritual struggle that human beings have with that most fearful experience of life — death. God said, you will die if you know the moral struggle between good and evil and become a species with conscience. Of course they will die. All species on the earth die. Flesh

---

[23] Romans 6: 23
[24] Romans 5: 12

deteriorates and after death, decays. There never has been flesh that lasts forever. So, the idea that before the Fall people lived forever is non-sensical. It would even have been non-sensical to our pre-scientific, ancient ancestors. There was much they didn't know, but they were not silly.

Modern Christians attempt to deal with this illogical aspect of the theology by referring to spiritual rather than physical death. However, the thrust of the whole passage is about the physical aspects of life — toil, childbirth, hardship and the body returning to the dust. The story is best understood as an origin myth about the contours of physical, human experience. Therefore, the theological assertion that "The wages of sin is death" must be called into question.

Let's step back for a moment into the broader story of earth's living species. Zoological studies have revealed that some animal species do grieve for their dead companions.[25] Nevertheless, because of their limited intelligence and language, while non-human species may form close relationships and experience grief, they do not take the next step and reflect upon the nature or origin of death itself. Even animals who experience loss and grief do not seek an intellectual understanding of death or attribute religious meaning to it. While not easy, life in the animal kingdom has a simplicity, a straightforward character

---

[25] In the late 19th century, research noted grief in chimpanzees. The more recent research by Marc Bekoff has described grieving behaviour by many animals including some non-mammals. These include wolves, chimpanzees, magpies, elephants, dolphins, otters, geese and sea lions.

about it, thanks to the limited nature of intellectual reflection.

In the context of mythology, the Genesis story explains how the human species became conscious — and afraid — of death. Death was not a fearful thing for other animals. In other words, if a species gained sufficient intelligence and the wisdom associated with moral reflection, it would also gain the self-reflective awareness of hardship and death. Instead of taking life simply as it unfolds and acting on instinct, this advanced species would have gained a new dimension of knowledge. But that very ability to reflect and ask questions about meaning would automatically bring the fears and anxieties that accompany unanswered questions.

The presence of good and evil, hardship, suffering, love and loss and the mysteries around death itself were the realities upon which this new species, the human being, reflected. Whether as people of faith we attribute this development to God's intentional creation, or as secular people, to a non-intentional evolution, the same reality applies. The first human beings, at the very time that they began to struggle with the complexity of life's choices and questioned its mysteries, realised that one day they would die. "If you eat of the Tree of the Knowledge of Good and Evil, you will die." Yes, you will know, you will comprehend that you are going to die. By definition then, being human means to experience existential anxiety.

Paradise Lost

The earth produced its bounty for human communities when they contributed some blood, sweat and tears of their own. Therefore, the natural desire to minimise frustration and pain led to the development of technologies and efficient patterns of work. This was particularly so for settled agrarian societies, the kind that existed when Genesis was written. People also contemplated the irony that the most natural thing in the world that brings great joy — childbirth — was inevitably so painful. At every turn, life, in all its wonder, was also a struggle for both men and women. Human beings questioned the origin and purpose of their struggles. They longed for explanations, as we still do today. Put another way, to know good and evil, to have wisdom, meant coming to terms with death and the inevitable hardships of ordinary living. Because humanity metaphorically ate from that tree, we have had to cope with the disturbing awareness of pain, suffering and loss ever since. It is easy to see how the Genesis origin myth reflects the challenges of the human condition and attempts to provide a meaning-filled story for human anguish and suffering.

The fact that 'sin' does not appear in the story supports this interpretation. Notice that the reason given for Eve's choice to eat from that tree was twofold — the fruit looked delicious, and she wanted to gain wisdom. In any other story we would assume that the desire for wisdom is a good thing. But we've been conditioned to think that in this story it is not, only because we've been taught that acting on this desire was a sin. Apparently, this mythological, human-like God did not want people to gain wisdom, or understand good and evil, did not want this intelligent species to develop a conscience. It's almost as though, in the mythological worldview, God accidentally went too far in the creating process. The other species were fine because they operated from instinct, not conscience. But in creating humanity, God had allowed a species to become too advanced. When Adam and Eve ate from the "tree of the knowledge of good and evil", they gained moral awareness. Their eyes were opened, just like the snake said would happen. (The snake was right about that.) They chose to act independently causing God to say, "See the man has become like one of us." Human beings moved from the realm of animal life where instinct governs behaviour to the realm of ethical choices.

This mythological, human-like God felt threatened by a species who made choices with the same open-eyed wisdom and possibilities that God did. The only thing marking humans as distinct from the gods themselves was their mortality. So, because God felt threatened, to keep human beings always a step away from divinity, they were barred from eating of the Tree of Life. To ensure that living forever never became an option for human beings, they were expelled from the garden altogether. They would remain flesh and bone, not gods after all. Only the gods live forever. The hierarchy of heaven was ensured and stable. Here we have the mythological explanation for why human beings have wisdom greater than the rest of creation but remain part of the world of flesh where death is inevitable.

The defining characteristic of humanity compared with the rest of the animal kingdom is the intelligent exercise of moral choice. The defining characteristic of humanity compared with God is that human life is limited by flesh — humans die. The Garden of Eden myth was never a story about sin and punishment. It is a story of how human beings became different from the animals, how they threatened the gods, how the hierarchy of the heavens was maintained and why the human condition inevitably involves pain and struggle. Genesis 2-3 is a typical origin myth from the ancient world. Who are we and how are we different? This is how.

The 'Garden of Eden' in the Matrix of the Fertile Crescent

Reading Genesis 2-3 as an origin myth is not an arbitrary choice, convenient for challenging traditional doctrines. It is wise to respect historical and literary research and allow our interpretation to be informed by knowledge and evidence. We know that death, the sheer struggle to survive, pain in childbirth, the complexity of gender relationships and the intellectual ability to exercise conscience have always been of the essence of the human condition.[26] Traditionally, we were taught that these aspects of life were punishment from God for Adam and Eve's sin. But human communal life on this planet has never been otherwise. Any life without these realities was not 'human' as we understand the term.

Further, there is convincing literary evidence that the Garden of Eden story is best understood in the tradition of other Ancient Near Eastern origin myths. Church members usually assume that the Bible's story of creation is unique. Bible study groups are rarely invited to compare the Genesis myth with other Ancient Near Eastern origin myths. Christians tend to assume that the Bible is self-explanatory, that it does not need any reference beyond itself.

Contrary to this, we learn a great deal more if we read the Garden of Eden story alongside another narrative poem from ancient Sumer,[27] the epic of Gilgamesh and Enkidu. The Gilgamesh Epic was discovered in 1853 in what is now modern-day Iraq. The whole text is readily

---

[26] These qualities of human life were not all a part of the forbears of Homo sapiens. The human life that I refer to here developed in the anatomically modern human from approximately 300,000 – 250,000 years ago according to the latest research.

[27] Sumer, in southern Mesopotamia, is considered the earliest human civilisation, dating back to approximately 4000 BCE. The Sumerians developed a writing script around 3000 BCE and produced the earliest literature known. It existed between the Tigris and Euphrates Rivers, located in what is now southern Iraq. *The Epic of Gilgamesh* was a long poem written in Sumerian cuneiform on twelve clay tablets that were discovered in the ruins of Uruk. Gilgamesh had been king of Uruk, the city referred to as Erech in Genesis 10:10.

available and can be read in its entirety online. For many generations, theological students have been taught to compare the Genesis Flood story of Noah with the Gilgamesh Flood story. But those training for ministry were not encouraged to read the Bible's creation story within that same literary and cultural matrix. And yet, to do so sheds light on a number of biblical mysteries.

Gilgamesh was a real-life king and warrior around 2700 BCE who became a legendary superhero. According to legend, Gilgamesh was created from heaven and Enkidu from the ground. Enkidu had been raised by animals and later became the companion of Gilgamesh on his adventures. After his friend Enkidu died naturally from illness, Gilgamesh was dismayed and set out on a quest to conquer death. Note that once again, the story originates in the deep human longing to understand the mystery of death. At the end of this section of the epic, Gilgamesh manages to obtain the root that he is told will give him eternal life. However, he loses it while washing himself in a pool. The root of eternal life is carried away by a snake! The snake moves off and sheds its skin — a symbol of rejuvenation or renewed life. It is interesting to note that in both this and the Adam and Eve story, a snake plays a role in the inevitable outcome — the human hero fails to obtain immortality.

From time immemorial, human beings have looked for meaning or explanations for the conditions and mysteries of their life. Searching their imaginations, they developed origin myths and religious legends to provide answers. In comparing the Adam and Eve story with the older Gilgamesh legend, we see that both stories are mythological tales to explain how it is that humans do not live forever. In both stories, the tantalising possibility of grasping immortality (through the Tree of Life in one and the magical root in the other) slips away from our heroes forever. No sooner was that possibility dreamed of than it was lost. In other words, immortality was never a possibility for human life at all. Coming to terms with death as part of life is integral to the psychological and spiritual development of the human species. As John Dominic Crossan points out,

> *Israel knew, as did the entire Fertile Crescent, that the Epic of Gilgamesh and Enkidu was not a tragic tale of "if only" Gilgamesh had not taken that cool swim, he would have been immortal. They also knew that Genesis 2-3 was not a tragic tale of "if only" Adam had not taken that first bite, humanity would have been immortal. Both these stories were metaphorical warnings against transcendental delusions of human immortality. They were parables proclaiming that death is our common human destiny.*[28]

---

[28] John Dominic Crossan, *Jesus and the Violence of Scripture: How to read the Bible and still be a Christian*, SPCK 2015 p. 53. Crossan is Professor Emeritus at DePaul University and has been President of the Society of Biblical Literature.

Even those, who choose to give this mythological tale pride of place in their worldview, need to understand the difference between consequences and punishment. According to the myth, God didn't like the development of human conscience, because God felt threatened by humanity who had "become like us." And consequently, we're told, God acted out of that sense of threat. (Surely that jealous, self-protective, human-like version of God should alert us to the nature of this ancient mythical story.) As the story goes, the *consequence* of human intellectual and moral development was a petulant reaction by a small-minded God. That reaction was to prevent humanity from becoming immortal. This mythical tradition, explaining death as our common destiny, was never a story about *punishment* for *sin*. We must rewrite the theology suggesting death was introduced into human life as a punishment for sin. In fact, death was never *introduced* by God or by anything or anyone else. Death became a reality at the very moment that the material cosmos came into existence. The material order is always changing, evolving, dying and being reborn. We know that death was always integral to human and animal existence.

Further, we should note that the word 'sin' is not mentioned in the story at all. Sin is first mentioned in the following chapter, where it is associated with Cain's murder of Abel. In Genesis, sin is related to violence and the taking of human life. If we want to use the religiously-loaded term, sin, we only need to read the morning papers to know it exists. But there are no grounds for connecting the idea of sin to people acquiring knowledge and becoming independent, moral beings. According to the story, both Eve and Adam desired to grow in wisdom. And so they should! Contemplating the inevitability of death was a natural consequence of evolving into an independent, intelligent species with the potential for self-awareness. The idea that humans die eternally because of this 'sinful' choice makes no sense from any logical, mythological, spiritual or scientific perspective.

We need to be freed from the unfortunate misreading of this ancient myth implying that our search for wisdom, knowledge, independent thinking, moral awareness and human initiative is somehow sinful or against the divine impulse. Without these qualities of life, we would not be human. There was no original sin in the Garden of Eden. There was no death penalty for sin. There was no Fall because nothing real had been lost.

Use of 'The Fall' in Christian Theology

Unfortunately, later generations of religious leaders read the concepts of sin and punishment into the Garden of Eden story and made it serve another purpose altogether. The character of this origin myth was dramatically changed and used by Paul to further his own theology. Since then, this beautifully-crafted story has not been preserved according to its original intention.

The apostle Paul established a direct link from the Adam and Eve mythology to Christian teaching. Paul (who wrote much of the New Testament) spoke of Adam being a "type of the one who was to come."[29] He set Adam and Jesus over against each other as 'types' in their responses to God. The new theology became: Adam disobeyed and was punished with death. Jesus obeyed and through his obedience saved human beings from death.

> *Not only so, but we also rejoice in God through our Lord Jesus Christ, through whom we have now received reconciliation. Therefore, just as sin entered the world through one man, and death through sin, so also death was passed on to all men, because all sinned ... Therefore, just as one man's trespass led to condemnation for all, so one man's act of righteousness leads to justification and life for all.* [30]

The issue is not whether to read the story literally or as a metaphor, because the core message of the story is the same either way — that humanity has been exiled from the presence of God forever as punishment for our sin. The church taught us that we lost our innocence because, rebelliously, we all want to "be like God". The tendency of humans to assert themselves at the cost of their innate innocence is traced to the Garden of Eden story. Traditional Christians believed that their common longing for a

---

[29] *Romans* 5: 14
[30] *Romans* 5: 11-12,18

relationship with God is the longing to restore what was lost in the Fall.

In the 16th century, the church reformer and theologian, John Calvin,[31] was directly influenced by the writings of Augustine of Hippo[32] (5th century). Calvin placed the emphasis back upon Augustine's notion of 'original sin' — that humans inherit Adam's guilt and are in a state of sin from the moment of conception. This inherently sinful nature (Calvin's doctrine of "total depravity") results in a complete alienation from God and the total inability of humans to achieve reconciliation with God based on their own abilities. Even the word 'reconciliation' implies that an existing relationship has been lost. Since Adam was the representative human being, all people inherit the guilt of his sin. Calvin's teaching, that redemption through Jesus's death is the only remedy for this terrible state of humanity, permeates the Christian community to this day. Acknowledging human and individual sinfulness was usually the starting point for evangelical preaching like that of the late Billy Graham.[33]

---

[31] John Calvin (1509 – 1564) was an influential leader of the second wave of the Protestant Reformation. He directly influenced the development of the church in Scotland.

[32] Augustine, sometimes St Augustine, (354 – 430) became Bishop of Hippo in North Africa. His teachings and writings had enormous influence on the church, including the Protestant churches from the 16th century onwards. He developed the doctrine of "original sin".

[33] Rev Billy Graham (1918 – 2018), an ordained Southern Baptist minister from USA, became prominent as an international preacher from the 1940's. It is estimated that over 3 million from a total Australian population of 10 million in 1959 flocked to his Australian crusades.

Paradise Lost

The church has taught that our sense of spiritual isolation comes from participating in the original disobedience of humanity and that the only way to restore a healthy connection with God is through the second Adam, Jesus. Therefore, any suggestion that there was no Fall — that humanity has always experienced self-awareness; that we have always made moral choices according to conscience; that we have always lived with natural hardships outside of a non-existent Paradise; that the mystery and fear of death have always been with us; and that independently seeking wisdom was never a mortal sin — radically undermines the evangelical tradition. *This reading of the Garden of Eden origin myth strongly suggests that our primary need is not for a saviour who will die to take the punishment for our sin. On the contrary, it suggests that we are not as hopelessly alienated from God as we have been led to believe.*

Liberal Christian preaching has shifted focus now to the unconditional love of God and the possibilities for all people to be healed by that love. Sin is regarded as the rejection of God's ways or as systemic injustice and original, inherited sin is simply not mentioned. But there are still questions that are largely ignored. If there was no original sin in which we all participate, and no divinely decreed punishment of death, what need is there for a counterbalance to Adam? What is the need for a saviour?

Think of it this way. Imagine that humanity once lived happily in perfect harmony with God and nature in an undefiled garden where there was no pain, suffering or death. But all that was lost because of the deliberate catastrophic choice and action of one person. Exiled from the garden, human beings became alienated from God and from nature. The world itself became a difficult place pitted against human survival. Restoring humanity's harmony with God would take the heroic action of another person to right the wrong. The God-Man, Jesus, was the hero who alone could restore what was lost by Adam, the anti-hero. But if we put the first part of that narrative in doubt, as we have, what are the implications for the second part?

According to the Old Story, the primary role of Jesus is that of saviour and redeemer — a saviour who saves us from death as punishment for our sin, and a redeemer who takes our punishment for us. Because he dies in our place, we no longer have to die. But of course, that's where the old tradition all goes awry. To state the obvious, we do all die. Death, with all its mystery, anxiety and grief, is our lot. Accepting the limitations of our human existence includes coming to terms with that reality. Believing in Jesus does not change that — we all still die.

The Christian tradition found a way around this obvious reality by spiritualising the idea of death, insisting that the story was never about physical death at all. The punishment for sin, they said, was alienation from God, like being thrown out of the Garden of Eden. According to this traditional view, unless someone redeems us, we will always be out-in-the-cold, as it were, alone and unable to enjoy the presence of God as we had once done before sin

Paradise Lost

entered the story. Therefore, Jesus becomes the redeemer who steps in and changes the story. Because of him, we will die physically, but we will be reunited spiritually with God after death. But where did the idea come from that *any* kind of death was the consequence of our sin? It came from the mis-interpretation of the Genesis story — an origin myth that never mentions sin, punishment or a Fall.

Furthermore, in all the teachings of Jesus that we have in the gospels, he never preaches on death as the penalty for sin. He talks a lot about loving God, loving our neighbour, having purity of heart, being peacemakers, welcoming the outcasts and disadvantaged, not judging others, giving money to the poor, sacrificing temporary pleasures to create the Kingdom of God here and now, being generous, being healed and healing. But *nowhere* does Jesus preach about all of us being eternally cut-off from God without a redeemer. There are only a few references in the New Testament that fit this doctrine, specifically at the last supper, a text that dates, not to Jesus himself but, to Paul.[34] If this were really the primary meaning of Jesus' life, wouldn't he have made it the focus of his teaching?

---

[34] For an exploration of whether the words at the last supper originate with Jesus, see *"Eat My Body, Drink My Blood"— Did Jesus Really Say That?* by James D. Tabor. Tabor is Professor in the Department of Religious Studies at the University of North Carolina and author of *The Jesus Dynasty*, 2006 and *Paul and Jesus: How the Apostle Transformed Christianity*, 2010.

An Alternative View of Humanity

Re-reading the Garden of Eden mythology has implications for the spiritual life and our relationship with others. If this ancient story is not about sin and punishment, it throws into question the idea that there is an imposed barrier between human beings and the divine. It suggests, instead, that outside of a mythical 'Paradise' is where human beings have always lived: a place where survival is fragile, pain and suffering are inevitable, relationships of love hold families and tribes together, people grieve over lost loved ones, rejoice at the birth of babies and cultural myths attempt to provide meaning for it all. This is our lot and it has always been so.

This is not to deny the existence of sin, however we name or define it. What is denied, in this re-reading of the Garden of Eden story, is that God pronounced that death was the punishment for human sin. Taking it one step further, if there was no original sin, no anti-hero, no death penalty and no need for a countering hero, then belief in a saviour is unnecessary for healthy human spirituality. No divinely imposed barrier prevents us from (metaphorically) re-entering 'the Garden'. In other words, there has never been anything, other than what we allow through our own attitudes, fears and pre-occupations, that separates us from God. Surely, it is beyond the non-existent Garden of Eden, within normal life on this planet, where human beings have always caught glimpses of the beauty of something mysteriously expansive — that which we call God.

Therefore, if the traditional interpretation of the storyline was never accurate, even metaphorically, there is no logic in the assumption that humanity is alienated from the divine. The story should be read merely as counsel to accept the natural contours of our flesh and mortality. Within our natural habitat there is, was, and always will be work, struggle, pain, love, happiness and grief. The idea of a heroic figure who reversed the consequences, either of our own choices or that of our common ancestor, is out of place. We need to look elsewhere for the significance of Jesus' life.

Without any artificial barrier between us and God, human beings have only ever needed to take a long, loving look at the everyday beauty of their lives and surroundings to restore their awareness of the divine presence. God is experienced within our mortal, messy lives, which is the heart of spiritual living. The new spiritual tapestry that we are weaving affirms this truth, while calling into question the basic doctrines of traditional Christianity.

Whatever our culture, religious tradition or lack therefore, I suggest that the challenges facing all human beings are remarkably similar. There are differences, it is true. Some cultures emphasise communal participation while some encourage individualism. Some teach us to connect closely with the land, while others emphasise our dominance over the earth. But in the end, we all must learn how to see through the eyes of others, to forgive rather than seek revenge, to grow in compassion and not bitterness, and to open ourselves to beauty rather than close our hearts. These are the everyday spiritual choices we all make as human beings, with or without a heroic saviour.

The spiritual mystics of both Eastern and Western religions speak similarly of inner experiences of connection, surrender and calm. The terminology may differ, but the inner dynamics of becoming a spiritual person cross over the differences in religion. Our common experience makes sense and aligns with the Garden of Eden story when it is interpreted as counselling us to accept the hardship inherent in the human condition.

Our imperfections and regrets should not lead us to view ourselves negatively as 'fallen'. Self-awareness should not burden us with toxic shame or guilt. Instead, we can be real about the whole of who we are — the wonder *and* the weakness. With all our sin, failures, achievements, love, courage and disappointments, it is possible for us to find the path of personal and communal growth. Self-awareness can help us to become less selfish, less fearful and more compassionate. As Ann Milliken Pederson says,

> *We were never created perfect in that first time and place, in that Garden that was our home. God said, "Good" and even "very good." But never, "Perfect" or "Done." The traditional story of the Fall implies that we fell once upon a time, from some kind of perfection that we will never have again until we reach our heavenly home. But what if we are always falling? What if those*

stories about Adam and Eve are meant to tell us that falling is built into who we are? [35]

Rather than being misled or embarrassed by the Garden of Eden story, we should place it squarely within the tradition of ancient origin myths, where it can be treasured for its wisdom concerning the human condition. We must reject the misunderstanding that we have been punished by a God who is distant and judging. Certainly, there are realities and actions that we might call 'sinful' and even 'evil' in the world. But we are not sinful merely for being human.

Christianity is losing credibility because observers notice that it is built on a foundation of guilt and fear, both promoted by religious doctrines. It is time we recognised that these doctrines can be traced all the way back to a misleading interpretation of myths, such as the Garden of Eden. We need to develop a spirituality on a different view of humanity and on gratitude that, within our imperfect lives, the divine impulse is always, faithfully present.

The path of connection to God — the pervasive power of ultimate goodness — is not through the death of one heroic God-Man, the counter-balance to sinful Adam. The path of connection to God is through an awareness of that relationship which is sometimes hidden but was never broken and never really 'lost'.

---

[35] From Ann Milliken Pederson's entry at the *Process and Faith* website. Ann is the author of *The Geography of God's Incarnation* 2013 and a contributor to P Hefner's book *Our Bodies are Selves* 2015. She is professor of Religion at Augustana College, South Dakota, USA.

CHAPTER THREE

Non-Violence and Peacemaking

> *Non-violence means not only avoiding external, physical violence but also internal violence of spirit. You not only refuse to shoot a man but you refuse to hate him.*
>
> Martin Luther King Jr.

Death and violence are part of life. We of the animal kingdom live by killing. Even vegetarians put the knife to living plants, and countless insects and worms are inadvertently killed in the harvest. It is simply not possible to live on this planet and not participate in the processes of killing and death. Making war or making peace deals with the next dimension of violence — the deliberate killing of other human beings. There is an assumption that Christianity is a peace-loving religion. However, a close examination of the biblical tradition and the central image of Christian faith — the cross — reveals that our religious tradition is problematic in relation to non-violence. In reality, the Judeo-Christian tradition contains one of the most gruesome war mythologies of all time. This chapter explores the complexity of the biblical tradition in the hope of salvaging a peace-building, life-giving thread of wisdom from that same heritage.

Ancient Tribal Traditions

Reading backwards from the ancient rites of battle, we can assume that the earliest meat-eating hunters occasionally found themselves in conflict with neighbouring tribes attempting to hunt the same herds. Hence, they developed their own mythologies of battle. Warriors were revered by their tribes because they ensured the survival of their own kin. We have no knowledge of any historical period that was devoid of violent conflict.

Religious mythologies have always attempted to provide some explanation for death, the deepest mystery of life. It is important to acknowledge that, in ancient times, tribally sanctioned killing was not synonymous with a blatant disregard for the value of human life. (In a similar way today, killing an enemy soldier in a declared war is not regarded as murder.) On the contrary, following an authorised killing, ancient tribes performed ceremonies to

A Spiritual Tapestry

honour the dead and to ensure their passage to the next life.

Historians have shown that not only hunting tribes, but also farming, crop-eating communities engaged in authorised killing. Because they were utterly dependent on the fruitfulness of the land, rites were performed for the pleasure and persuasion of the fertility gods. These included re-enactments of sexual acts, either actual or symbolic, and the sacrifice of animals. The sacrificial blood was returned to the ground, nurturing the life force of mother earth and increasing her fruitfulness. And in some tribal cultures, even human beings were sacrificed in the belief that this would ensure a good harvest.

With our scientific viewpoint, we moderns find these ancient practices abhorrent. Such a tragic waste of life. But the ancients believed utterly in their cultural myths. For them, such violent acts were not senseless slaughter, but holy acts infused with great respect for the sacrificial victims. These practices continued for millennia.[36] When people or animals were ritually sacrificed, they were honoured for giving their lives for the life of the tribe. The sacrificial victim was purified, and it

---

[36] The ancient Aztecs believed that if human beings were not regularly sacrificed to the gods, the sun itself would not shine and the world would fall apart. To obtain sacrificial victims, the Aztecs constantly waged war on their neighbours and their warriors were regarded as priests. Human sacrifice was also practised occasionally by the Vikings in northern Europe. Archaeological evidence also suggests that human sacrifice was practiced there in the pre-Viking age.

Non-Violence and Peacemaking

was believed they either returned in another life form or were united with the gods after death.

The Old Testament reflects the practice of child sacrifice in ancient Mesopotamia when Abraham intended to kill his own son, Isaac, to please his God.[37] According to the story, Abraham's God changed his mind, allowed Isaac to live and accepted a lamb sacrifice instead. Abraham had no expectation that his God would intervene and change the instruction. He was willing to kill the vulnerable and innocent boy. This legend appears to reflect the historical period during which the Semitic cultures transitioned from human to animal sacrifice.

When this story is read in churches today, it becomes an example of how our normal ethical values are set aside by our religious indoctrination. Most Christians are not horrified by the thought that the God they worship had originally told Abraham to kill his son as a child sacrifice. They are not alarmed that Abraham, the 'father of faith', was willing to perform such a violent act. They are not disturbed that Abraham placed obedience to his deity before his protective instincts as a father. We have heard the story many times, so we know how it ends. Therefore, we dismiss the idea that Abraham was ready to kill a child at the instruction of an apparent 'God'.

Instead, most Christians accept the story unquestioningly as a lesson in trust and hold Abraham in esteem for putting God before all else. Worse even, we tend

---

[37] Genesis 22: 1 - 14

to focus on the risk Abraham was taking regarding his own future. If he killed his long-awaited son, then he may not have the descendants he believed were promised to him. We make the story all about Abraham. The child's well-being, his insignificance as a person and his potential killing in the name of God are completely overlooked. Horrid things are accepted because we are told they come from God who knows the bigger picture better than we do. In the worst instances of uncritical religious belief, this is what faith looks like — a blind acceptance of things that should never be accepted, disguised as trust in God.

There seems little awareness in the Christian community that ancient Israel's conception of God developed over time. Although the story of Abraham was written down hundreds of years later, it refers to the prehistoric period in Israel's past. Abraham emerged from ancient Mesopotamia with the mental image of a 'God' who previously had been worshipped with fertility rites and child sacrifices. The potential sacrifice of Isaac is set hundreds of years before Moses, the exodus, or the ten commandments. There was no Israel and no concept of an ethical God. Tribal fertility gods were very human-like in their motives and desires.

Isaac was spared in the end, and we sense relief when a lamb is killed instead. With that feeling of relief we question the tradition no further. But we shouldn't pretend that all is well. When will the faith community debate the ethics of killing animals, not for food, but to please, persuade, or appease a God? Many Christians assume their own concept of God is the one portrayed throughout the Bible. However, there is no *one* image of God in the Bible. We do not belong to these ancient cultures and we are right to question their worldview and the way they imagined God.

The Sacrifice of Jesus

The shedding of blood is still understood to be necessary in the Christian church today, not to secure fertility or victory in battle, but to atone for sin. The church proclaims that God sent his only Son to die, not naturally but to be killed, so that the shedding of his blood as a sacrifice would provide forgiveness and salvation for those who believe in him. Christians celebrate the fact that no longer must the blood of lambs be shed, because the blood of Jesus has sufficed. God's demand for punishment has been appeased. These same Christians are then horrified when they read of ancient human blood sacrifices to appease pagan gods. Thanks to a religious, intellectual blind-spot, Christians tend not to make the natural comparison between their God and the ancient tribal gods regarding the shedding of blood.

The ancient Hebrew tradition[38] of making atonement for sin, through the blood sacrifice of a lamb on

---

[38] See the detailed instructions for the atonement sacrifices in Leviticus 16. The blood of a bull is offered to atone for the sins of the priest and the blood of a lamb to atone for the sins of the people. After praying over it, another "scapegoat" is sent out into the wilderness to carry away the sins

a temple altar, is thought to be perfectly acceptable. It is one simple step from accepting this practice to accepting the role of sacrifice in Christian theology. According to traditional Christian teaching, God demands a blood sacrifice to atone for human sin. The church teaches that the sacrificial lamb within Judaism on the Day of Atonement was always intended as an interim measure until the perfect human being would become the ultimate sacrifice once and for all. That person was Jesus, God's only perfect Son. Consequently, throughout the history of the church Jesus has been referred to as the "Lamb of God."

The broken body and the shed blood of Jesus are the focus of the most holy commemorative act of the church — the Eucharist or Holy Communion. Familiarity with a story or teaching means we are more likely to accept it. Those who have grown up within the church have always believed that the killing of Jesus is central to our relationship with God. As noted in the previous chapter, this whole theology is based on the Genesis story of the 'Fall'. Church members are taught that God pronounced death as the punishment for human sin. We all sin and consequently we all should die as God decreed, but Jesus has taken our place and his death acts as a ransom for us — a ransom paid to God. This idea is not found within the body of teaching that originated from the historical Jesus. Rather, it seems to have gained traction by the second half

---

of Israel. In practice this goat is pushed off a cliff to make sure it does not return to the people.

of the first century. By then, the meaning of being faithful to God had changed from loving one's neighbour and caring for the vulnerable, as Jesus had emphasised, to 'believing in Jesus' himself. Arguably, the historical Jesus never intended or anticipated this massive shift in the significance of his life.

Outsiders might wonder how educated people in the twenty-first century could believe in blood sacrifices for sin. It seems so out of place given our scientific worldview. Perhaps the answer lies in the psychological complexity of the concept of atonement. The fact is, all well-adjusted human beings experience feelings of guilt. We are aware of our failings and the way we occasionally disappoint ourselves and others. We know we are not perfect. Nevertheless, we naturally want to be reconciled to that good, loving Other, the One we call God. We want to feel forgiven. Non-religious people might simply say they want to feel 'OK'. Whatever language we use, these are natural feelings for all of us at times. Participating in a ceremony, in which we are proclaimed "forgiven", accepted, renewed and reconciled to God, has a natural appeal, even today.

Because the crucifixion has been domesticated within the church, we tend to gloss over the violence that is at the heart of the Eucharistic tradition. A ceremony in which one sips wine and eats a small morsel of bread seems far removed from the violent act that it symbolises. Jesus' death as a willing sacrifice for us is presented as a symbol of God's love. It feels good to be loved. Consequently, we have jettisoned any thoughts of violence from our participation in this affirming ceremony. Accordingly, modern Christians are not encouraged to face squarely what the ceremony is really all about — the violent shedding of blood and death required to appease the wrath of God.

To be clear, the death of Jesus is not at issue here. There is adequate historical evidence that Jesus was indeed crucified. It is the interpretation given to his death that is at issue. Why was Jesus killed and what impact did his death have upon his followers? Within traditional Christian teaching, his crucifixion is described as the will and plan of God. Further, it is popular for Christians to believe that Jesus himself knowingly chose the cross as a willing 'lamb to the slaughter' to redeem us from God's punishment. However, there is evidence to the contrary, usually overlooked, in the New Testament itself.

According to the Gospel narratives, although Jesus understood the risks, he did not accept his execution as inevitable. The indications are that he hoped to avoid being arrested until the very end. In Jesus' last week he publicly challenged the Roman and temple authorities. Arguably, Jesus used the people as protection, knowing that the authorities considered it too risky to arrest him in front of a large Jewish crowd.[39] The Romans did not want another riot on their hands coinciding with a Jewish religious festival. At night, he escaped to Bethany and hid out with

---

[39] Matthew 21:46

his close friends there.[40] In fact, without his overnight whereabouts being given away by one of his own group (the betrayer) Jesus may well have escaped Jerusalem alive.

Accepting the risks associated with political dissonance under the brutal rule of Pilate is quite contrary to the idea of deliberately courting death because God willed it. When we look at all the documented teachings of Jesus, providing a blood sacrifice for sin seems to have been far from his mind. Jesus was not working from the premise that his mission in life was to be killed.

A Violent God

Since childhood, we have been taught that the God of the Bible is good and loving. Therefore, we reasoned that whatever God asks must be good and ultimately loving, even if it appears harsh to us. Typically, we ignore what is in plain sight by reasoning that we are merely creatures who cannot fathom the ways of God. And so, we failed to critique the mythology of violence in which we have been immersed all our lives. A faith-filled person doesn't recognise the need to question the nature of the God they worship. We do not see ourselves as barbaric human beings who worship a violent God. We want to believe that God's love for us is unconditional. Therefore, we rationalise away the idea that God would not forgive us unless either our blood or some other innocent's blood was shed in our place.

---

[40] Matthew 21:17

A Spiritual Tapestry

The central creeds of Christian faith do not teach that it was always the nature of God to forgive. They do not teach that God's love for us is unconditional. They do not teach that the longing for our growth, healing and happiness is integral to who God is. Rather, our faith teaches us that God's wrath, God's demand for punishment applies to all of us — that without our punishment being satisfied by the killing of Jesus, we sinful people are unacceptable to a perfect God. So, who or what is God? If we are to weave a credible, nurturing spiritual tapestry for our lives from the Christian tradition, we cannot avoid these questions. In chapter one we looked briefly at two different images of God. Now we must look at the nature of God as presented in the biblical tradition, and particularly God's use of force or violence.

Is God the one who lures us towards love, compassion and beauty? Is God the one who is present to us in all our struggles, frailty and learning? Is God the one who laughs with us in our joys and weeps with us in our disappointments and loss? Is God the one who beckons us on to new beginnings when we turn towards selfishness and cowardice? Is God the one who woos us towards forgiveness when we want revenge? Or, is God the one who judges us as sinful and tells us we are unworthy? Is God the one who says we must be punished with death for our failures? Is God the one who will only forgive us if blood is shed? When we stop and think about them, we cannot really accept both of these diametrically opposed concepts of God. So, Christians either accept the conditional, demanding, violent aspect of God's nature, or simply don't think about it.

There was a time in the history of the Christian church, in fact the greater part of that history, when the wrath of God was at the forefront of its teaching. There was a time when our sin and the punishment we deserved were regularly hammered home to us from the pulpit. There was a time when our prayer to Jesus, 'the Saviour', followed an awareness that without him we were destined for hell. There was a time when fearful church members hoped only that their belief was strong enough to save them from God's condemnation at the time of their death and judgement. This is still the case for many.

It is important to recognise the different streams of thought that sit alongside each other within the Bible. There is no one, consistent, biblical view of God. I frequently hear Christians say that the God of the Old Testament was a God of punishment, but the God of the New Testament is a God of love. That simplistic distinction is problematic. Firstly, it negatively and unfairly characterises the religion of the Jews as harsh and that of Christians as loving. History proves otherwise. Secondly, a closer scrutiny of the texts themselves does not support the idea. Both violent and non-violent themes coexist within both sections of the Bible. We must choose which image of the divine will shape our lives — a violent or a compassionate God?

A Spiritual Tapestry

The Mythology of Violence in the Old Testament

In the ancient Near East, from the eighth millennium BCE onwards, communities survived by farming crops on the fertile river plains. By the sixth millennium BCE, and especially in the fifth, walls began to appear around these towns, suggesting they protected themselves from raiding warriors. The two most important raiding races were the cattle-herding Aryans of Eastern Europe and the Semites from the south, with their flocks of goats and sheep.[41] Battle legends survived for many generations and some eventually found expression within the writings of the Hebrew tribes.[42] Most likely written in the late seventh century BCE, the book of Deuteronomy tells the tale of their much earlier (1300 - 1200 BCE) conquest of the land of Canaan. The Bible has several examples of battle legends like this one:

> *When the Lord your God brings you into the land you are entering to possess and drives out before you many nations — the Hittites, Girgashites, Amorites, Canaanites, Perizzites, Hivites and Jebusites, seven nations larger and stronger than you — and when the Lord your God has delivered them over to you and you have defeated*

---

[41] As described by Joseph Campbell, *Myths to Live By*, Penguin Compass 1972, p.173.

[42] By 2500 BCE Semitic-speaking peoples had become widely dispersed throughout western Asia. In Phoenicia they became seafarers. In Mesopotamia they blended with the civilization of Sumer. Later, the Hebrews settled with other Semitic-speaking peoples in Palestine.

Non-Violence and Peacemaking

them, then you must destroy them totally. Make no treaty with them and show them no mercy.[43]

Another example from the Book of Joshua[44] is typical of the war mythology of the time. Describing the defeat of Jericho, it says,

When the trumpets sounded, the army shouted, and at the sound of the trumpet, when the men gave a loud shout, the wall collapsed; so everyone charged straight in, and they took the city. They devoted the city to the Lord and destroyed with the sword every living thing in it — men and women, young and old, cattle, sheep and donkeys... Then they burned the whole city and everything in it, but they put the silver and gold and the articles of bronze and iron into the treasury of the Lord's house. [45]

Two chapters later, we read about the conquest of the city Ai:

Then the Lord said to Joshua, "Hold out toward Ai the javelin that is in your hand, for into your hand I will deliver the city." So Joshua held out toward the city the javelin that was in his hand. As soon as he did this, the men in the ambush

---

[43] Deuteronomy 7: 1 - 2

[44] Although the book of Joshua was probably not completed until late in the sixth century BCE, this passage dates possibly from the seventh century BCE. It describes legends of the conquest of Canaan purported to have occurred around 1200 BCE. Scholars do not regard it as having much historical value.

[45] Joshua 6: 21,24

rose quickly from their position and rushed forward. They entered the city and captured it and quickly set it on fire. The men of Ai looked back and saw the smoke of the city rising up into the sky, but they had no chance to escape in any direction; the Israelites who had been fleeing toward the wilderness had turned back against their pursuers. For when Joshua and all Israel saw that the ambush had taken the city and that smoke was going up from it, they turned around and attacked the men of Ai. Those in the ambush also came out of the city against them, so that they were caught in the middle, with Israelites on both sides. Israel cut them down, leaving them neither survivors nor fugitives. But they took the king of Ai alive and brought him to Joshua.

When Israel had finished killing all the men of Ai in the fields and in the wilderness where they had chased them, and when every one of them had been put to the sword, all the Israelites returned to Ai and killed those who were in it. Twelve thousand men and women fell that day — all the people of Ai. For Joshua did not draw back the hand that held out his javelin until he had destroyed all who lived in Ai. But Israel did carry off for themselves the livestock and plunder of this city, as the Lord had instructed Joshua. So Joshua burned Ai and made it a permanent heap of ruins, a desolate place to this day. He impaled the body of the king of Ai on a pole and left it there until evening.[46]

We know the account of these conquests is not totally accurate because archaeological evidence shows that the walls of Jericho had come down long before the Hebrews began their raids. Nevertheless, they form the basis of a war mythology in which God is solely on the side of the Hebrews and all others are enemies. In contrast to the fertility rites of some cultures, here there is no respect for human life or honouring the life of victims. The God described by the early Hebrews was a tribal warrior God who showed no mercy to the enemies of the tribe. Not only were the fighting men killed, but the old and infirm, the women and the children were all slaughtered. Leaving the impaled body of the king on a pole outside the desolate ruins of the city was the ultimate act of contempt for the enemy. When this happens in modern times we call it genocide and those doing the killing, at the behest of their God, can be charged with crimes against humanity. Sadly, still today we witness horrific crimes against humanity in the name of a God or a national religious identity.

Renowned scholar and author, Joseph Campbell, studied the mythologies of numerous ancient cultures around the world. In referring to the Judeo-Christian tradition, he justifiably concluded, "we have been bred to one of the most brutal war mythologies of all time."[47]

---

[46] Joshua 8: 18 - 29
[47] Joseph Campbell, *Myths to Live By*, Penguin Compass 1972 p. 175.

A Spiritual Tapestry

Violence permeates many of the stories of the Bible. At times the origin of the violence is the human heart and is condemned, such as the first murder by Cain of his brother in Genesis 4. At other times, God is the one sanctioning the bloodlust.

We hear what we want to hear. And once we see what we want to see, we tend to look no further. That is the case with one of the oft-quoted verses of the Bible: *"Vengeance is mine," says the Lord.*[48] The values expressed in this text are ambiguous at best. The 'lighter' interpretation of this verse is that it urges us to refrain from taking revenge on those who have harmed us. It is as though, fuelled by anger, and armed with a weapon about to strike, our hand is stayed by God. We hear the teaching as, "Do not take justice into your own hands." The benefit of this interpretation is that it may reduce revenge violence. When the desire for pay-back rises in our blood, we are counselled to let it go and wait for nature to take its course. We are comforted by the belief that in the fullness of time, God will punish those who do us harm. Christians tend to remember this verse when they are wronged and hear it as spiritual direction to have patience and believe that justice and punishment will ultimately befall wrongdoers.

The 'darker' interpretation of this well-known text is obvious. It enforces the view that God is a vengeful God. It encourages us to trust that there will be vengeance — at

---

[48] Deuteronomy 32:35

the hands of God. Although it discourages personal violence and pay-back, it does not encourage change or a softening in the human heart. God is the one who will punish those who hurt us. God alone has the right to be violent and harsh. We are meant to be encouraged, knowing that one day the people we blame for having wronged us will get their 'just rewards'. There is no forgiveness within this value system.

This vengeance tradition is present in the three Abrahamic faiths through similar verses in each of their sacred writings. Surely, on balance, it is a tradition that does more harm than good. It entrenches the notion that God is vengeful rather than forgiving. It encourages a holier-than-thou attitude in those who believe that God is on their side and against their enemies. In stark contrast to Jesus' teaching on forgiveness, this theme of vengeance lacks a moral vision. It does nothing to build peace. By and large, predominantly Christian nations believe no less than others that their societies occupy the moral high-ground. But how small must our image of the divine presence be if we can believe that 'God is on our side'?

The Mythology of Violence in the New Testament

Although the convictions of the historical Jesus were quite contrary to this theme, the mythology of violence and conquest is continued to some extent in the New Testament. In a host of instances, a proclivity for anger towards and judgement and punishment of outsiders is written back into the story of Jesus. Occasionally, the authors of the Gospels put harsh, aggressive images onto the lips of Jesus himself. Many Christians still believe that at the end of the world there will be a gruesome, violent punishment for all who do not believe in Jesus as their 'Saviour'. This traditional belief is consistent with the theology of the 'Fall', 'the cross' the sacrificial lamb, the 'Judgement' and heaven and hell. And yes, it is in the Bible.

We cannot ignore the way the New Testament itself concludes. The Revelation of John of Patmos gives us that wonderful vision of a new heaven and a new earth — the new Jerusalem in which there will be no need for sun or moon because the glory of God will be its light, no more mourning or crying, with every tear wiped away (Revelation 21: 22,24). This is the glorious hope that we love to hear sung in the much loved "The Holy City".

Unfortunately, this dream of a peace-filled future is placed within another horrifically violent tradition. The vision of harmony and happiness is apparently only realised through merciless judgement and vicious punishment. We read of God's great feast where vultures feed on human flesh, of seven painful plagues thrown by angels onto unsuspecting human beings and how the 'vintage' of the earth is thrown into the wine press of the God's wrath. "And blood flowed from the wine press, as high as a horse's bridle, for a distance of about two hundred miles" (Revelation 14: 20). Even if we read this description of killing as metaphorical, the intent, the attitude of heart behind this imagery is cruel and unforgiving. It is a bloody tale, not merely of punishment but cruelty by a pitiless God. The desire for revenge through the slaughter of opponents could not be fiercer.

The fact that this bloodletting is described as the action of God rather than humans should not make it more palatable. Unfortunately, the acceptance of violence is sometimes stronger within the church because Christians feel they cannot question the 'ways of God'. In an age of Islamist terrorism, we worry how other fundamentalist religious groups read their scriptures. We hope they will be discerning about which parts of their sacred writings guide their actions. For example, we want all Muslims to focus on the peace-loving traditions within Islam and reject the passages that speak of the punishment of non-believers. The fact is, Christians need to do the same. We also need to acknowledge the destructive power of some of our own scriptural passages. If we fail to reject such bloodthirsty biblical imagery, we will have sacrificed all semblance of decent values in our commitment to an ancient warrior God.

In Revelation we are dealing with apocalyptic metaphor, most likely expressing an early second century Christian reaction to the violence of Rome. Such sentiments are perhaps understandable, coming from those whom the Roman Empire had oppressed. However, they are a far cry from Jesus' teaching of non-violence and forgiveness. Whether we read them literally or metaphorically, these gruesome images of suffering and revenge do not emanate from a merciful God. By the early second century, the image of the humble Jesus riding on a donkey into Jerusalem on Palm Sunday, had given way to that of the triumphant Christ riding on a horse with a sword coming out of his mouth.

Sadly, this is exactly the reversal of fortunes that many Christians enjoy — the moment of triumph when the world, who rejected Jesus, is proved wrong. Any of us who have been wronged may be able to understand that desire to be validated. However, do we identify the divine impulse as the one beckoning us towards forgiveness or vengeance? The vision of John of Patmos is steeped in the desire for victory and revenge. Unfortunately, the church throughout the centuries was comfortable adopting this same theology of judgement and gruesome punishment. It is a tradition, however, that has no place in the new spiritual vision for our lives.

Two Competing Spiritual Visions

Phrases such as "love your enemies and pray for those who persecute you" and "turn the other cheek" are diametrically opposed to, "The Son of Man will send out his angels, and they will weed out of his kingdom everything that causes sin and all who do evil. They will throw them into the blazing furnace, where there will be weeping and gnashing of teeth" (Matthew 13: 41-42). Which is the real Jesus? Biblical scholars conclude that the first two are consistent with the life and message of the historical Jesus. Unfortunately, the faith *of Jesus* became twisted and almost lost within what later emerged as the faith *about Jesus*. Instead of the simplistic approach which asks, "Is it biblical?" it is imperative that Christians learn to distinguish between the passages that express an ungodly acceptance of violence and Jesus' own radically non-violent convictions.

We do not need to excuse God for condoning violence or revenge. Explaining the necessity for violent punishment as a form of justice, as many do, simply does not square with the concept of mercy or forgiveness. Instead, let's admit that such passages do not express the divine impulse, but the lesser attitudes and agenda of some of the biblical authors. John Dominic Crossan attributes the violent tradition to the influence of civilisation. He suggests that the discordant texts of brutality are not due to human nature but to the overarching prevalence of social norms. Addressing the presence of both violent and radically non-violent themes in the Bible, Crossan writes,

> *The struggle is not between divine good and human evil but between, on one hand, God's radical dream for an Earth distributed fairly and non-violently among all its peoples and, on the other hand, civilization's normal dream for me keeping mine, getting yours, and having more and more forever. The tension is not between the Good Book and the bad world that is outside the book.*

A Spiritual Tapestry

> *It is between the Good Book and the bad world that are both within the book.*[49]

Turning to the birth narratives of Jesus, we hear a different sentiment — a longing for peace and all that peacemaking entails. The Messiah is pictured as poor and humble, born in an animal shelter. There is no place for such an infant within the power structures of civilised society. And yet, other New Testament authors longed for triumph over their oppressors. In their preference, the image of the Prince of Peace became the all-conquering hero who is worshipped with songs of triumphalism. These two competing spiritual visions have survived side by side within the scriptures. Sadly, those who assumed authority in the Christian church, for the best part of two thousand years, preferred the vision of power and victory.

In the twenty-first century these two traditions remain intertwined. Within the fundamentalist stream of Christianity, the violent punishment of unbelievers is still promoted. Even today, books are dedicated to threatening people with what will happen to them at the second coming of Christ if they do not believe in Jesus to save them or if they turn others away from the true doctrines. Interestingly, for many of these literal thinkers, it seems almost more important that we believe in a six-day creation and the second coming of Christ rather than have affirming personal experience of a loving and forgiving God.

---

[49] John Dominic Crossan, *Jesus and the Violence of Scripture: How to Read the Bible and Still be a Christian,* (SPCK 2015) p.31.

Many Christians seem to assume that both the judgemental and the compassionate visions of the spiritual life are valid because both are represented within the Bible. Therefore, they attempt to make these incompatible concepts fit together within the one belief system. This forced union of opposing visions is made easier in many churches now, because the cruel, violent tradition is largely ignored. The texts of violence are not read during worship services in mainstream churches and do not figure in daily reading guides for Christians. These passages are avoided, not because they have been officially rejected as ungodly, but because they are embarrassing. Preachers don't know what to do with them. The church has not given its leaders the freedom to say, "This biblical passage does not express godly values and is unlikely to have been inspired by God." If the clergy admitted that publicly, it would naturally follow that Christian congregations would begin questioning other texts and teaching. Therefore, the bloodthirsty, vengeful texts are largely unknown to those church goers who do not read the Bible for themselves. In fact, many Christians assume that this kind of violent scriptural text exists only in Islam.

When the divine violence in the Bible is acknowledged, it is usually understood as necessary for God's justice. The argument is put forward that a just and holy God cannot coexist with or ignore human sin. To escape the justified wrath of God, one needs only to believe in Jesus, after which the mercy and forgiveness of God flow generously. But do we really need to fit these contrary views of the world together? If our image of the God we worship is one of unconditional love, then why should we make room in that theology for vengeance and violence? It is simply not necessary.

These two contrasting religious attitudes developed and coexisted within different Christian communities from the beginning. The biblical authors were mere human beings. Some were immersed in a self-justifying, vengeful value system and some in a humble, peacemaking ethic. Some understood the scope of the non-violent vision of Jesus and some did not. Perhaps all the biblical authors believed they were representing a valid, faithful interpretation of their community's experience of God. But throughout history and across cultures, diverse people have believed that they understood divine revelation. Those ancient tribes who sacrificed young adults and children to their fertility gods also believed they were being faithful to *their* God's will. We do not have to explain why God would be so cruel, once we accept that such cruelty and such texts never had anything to do with God.

Peace-building in the Old Testament

Where, then, in the Old Tradition can we find the threads of peacemaking and compassion that are worthy to be woven into the new spirituality? The Torah stands on two central traditions — 1. The slaves' exodus from Egypt and wandering in the wilderness as their formative experience of liberation and 2. The ten commandments as their foundational communal ethic. The peace envisaged by the nomadic former slaves was built upon equality and distributive social justice. (In chapter four we will look more closely at the values of justice and care that shaped Israel in the wilderness.) Turning to the ten commandments, perhaps the most widely known passage in the whole Old Testament, we find a total rejection of violence.

"Thou shalt not kill"[50] is unequivocal in its anti-violent stance. The simple clarity of this instruction profoundly expresses the unassailable value of human life. It stands in stark contrast to the vicious war mythology that governed the conquest of Canaan. The first four commandments address the people's relationship to God and the next six how the Israelites should live with one another. The latter are based upon an inherent respect for the other person — their life, their relationships, their right to dignity and honesty, and their property. Respect for the other person is a very good place to begin in the peace-building process.

Given the number of wars that have been fought over territory, plant resources, oil, minerals and fertile land, the commandment to not covet anything that belongs to one's neighbour is as pertinent now as ever. We could do worse than attempt to live by these straight-forward guidelines for life. Yes, we know the Israelites, just like the

---

[50] Exodus 20: 13

rest of us, failed to adhere to this ethical vision. But if our laws can express the inherent value of life and respect for others, they add a worthy dimension to our lives.

Although we may prefer to word these behavioural instructions differently for the twenty-first century, there is an important place within spirituality for clear moral imperatives. A spiritual vision for life is not a collection of 'do's and don'ts'. Nevertheless, codes of ethics or laws that express the values we hold most dear can be a help to communal life. We know that regulations do not inspire us to step out in faith into unknown adventures, but they have a place as a basic requirement of love and respect for others. And in this case, amidst all the murders and crimes against humanity also recorded in the Old Testament, the commandment against killing and selfish aggression offered the ancient Hebrews an alternative vision.

Moving beyond Israel's central commandments, we can also find some beautiful images of peace in the Old Testament. This passage is from the prophet Isaiah.

> *The wolf will live with the lamb,*
> *the leopard will lie down with the goat,*
> *the calf and the lion and the yearling together;*
> *and a little child will lead them.*
> *The cow will feed with the bear,*
> *their young will lie down together,*
> *and the lion will eat straw like the ox.*
> *The infant will play near the cobra's den,*
> *and the young child will put its hand*
> *into the viper's nest.*

Non-Violence and Peacemaking

*They will neither harm nor destroy
on all my holy mountain,
for the earth will be filled with the
knowledge of the Lord
as the waters cover the sea.*[51]

Isaiah's vision reads like a utopian dream. Even those of us do not believe in utopia find it inspiring. A vision does not have to be believed literally to inspire. As a poetic expression of harmony, this text gives us an alternative set of values towards which we can move. *They will neither harm nor destroy on all my holy mountain* gives voice to the longing for a positive peace. The same prophet penned this other vision of a world without war.

*Many peoples shall come and say,
"Come, let us go up to the mountain of the
LORD, to the house of the God of Jacob;
that he may teach us his ways
and that we may walk in his paths."
For out of Zion shall go forth instruction,
and the word of the LORD from Jerusalem.
He shall judge between the nations,
and shall arbitrate for many peoples;
they shall beat their swords into plowshares,
and their spears into pruning hooks;
nation shall not lift up sword against nation,
neither shall they learn war any more.* [52]

---

[51] Isaiah 11: 6-9
[52] Isaiah 2: 3-4

The ploughshare, an agricultural tool, represents human inventiveness to feed and generally benefit the community. The sword represents human inventiveness for killing and war. Since World War II all nations have been keenly aware of the unutterably destructive force of nuclear weapons. The 'Megatons to Megawatts Project' is about the dismantling of nuclear weapons and the redirection of their power to civilian power stations. At the time of writing, the USA is attempting to convince North Korea to embark on a unilateral denuclearisation program. The rest of the world looks on warily, aware that the vision of peace is not strong even in the nation doing the persuading. And the people for whom this passage was originally written, the Israelites, now the Jewish nation, do not promote peace on 'the mountain of the Lord' (Jerusalem). Thousands of years after Isaiah's prophecy, the vision of warring tribes beating swords into ploughshares has not yet been embraced.

We know that peace is not merely the absence of war. Conflict and hatred can smoulder for years, even generations, without any official war taking place. Countless historical examples have demonstrated that unless there is both an improvement in the living conditions of communities in conflict and some work towards reconciliation, violence will inevitably resurface. Signing a peace accord or treaty is only the first step in peace-building. We only need think of the modern Israel / Palestine conflict, the Bosnia / Serbia conflict, or the Northern Ireland / England conflict to see how peace

Non-Violence and Peacemaking

depends upon more than a cessation of violence. The question is, does the peace-building vision in the Old Testament recognise this reality?

A later passage from Isaiah, probably from a different prophetic author about the time of the restoration of Jerusalem following the exile, offers the most promising vision of a comprehensive peace in the Hebrew Bible. Although idealistic, it fleshes out the communal requirements for a lasting peace.

> *For I am about to create new heavens*
> *and a new earth; the former things shall not be*
> *remembered or come to mind.*
>
> *But be glad and rejoice forever in what I am*
> *creating; for I am about to create Jerusalem as*
> *a joy, and its people as a delight.*
> *I will rejoice in Jerusalem, and delight in my*
> *people; no more shall the sound of weeping be*
> *heard in it, or the cry of distress.*
> *No more shall there be in it*
> *an infant that lives but a few days,*
> *or an old person who does not live out a lifetime;*
> *for one who dies at a hundred years will be*
> *considered a youth, and one who falls short of a*
> *hundred will be considered accursed.*
>
> *They shall build houses and inhabit them;*
> *they shall plant vineyards and eat their fruit.*
> *They shall not build and another inhabit;*
> *they shall not plant and another eat;*
> *for like the days of a tree shall the days of my*

> *people be, and my chosen shall long enjoy the work of their hands.*
>
> *They shall not labour in vain,*
> *or bear children for calamity;*
> *for they shall be offspring blessed by the Lord —*
> *and their descendants as well.*
> *Before they call I will answer,*
> *while they are yet speaking I will hear.*[53]

The poetry is inspiring, beautiful and captures the essential qualities that make for peace — full lives that are not cut short by violence or disease; the freedom to build and live in one's own home without eviction or crippling rent; social justice where ordinary people can enjoy the fruits of their labour; no exploitation by absentee landowners; and a nurturing relationship with a God who listens. Whenever a society is depressed by economic injustice and the people robbed of the enjoyment and benefits of their work, the seeds of violent up-risings are sown. This principle applies both to civil practices within nations and to the way we treat our enemies following wars. There is no point in dreaming of peace unless we are willing to work for social justice and freedom for everyone.

Unfortunately, the following verses, appearing just prior to the image of the wolf living with the lamb, show how the vision of peace was intertwined with the assumption of God's judgement and punishment. Notice how the spiritual leader will "slay the wicked."

---

[53] Isaiah 65: 17-24

He will not judge by what he sees with his eyes,
or decide by what he hears with his ears;
but with righteousness he will judge the needy,
with justice he will give decisions for the poor
of the earth. He will strike the earth with the
rod of his mouth; with the breath of his lips
he will slay the wicked.
Righteousness will be his belt
and faithfulness the sash around his waist.[54]

How wonderful that the needy and the poor will be given justice. And perhaps we are tempted to agree that we do not want 'the wicked' living in our peaceful society. But who are the 'wicked'? The Hebrew Bible provides only rare texts that distinguishes between the righteous and the wicked and this is not one of them. Without a theology of the creative transformation of us all, religion frequently divides humanity into two groups — the faithful and the wicked. But we know we don't fit into those simplistic categories. If this vision of peace presented a mature view of all human beings having the potential for both good and evil, the image of the wicked being slain would be redundant.

The dualistic thinking of the righteous vs wicked, God's people vs God's enemies permeates most of the Old Testament. (In the first story in chapter eight I will explore one of those rare moments in the Old Testament when this dualistic worldview is challenged.) Sadly, the vision of

---

[54] Isaiah 11: 3-5

peace in Isaiah still excluded enemies or those considered wicked. Perhaps this limitation in the scriptural vision of peace still contributes to so many failed attempts at peacemaking around the world. Real peace-building requires us to let go of our self-righteousness and embrace, as equals, those who live differently.

In a similar vein, we read in Zechariah 2 the vision of the rebuilt Jerusalem following the Israelites' return from exile in Babylon. In it we catch just a glimpse of a larger hope, a city without walls.

> *Then the angel who talked with me came forward, and another angel came forward to meet him, and said to him, "Run, say to that young man: Jerusalem shall be inhabited like villages without walls, because of the multitude of people and animals in it. For I will be a wall of fire all around it, says the LORD, and I will be the glory within it."*[55]

For a moment, the prophet envisages a city whose welcome of outsiders was wholehearted and who did not live by fighting. Walls are a fortification for war. A city without walls is a city built for peace. The hope of living without war was somewhere deep in the ancient Israelite spiritual dream. But again, it did not last. The vision of becoming a community without war could not win over those who saw life in more practical, military terms. In Nehemiah we read that Jerusalem was rebuilt with walls

---

[55] Zechariah 2: 3-5

all over again. "Then I said to them, 'You see the trouble we are in: Jerusalem lies in ruins, and its gates have been burned with fire. Come, let us rebuild the wall of Jerusalem, and we will no longer be in disgrace'" (Nehemiah 2: 17). No thought of any other way to be a city or nation. It seems that the ancient Israelite commitment to peace, as in any other nation then or now, was limited by the urge of self-protection and the assumed need of preparation for war.

We operate from the same urge and the same assumptions today. Our walls are our ships, submarines, fighter planes and nuclear weapons or our alliances with those who have them. We also have not been able to conceive of other ways to be a nation. We dare not rely on our abilities in developing international relationships for peace and understanding. Rather than weapons being a 'back-up plan' if our commitment to peacebuilding fails, our defence forces and alliances are regarded as the front line of our national security. I remember once seeing a prophetic vision printed on, of all things, a linen tea-towel that a young mother had hung on her wall. It read, "I dream of a day when our schools and hospitals have all the resources they need while the military holds cake stalls to raise money for submarines."

On balance, the Old Testament is weighted towards war and violence. God is frequently depicted as the divine warrior who fights on the side of Israel and defeats her enemies in battle. Nevertheless, there are threads of hope to retain for our new spiritual tapestry. Rare texts that value peace include the commandment against killing, the vision of ultimate harmony in Isaiah, and the momentary hope of rebuilding Jerusalem as a city without walls or war. There are strong indications in both the Prophets and in Exodus that some ancient Israelites dreamed of social justice as the basis of a peaceful society. Furthermore, they understood this vision of peace and justice as the way of God.

Peace-building in the New Testament

We find many more threads of peacemaking in the stories of Jesus, the 'Prince of Peace'. Although the faction of Christianity that came to dominate the church for two millennia focussed on belief in the divinity of Jesus, the values and teachings of Jesus have remained as a minority report within the New Testament. Within these preserved stories we discover what mattered to Jesus himself. It is to these stories and teachings that we now turn for inspiration on peacemaking.

Within this alternative tradition, the historical Jesus was passionate about seeking justice for the poor and oppressed. He prophetically challenged the Roman overlords, not with violence, but with words and ideas. He urged the people to return to the wisdom and strength of their inner lives. He taught that what is in the heart matters more than outward religious observance.

Non-Violence and Peacemaking

Jesus' teaching aimed to revitalise the spiritual foundations of Judaism. From the sacred Jewish writings in which he was trained, he focussed on the most radical commands to love God and neighbour. He refused to condemn the ordinary man and woman and urged an endless attitude of forgiveness. He showed respect for the humble person and preached about the spiritual dangers of wealth. Most importantly for this discussion, and consistent with all these convictions, Jesus practiced a radical ethic of non-violence.

Some have suggested that Jesus acted violently when he drove the money-lenders out of the temple.[56] However, three Gospels do not mention a whip in their description of this event and even in John, there is no implication that Jesus used a whip on a person or even an animal. The incident is best understood as a calculated prophetic action designed to condemn the corrupt temple system. Jesus taught his followers not to take up arms but to protest at injustice with symbolic action and non-violent solidarity. He warned that hatred is as sinful as murder, and that peacemaking is a godly calling. Most radically, Matthew's Jesus says,

> *You have heard that it was said, 'Love your neighbour and hate your enemy.' But I tell you, love your enemies and pray for those who persecute you, that you may be sons of your Father in heaven. He causes His sun to rise on*

---

[56] John 2:13-16; Matthew 21: 12-13; Mark 11: 15-19; Luke 19: 45-48

> *the evil and the good and sends rain on the righteous and the unrighteous.* [57]

Vengeance breeds vengeance and leads to an escalation of violence. Although taking up arms was always a possibility in the atmosphere of heightened tension and military oppression in which he lived, Jesus did not want to see an eruption of violence in his homeland. At the time of his arrest we read,

> *Then they came and laid hands on Jesus and arrested him. Suddenly, one of those with Jesus put his hand on his sword, drew it, and struck the slave of the high priest, cutting off his ear. Then Jesus said to him, "Put your sword back into its place; for all who take the sword will perish by the sword.*[58]

When our lives are threatened, most of us would consider fighting. But committed to non-violence, Jesus would not fight nor allow others to fight for him. He had cast a vision of an alternative kind of society that was not based on physical force and he lived by that vision until the end. A few of his followers had grasped the vision. But it made no significant dent in the military mindset of those who put him to death.

As he was dying in excruciating pain, Jesus famously prayed for his oppressors, "Father forgive them, because they do not understand what they are doing." In

---

[57] Matthew 5: 43-45
[58] Matthew 26: 50-52

this extreme circumstance, he chose to let go of the need for validation and the desire for revenge. Without intending to speak for Jesus, his profound prayer of forgiveness was, in effect, expressing this kind of sentiment towards his enemies: *I understand that you do not see the vision of God's kingdom as I see it. You are operating from another perspective, that I oppose. But you are also human beings and I do not want you to suffer so that I can have revenge. I long for God to be present to you and to me. I will not hold on to the emotional pain of fury that would rob me of my identity at the end of my life. I will not become the cause of more hatred and bloodshed. Therefore, I forgive you. I let go all anger and blame and I ask God to forgive also."* None of us who claim to be followers of Jesus can live from an ethic of vengeance, blame or hatred.

And so, we have two contrary streams of thought expressed in the New Testament, one focussed on sacrifice, judgement, religious identity and supportive of organisation and hierarchy; the other committed to non-violence, social justice and supportive of non-hierarchical community. The first evolved into the dominant theology of the church and the second into a values-based vision for life that has remained as a minority report concerning the life of Jesus. These two theologies are vastly different and have always been in tension with one another in Christian thought.

The first stream of thought mentioned above projected the image of a powerful God, focussed upon Jesus' death as a blood sacrifice and emphasised his triumphant resurrection. It proclaimed the ultimate victory of God, Jesus and the church over all others through earthly and heavenly rule. Its adherents developed the doctrines of the divinity of Jesus, the Christ and the Trinity. Failure to believe its creeds meant exclusion from the community of the 'saved'. It produced a theology of unique claims to truth that supported a powerful religious institution for two thousand years.

The second stream of thought mentioned above was prominent within the very earliest group of Jesus' friends and followers. James, the brother of Jesus, provided leadership for the group, which was based in Jerusalem. They embraced the values and teachings that they had learned while on the road with Jesus. They practised a communal life in which women, the poor, the wealthy and the outcasts were all included fully.[59] They called their renewal movement 'the Way' and referred to themselves as 'followers of the Way'. This way of life was built on an integrated set of values that included forgiveness, humility, compassion, social justice and spiritual transformation. They attempted to live by the faith *of Jesus* rather than making him the focus of their faith. They continued to worship at the synagogue and, rather than turn away from Judaism, they sought to revitalise it through the spiritual insights of Jesus. They kept Jesus'

---

[59] Although the description of this communal life in Acts 4 is probably a very romantic, idealised version of the reality, it nevertheless points to the values of the early disciples in Jerusalem.

Non-Violence and Peacemaking

teachings alive orally until some of their stories were later incorporated into the Gospels.

Biblical scholar, Lorraine Parkinson, has shown that both streams of thought developed as far back as the first century.[60] The second, values-based tradition of the disciples was overwhelmed by the development of the creedal, authoritative religion that became traditional Christianity as we know it. But the disciples' understanding of 'the Way' was never fully lost and is kept alive through the stories of Jesus within the scriptures. This alternative tradition urged and continues to urge a commitment to non-violence and peacemaking. This is the visionary thread I want to incorporate into the new spiritual perspective.

Non-Violence, Peacemaking and Us

The spiritual tapestry I seek to weave is not intended to be naïve or impossible to live by. Because some level of aggression is always present in communal life, a vision for non-violence and peacebuilding can seem unreachable. Must our commitment to non-violence be absolute? If Jesus promoted an ethic of non-violence, does that mean God always leads us away from the possibility of injuring another person? There are some that would answer emphatically "Yes". According to the new image of

---

[60] Lorraine Parkinson, *Made on Earth: How Gospel writers created the Christ*, Spectrum, 2015.

God presented in chapter one, God always interacts with us persuasively, not coercively. Violence harms a person physically, restricts their freedom and, by definition, is contrary to the nature of God.

However, there are some who hold that God's power is non-coercive, but who also concede that on rare occasions a violent act may be required for the greater good. For instance, we may intervene with physical force to prevent a person being harmed by an impending accident. Or more pointedly, if all other measures have failed, violence may be necessary to prevent the murder of others. For instance, Christian theologian, Dietrich Bonhoeffer, was part of a plot to kill Hitler. (The plot failed, and he spent the rest of his life imprisoned.) This same moral logic is used by people of faith who fight in wars, believing their actions are protecting ordinary people from the violence of aggressors. In these cases, the choice to use violence would be 'the best for the impasse',[61] an awful choice but still the best option in a dreadful situation.

Perhaps total non-violence is impossible. However, we can be counselled by the conviction of theologian, John Cobb, who refers us to process philosopher, Alfred North Whitehead.

> *Whitehead pointed out that "life is robbery." For one creature to live, other lives are sacrificed.*

---

[61] This was the term coined by process philosopher, Alfred North Whitehead. It refers to the best option towards which we are lured by the 'initial aim of life' in a given situation, even though that option looks meagre because the context is so limited.

Certainly, human life involves enormous killing of other creatures. That is the kind of world we live in. But Whitehead goes on to say that the robber needs justification. The fact that we must destroy to live does not mean that the destruction is not evil. Because it is evil, we should minimize it.[62]

Killing other human beings must be a desperate last resort once all other options to save others are exhausted. We know Jesus lived by a non-violent ethic and it cost him his life. Too often we hasten to fight, at least verbally, when we feel affronted. Too often we hope our armed forces will crush our enemies rather than publicly question the need for war. Choosing the non-violent path is often the most unpopular stance. Looking for opportunities to improve global social justice as a way to decrease violence does not win many votes in our nation. Recognising that there are no easy answers when faced with aggression from others, we must at least consider all non-violent possibilities if we claim to follow Jesus. This challenges us to counter our natural tendency to fight. Perhaps the moral challenge to 'turn the other cheek' is a practical option for all of us, individually and communally, more often than we would prefer to admit.

History is littered with 'saints' who demonstrated this radical non-violent spirit — Mohandas Gandhi, Martin Luther King Jr and Nelson Mandela are well-known names

---

[62] John Cobb, *Ask Dr Cobb*, January 2000 at https://processandfaith.org

amongst many lesser-known others. Enormous change has been achieved in real terms for millions of people through non-violent resistance. At times these courageous leaders have had to 'walk a tightrope' as it were — resisting authority but needing to quell the tendency of the oppressed community to lash out with force when tensions were high.

Gathering together threads of wisdom from the Christian tradition to incorporate into a new spiritual tapestry requires discernment. That has been starkly evident in this chapter. Honesty forces us to acknowledge the presence of an unacceptable level of violence that touches the heart of the old tradition. The desire for revenge, outright bloodlust, the divine stance of judgement and punishment, and the linking of forgiveness and mercy to the shedding of blood are very prominent in both the Old and New Testaments. Some Christians will continue to explain how these mythologies are consistent with a loving God. But the rest of us sense in our spirits that this religious worldview is *not* holy. These values do *not* speak to us of a God of goodness, hope and beauty.

At the same time, we can treasure other biblical passages that challenge us to forgive, to respect the other, to refuse to engage in unnecessary killing, and to do what is needed to build peace. Both the Old and New Testaments provide glimpses of how peace can be built upon forgiveness and social justice. Jesus, the 'Prince of Peace', lived according to his own values of non-violent resistance to evil and radical forgiveness of enemies.

CHAPTER FOUR

Abundance, Scarcity or Enough?

> *Give us today our daily bread
> and forgive us our debt
> as we forgive the debts of those
> who are indebted to us.*
>
> The Lord's Prayer

If our faith has nothing to say about poverty and the global concentration of wealth, it is unable to address a major social / moral crisis of our time — the widening gap between the rich and poor. The new spiritual paradigm emerging from the tatters of the old Christian tradition speaks directly to this dilemma. Our spiritual perspective participates in one or the other of two competing worldviews regarding power, the distribution of resources, and communal relationships.

There are the two worldviews that vie for our allegiance, 1) The *Empire of Power* assumes scarce resources and encourages the self-protective inclination to accumulate at the expense of competitors. Consumerism, integral to this dominant perspective within our society, produces addictions, alienation and anxiety.

2) The *Great Economy* or *Kin-dom of God* assumes an abundance of resources as gift and urges generosity towards others on the assumption that sharing resources benefits the whole society. This gift-economy develops community, compassion and gratitude.

This is not a party-political argument over the economy. The fact is, most political parties derive their philosophy from shared assumptions of scarce resources, class struggle, business competitiveness, the individual's aspirations to material wealth and the necessity for continual economic 'growth'. How to facilitate those essential economic processes and balance them with the needs of the whole society is hotly debated between parties. But the assumption of competition — that for some to win others must lose — is regarded as inevitable by a majority in both the right and the left.

Even mainstream economists say that our world capitalist economies, based on these assumptions, are heading for crisis and we need a 'new narrative'. According to American economic journalist and author, William Greider,

Abundance, Scarcity or Enough?

Above all, we need a new narrative of American capitalism. Our nation tells itself a strangely masochistic version of the American dream: If you want to be truly happy, you need to be truly rich. Most understand this is a mirage. In our new condition beyond scarcity, the economy of "more" has turned upon itself, tearing the social fabric and weakening family and community life, piling up discontents alongside the growing plenty. We need a new story, suitable for a new abundance. As it presently functions, capitalism encourages human pathologies — embodying irresponsibility as a central requirement in its operating routines... What we are after is more room for life itself. More power for ordinary people to control their lives and work. More equity in the distribution of rewards. More nurturance of society's softer assets: babies and children, the fate of the Earth and other living things, the grace notes of community life.[63]

When economists and thinkers outside of the faith community say our society needs a new narrative, we should take note.

---

[63] William Greider (1936 -) is an American economics journalist and author. His books include *Secrets of the Temple: How the Federal Reserve Runs the Country*, 1987; *Who Will Tell the People? The Betrayal of American Democracy*, 1992; *Fortress America: The American Military and the Consequences of Peace*, 1998; and *The Soul of Capitalism: Opening Paths to a Moral Economy*, 2003. The above quote comes from *Beyond Scarcity: A New Story for American Capitalism*, an excerpt from *The Soul of Capitalism* which appeared in a 2003 issue of *Business Ethics*.

A Story of Abundance

In this chapter, I draw upon one of the old stories of the Judaeo-Christian tradition to indicate how a new narrative might be imagined. The new spirituality that we are exploring links directly into this longing for what Greider called, "the grace notes of community life".

Those who went to Sunday School as children will know the story. Please read it closely now, with adult eyes. The core message is not usually taught in Sunday Schools, nor even in most churches.

> *The whole congregation of the Israelites set out from Elim; and Israel came to the wilderness of Sin... The whole congregation of the Israelites complained against Moses and Aaron in the wilderness. The Israelites said to them, "If only we had died by the hand of the Lord in the land of Egypt, when we sat by the fleshpots and ate our fill of bread; for you have brought us out into this wilderness to kill this whole assembly with hunger."*

> *Then the Lord said to Moses, "I am going to rain bread from heaven for you, and each day the people shall go out and gather enough for that day. In that way I will test them, whether they will follow my instruction or not. On the sixth day, when they prepare what they bring in, it will be twice as much as they gather on other days." So Moses and Aaron said to all the Israelites, "In the evening you shall know that it*

was the Lord who brought you out of the land of Egypt, and in the morning you shall see the glory of the Lord, because he has heard your complaining against the Lord...

In the evening quails came up and covered the camp; and in the morning there was a layer of dew around the camp. When the layer of dew lifted, there on the surface of the wilderness was a fine flaky substance, as fine as frost on the ground. When the Israelites saw it, they said to one another, "What is it?" [manna] For they did not know what it was. Moses said to them, "It is the bread that the Lord has given you to eat. This is what the Lord has commanded: 'Gather as much of it as each of you needs, an omer to a person according to the number of persons, all providing for those in their own tents.'"

The Israelites did so, some gathering more, some less. But when they measured it with an omer, those who gathered much had nothing over, and those who gathered little had no shortage; they gathered as much as each of them needed.

And Moses said to them, "Let no one leave any of it over until morning." But they did not listen to Moses; some left part of it until morning, and it bred worms and became foul. And Moses was angry with them. Morning by morning they gathered it, as much as each needed; but when the sun grew hot, it melted.

On the sixth day they gathered twice as much food, two omers apiece. When all the leaders of the congregation came and told Moses, he said to them, "This is what the Lord has commanded: 'Tomorrow is a day of solemn rest, a holy sabbath to the Lord; bake what you want to bake and boil what you want to boil, and all that is left over put aside to be kept until morning.'" So they put it aside until morning, as Moses commanded them; and it did not become foul, and there were no worms in it. Moses said, "Eat it today, for today is a sabbath to the Lord; today you will not find it in the field. Six days you shall gather it; but on the seventh day, which is a sabbath, there will be none."

On the seventh day some of the people went out to gather, and they found none. The Lord said to Moses, "How long will you refuse to keep my commandments and instructions? See! The Lord has given you the sabbath, therefore on the sixth day he gives you food for two days; each of you stay where you are; do not leave your place on the seventh day." So, the people rested on the seventh day.

The house of Israel called it manna; it was like coriander seed, white, and the taste of it was like wafers made with honey... The Israelites ate manna forty years, until they came to a habitable land; they ate manna, until they came to the border of the land of Canaan. An omer is a tenth of an ephah.[64]

I presume we have moved beyond questions of whether these events really happened. This story represents the imagination of early Israel as her people reflected upon their journey of discovery as a community of faith. In our day, church members have been taught that this is a story about trusting God to provide for our needs. Although this feel-good message is comforting, it misses the central point.

The bedrock of Israel's self-identity has always been her ancestors' journey from slavery in the Egyptian Empire to freedom, with land and a God of her own. But that was a difficult transition to make. It required those early generations to examine and reject the values of their earlier oppressors. They needed to develop a new perspective, not only about God but about how God wanted them to live with each other.

How should their social life be ordered? They had escaped from a hierarchical society where they had experienced the injustices inflicted on those at the bottom. Did their God now want them, in freedom, to create another hierarchical society where others would experience the horrors of slavery?

If not, they would need a *new story*, new values and a new vision. The lost, homeless, Hebrew slaves had to learn two lessons, beyond how to find sustenance in the

---

[64] Exodus 16: 1 – 36 excerpts

harsh wilderness environment. This legend of the gift of manna during their homeless wanderings was their first experience of creating a 'new story', a different society with vastly different values from that of the Empire. Their 'new story' has an important place in *our New Story*.

The First Principle of the New Story – Fair Distribution

According to the legend (which was committed to writing hundreds of years after the events it describes) God first instructed the Hebrews on the fair distribution of resources. Each morning they were to gather only enough bread-like substance to feed their household for that day. If they had a large family to feed, they could gather more than those with small families. And none of them could gather more than what they needed for that day alone. Tomorrow would be another day and there would be another day's manna. They were not allowed to hoard more than they needed. And when some of them tried it, they found the substance melted and was wasted. So, their first lesson was against the accumulation of wealth. The material gifts for life and sustenance should circulate, not accumulate.

Perhaps the most inspiring sentence of the story is "… Those who gathered much had nothing over, and those who gathered little had no shortage." This is not a miracle about bread falling from heaven. This is a miracle about the restraint of greed, fair distribution and no-one going hungry. It doesn't matter if it ever happened exactly as the book of Exodus tells it. The narrative, composed many generations later, conveys the message of how to create a different society from the Empire of Power. According to this early Hebrew legend, *there is such a thing as having too much and there is such a thing as having too little.*

Both extreme affluence and poverty are contrary to the ways of God. We are not all alike and we find ourselves in different circumstances. Some have greater needs than others. But a vision of equality means each person in a community has the natural right to whatever is needed for their sustenance and the adequate care of their household. Restraint by those who had the strength and possibility to gather an excess of manna, meant that there was enough to go around. Even those who were weak and took longer to gather what they needed, didn't miss out because others accepted the principle of fairness.

How relevant this story still is these thousands of years later! Today, whole societies suffer from systemic poverty and sections of our own community struggle to pay power bills or purchase their children's school needs because of the unequal distribution of resources. Perhaps the practical answers to poverty may only be understood by those with economic training. But the will to find a solution comes from all of us who understand the moral imperative of sustenance and dignity for all. As a political / economic worldwide community, we need to consider the alternative values of human equality, fair distribution and restraint on overconsumption. Do we really believe in fairness when we set a fair wage? Have we lost our distaste of overconsumption? The rich get richer and the poor get poorer in the Empire of Power. That is normal in societies governed by the dominant beliefs of Empire. But an alternative spiritual vision challenges that ugly reality.

Before moving on, it is worth taking a look at the second account of this legend in the book of Numbers. According to this version, again the people were dissatisfied, complaining that life in Egypt was better than what they had in the wilderness. They preferred the food they were given as slaves to the food they were able to gather as free people. But notice that in this version of the story there were no limits on their gathering.

> *Now a wind went out from the Lord and drove quail in from the sea. It scattered them up to two cubits deep all around the camp, as far as a day's walk in any direction. All that day and night and all the next day the people went out and gathered quail. No one gathered less than ten homers. Then they spread them out all around the camp. But while the meat was still between their teeth and before it could be consumed, the anger of the Lord burned against the people, and he struck them with a severe plague. Therefore, the place was named Kibroth Hattaavah,*

because there they buried the people who had craved other food.[65]

Here, they didn't gather the quail only in the evening but all day. They didn't gather only what was needed for their own household, some little and some more according to the size of their family. No, all of them gathered at least ten homers. They all just took as much as they could, irrespective of their need. There was an excess of quail and no restraint by the people. Overconsumption ran riot. But it all turned sour. The punishing God of their imagination punished them with a plague because of their complaints, lack of gratitude and lack of restraint.

Symbolically, the place was called "Kibroth Hattaavah" which means *graves of craving* or *graves of greed*. In this version of the story the people did not learn about fair distribution and enough for everyone. They were driven by greed as the Egyptians had been. Their fight for the accumulation of scarce resources was based on the same worldview as the Empire of Power from which they had escaped. They remained slaves to the driving force of greed. In this alternative version of the legend, God still provided for the people's needs. But the people did not understand the principle of gift and abundance. Scarcity governed their mindset, and greed, rather than fairness, governed their actions. It is a sombre tale, pointing to the destructive nature of communal life, if restraint is not learned.

---

[65] Numbers 11: 31 - 34

The Second Principle of the New Story – Take Time Out

The next lesson that the first generation of free Hebrews learned came though the instruction to rest for a day. On the sixth day they could gather enough food for two days and it wouldn't melt or rot at the end of the day. They could take measures to preserve it by cooking so that they didn't need to work at gathering on the seventh day. That was to be a day of rest. Those who tested it out went out to gather and found no manna. So, at this early stage, God enforced the Sabbath concept by refusing to play the game any other way. But why force people to take a rest?

The wisdom of the Sabbath concept has largely been lost within institutional religion. In Judaism it devolved into an oppressive set of regulations about what one can and can't do on the Sabbath. There are a few stories in the New Testament about Jesus breaking the Sabbath rules to make the point that the vision of the Sabbath had been lost. Ironically, the Christian church also became obsessive-compulsive about the Sabbath rest. That has changed now. However, only last century in the Methodist Church in Australia, for example, families were burdened by rules surrounding the Sabbath. Members were not allowed to play social tennis or other recreational sports on a Sunday afternoon, even if they had attended church in the morning. A Christian mother dared not wash on a Sunday, even if she needed to deal with a baby's soiled nappies. Enforced rest became stressful for some and did not include recreation. It seems religion had lost sight of the original wisdom of the Sabbath.

What contribution can this legendary introduction of the Sabbath make to a renewed spiritual perspective in our own day? Notice, firstly, that this wasn't a story about going without. The people did not fast on the seventh day but gathered twice as much on the previous day so there would still be enough to eat. It was a story about placing limits on labour and production. At regular, weekly intervals, the people were required to stop work. Even if we are only gathering from what nature freely offers, it is easy to presume that we are providing for our own needs. Being forced to rest, while still having enough to survive, reminds us that *we* do not create wealth, that the good things of life are *gifts from beyond ourselves.*

The produce of the earth is abundant and generous. We do not create it, we gather it. In our industrial society, although vast stores of non-living commodities are produced by human labour, our bodies are still nourished organically from nature, even when it is farmed. The abundant gifts of the natural world are what we sow, fertilise, collect and distribute for the sustenance of human life. The 'rest' of the Sabbath was a lesson in remembering that giftedness of life. We all receive from this bounty in one way or another.

Sabbath rest is a correction to the arrogance that assumes we provide for ourselves. We do not. We do not make the sun shine, or the rain fall, or the rivers run. We do not create the beaches and the ocean in which we delight to swim. We do not create the rainforests in which we walk or the mountains that we climb for refreshment. We work, we gather, we process, we sell, we buy at the market. But we do all these within the sustaining framework of the natural world which we do not create or earn. Recovering an awareness of that gift is central to the new spirituality. Accepting the limits of our own strength and ability, we pause to reflect upon the giftedness of life itself. Gratitude is the benefit to the soul from 'taking time out'.

During earlier decades in the Australian community, governments legislated support for the church's commitment to the Sabbath (Sunday as opposed to Saturday in Judaism). In that social context it was easier to take time out for rest. Shops, businesses, government departments and banks all closed for the day. There was a time when even sporting competitions were played only on Saturdays. It is definitely not as convenient these days to set aside time for rest and reflection on the giftedness of life. Without external regulations, individuals need to choose their own way of halting production and calling 'time out' for the soul.

'Holding out' for annual leave, then rushing away on a non-stop overseas holiday rarely benefits the soul in the same way as pausing for rest at regular intervals throughout the year. Stress levels are high in our cities and so many seem to be time-poor. It has become almost countercultural to have a day of simple leisure without any pressing demands.

The ancient Hebrews perceived correctly that we all need to break the cycle of work regularly, to give ourselves the mental and physical gift of rest and reflection. The original concept of Sabbath acknowledged the limits of human effort. We are not superhuman. However able or focussed we are, we need the humility to recognise our limitations and live within them.

Whatever income our efforts are earning, we need to recognise when enough is enough. Working one more day beyond personal exhaustion or demanding staff work overtime to increase profits is not healthy or just. Workers are exploited by companies who do not respect their needs for rest and refreshment. According to the ancient story, the people were instructed not to gather food on the seventh day, to take a rest. There is wisdom in recognising that production and consumption are not the whole of life. We need to make space for what William Greider calls the "softer assets: babies and children, the fate of the Earth and other living things, the grace notes of community life."

If we are totally driven by production, profits and growth, our lives will be out of kilter. Those who are self-employed, manage the business, or take casual work must themselves decide when to stop. If we wait until we think we have plenty stored up for a rainy day before taking time off, we will suffer from a depletion of soul. Employees with permanent work and paid weekends are better off in this regard. Yet still, accounts of people's weekends can sound like a self-imposed, non-stop rush of duties and activities with little space for refreshment of body and soul. It seems that even our children now have crowded diaries, filled by parents who do not model regular rest and relaxation.

A frantic consumption of entertainment does not equate to the inner letting-go of demands upon our person. We take pride in telling others we are busy, as though our worth is measured by the demands upon our time. Consequently, we are in danger of losing the ability to breathe. However and whenever we observe it, Sabbath is for breathing, breathing deeply.

Social Justice in the New Story – The Sabbatical Year, Gleaning and The Jubilee

Later in the story of ancient Israel, once the community settled and became farmers, the people observed (or intended to observe) some further provisions for social justice. Most readers will be familiar with the 'ten commandments'. But they are merely a part of a much larger body of instructions that are said to have come from God. These instructions are a mixed bag. A longing for equality, fairness and justice for the poor and marginalised sit alongside the practice of war and conquest. That's to be expected as these writings describe the religiously interpreted experience of a community with an ancient worldview. We don't know how well their social justice instructions were observed, but they remain in the Bible as a witness to the vision of an alternative, fair and just society.

Abundance, Scarcity or Enough?

You shall not oppress a resident alien; you know the heart of an alien, for you were aliens in the land of Egypt. For six years you shall sow your land and gather in its yield; but the seventh year you shall let it rest and lie fallow, so that the poor of your people may eat; and what they leave the wild animals may eat. You shall do the same with your vineyard, and with your olive orchard. Six days you shall do your work, but on the seventh day you shall rest, so that your ox and your donkey may have relief, and your homeborn slave and the resident alien may be refreshed.[66]

The principle of the seventh day of rest was extended to the seventh year, a sabbatical year. We know the benefit to soil enrichment of allowing cultivated land to lie fallow for a time. This is still practiced in one way or another by many farmers today. But in the text, the fallow year was expressly about providing for poor people and undomesticated animals. The Bible is close to silent on animal welfare, but this provision recognises the rights of wild animals and presupposes the adequate care of domesticated animals. And it was expected that there would always be members of society who struggled to provide for their needs. Therefore, the sabbatical year was an inbuilt provision to avoid the excesses of poverty. The laws of ancient Israel encouraged a communal responsibility to provide for the vulnerable in its midst.

---

[66] Exodus 23: 9 - 12

Interesting, also, is the provision for the "resident alien" or undocumented immigrant. The Hebrews were reminded that they also were once refugees when they fled from the tyranny of the Egyptian Empire. They must not forget it. The oppressed must not become the oppressors. Even the homeless amongst them have the right to sustenance from the abundant gifts of the land. The new society they were called to create was not egalitarian in the narrow sense of eliminating the rich and the poor altogether. But it did place limits on the gap between the two. In contrast to the brutality of the Egyptian Empire, this new community was envisioned as one where poverty would never become so extreme as to threaten life.

The laws on 'gleaning' were very specific: "When you reap the harvest of your land, you shall not reap to the very edges of your field or gather the gleanings of your harvest. You shall not strip your vineyard bare or gather the fallen grapes of your vineyard; you shall leave them for the poor and the alien."[67] The poor must never be abandoned. No-one should go hungry. According to the story of Ruth, gleaning was indeed practiced. When the widowed Ruth and her mother-in-law, Naomi, travelled away from their home, they were two women with no means of support. So, they fed themselves through gleaning, with permission, in the fields of Boaz.[68]

---

[67] Leviticus 19: 9 - 10
[68] Ruth 2

Abundance, Scarcity or Enough?

In our capitalist culture today, landowners would undoubtably be alarmed if told that their harvest was not entirely theirs, that a portion of it belonged to the poor and the homeless itinerant. A society that values the just care of all its members will accept that a portion of production and profits belongs to those without means. This philosophy is the basis of a progressive tax system. Unfortunately, many businesses that reap enormous profits do not accept their responsibility towards the rest of the community. This is a very active debate in Australia at the time of writing. But rarely do we hear the debate taken into the realm of a philosophical vision.

Those who promote an alternative vision of society, who accept the responsibility of providing for all its people, its foreign itinerants and its animals, come up against the assumptions of the Empire of Power. In the dominant, consumer culture, it is assumed that the earth's resources are scarce and so we must compete with our neighbours to get as much as we can. If I am to win, you must lose in this harsh, unforgiving, dog-eat-dog world. Ironically, some who do manage to store up riches for themselves still experience personal insecurity. In the ancient Israelite legend, accumulating manna for tomorrow was not allowed. It was not necessary, given the on-going renewal and seasonal nature of the land, and it did not provide for the needs of the soul. Unless we can appreciate life and its abundant nourishment as a gift, we will be unable to face the insecurities of life with a sense of peace.

Finally, the ancient Hebrew society included a remarkable tradition known as the Jubilee. Again, we do not know if this tradition was ever fully practiced, although we do know that it had faded out by the time of Jesus. The Jubilee attempted to address the problem of debt leading to loss of family and tribal lands. Those who fell hopelessly into debt were often forced to surrender their land to their creditors. Over the generations, that resulted in wealth being concentrated in the hands of a few landholders. After losing their land, the poor could be forced into indentured labour, further widening the inequality gap. The concept of the Jubilee was based on the conviction that these changes in fortune should not have permanent consequences. After forty-nine years, the land should be returned to its original owners and the indentured labourers set free. Only Israelites were covered by this provision. Unfortunately, foreigners were beyond the protection of Israel's law. The following excerpts from Leviticus provide a glimpse of this social justice vision.

> *You shall hallow the fiftieth year and you shall proclaim liberty throughout the land to all its inhabitants. It shall be a jubilee for you: you shall return, every one of you, to your property and every one of you to your family... You shall observe my statutes and faithfully keep my ordinances, so that you may live on the land securely. The land will yield its fruit and you will eat your fill and live on it securely... If any who are dependent on you become so impoverished*

> *that they sell themselves to you, you shall not make them as slaves. They shall remain with you as hired or bound labourers. They shall serve with you until the year of jubilee. Then they and their children with them shall be free from your authority. They shall go back to their own family and return to their ancestral property...You shall not rule over them with harshness, but shall fear your God.*

The Jubilee was an attempt to wipe the slate clean, to hit the reset button in the social structure of ancient Israel. The philosophical underpinning of the Jubilee was the belief that the land belonged to God and that the produce of the land was a gift from God. Wealth was never intended to accumulate in one place, or in the hands of a few. The self-identity of the freed Hebrew slaves was being shaped by the perception that they were sojourners in a land that no human being permanently owned. Every fifty years the rich, who reaped the rewards of others' unfortunate circumstances, were reminded that they had no personal right to accumulate wealth and property at the expense of the poor.

Many have criticised the idea of the Jubilee as hopelessly utopian. But economist Michael Hudson[69] maintains that this legislation was an advancement on similar laws in the ancient world. Whereas in Babylon

---

[69] Michael Hudson (1939 -) is a professor of economics at the University of Missouri, a researcher at the Levy Economics Institute, a former Wall Street analyst, political consultant, commentator and journalist.

attempts to make life equitable were at the whim of the kings, the law of Leviticus was fairer and doable. After studying debt in the Bronze Age, Hudson concluded that the stability of ancient states depended on the number of free people. He argued that freeing bondservants and cancelling rural debt preserved social balance and economic stability.

More recently, inspired by the biblical concept of the Jubilee, *Jubilee 2000* was an international movement that called for the cancellation of third world debt by the year 2000. The primary organising energy for *Jubilee 2000* came from the churches and Christian youth groups. The movement gained the support of some governments such as the UK and USA and the debt of some third world countries was significantly reduced. Later in 2005, debt relief for the poorest countries in the world was a focus of the *Make Poverty History* campaign. Unfortunately, given that our worldwide economic system and the philosophy that undergirds it has not changed, the crippling effects of debt remain a huge global challenge. The year of Jubilee may never have been enacted in full, and yet it stands as a prophetic witness to an alternative, spiritually healthy socio-economic vision.

Summarising the Economic Vision of Abundance

In summary, if the ancient Hebrews were to form a new community after fleeing slavery in Egypt, they needed a new social narrative. Their view of the world needed to offer an alternative to the harsh, oppressive values of the Empire of Power. And so, we find within the writings of ancient Israel the teaching that we humans are merely sojourners in our land — a land that ultimately belongs to God. This perspective is echoed in many indigenous cultures around the world. Australian Aboriginal people have the saying that "The land does not belong to us. We belong to the land." Their people's connection to a specific place is sacred. Precious memories of generations are enshrined in that place, with its waters, trees, rocks, mountains and rivers. In our modern Western culture, we have so often become alienated from any sense of place. Rediscovering a sense of place is a significant and healing dimension of the new spiritual tapestry.

The flow-on effect from this perspective on the land is social justice in the community. Life is a gift and the abundance of the land is for everyone. The legend of the Hebrews wandering in the wilderness, gathering manna for the day, expressed the conviction that, in material provisions for life, there is such a thing as too much and too little. Greed should not dictate how we relate to each other. Sabbath Economics[70] imagined a just society where everyone gathered enough for the needs of their own household and, beyond that, did not store up or attempt to accumulate excess. The gifts of the land were intended to

---

[70] The term, Sabbath Economics, was coined by biblical scholar, Ched Myers, to describe some of the principles mentioned in this chapter.

circulate in the community. A just society meant that limits would be placed on production and the need of labourers for rest and refreshment should be respected. Taking regular time off, one day a week, acted as a reminder that the land, its bounty, and the whole of life was a gift. Gratitude for the gift was the spiritual outcome of this social vision.

The basic needs of all people, including the poor, the widow, the orphan and the foreigner, must be respected. Hence, the crops of a field did not belong exclusively to the landowner. A portion should be left alone so that those who had need could glean the fields and be fed. According to the concept of the sabbatical, every seven years the land should be rested. The landless, the poor and the animals were provided for. The provision of the Jubilee was a daring, prophetic redress against the excesses of wealth and poverty. After every forty-nine years, in the year of Jubilee, debts were cancelled, allowing for a redistribution of wealth. The reset button was hit so that the rich did not get richer and the poor did not get poorer. The scope of the vision was vast — a significant alternative to the Empire's assumption of scarcity and ruthless competition.

Jesus and the New Economic Vision

What did Jesus think about the land as gift? Did the instruction not to accumulate wealth matter to Jesus? Did the use of power and money figure in Jesus' understanding

Abundance, Scarcity or Enough?

of repentance? Let's look briefly at a couple of stories from the New Testament that suggest a 'yes' answer.

Mark 2 has a little cameo account of Jesus and his disciples walking through a grain-field on the Sabbath.[71] They began to pluck heads of grain and were taken to task for doing so by the Pharisees. The ensuing debate seemed to be around what is permissible on the Sabbath. Preachers have tended to use the story as evidence that Jesus is Lord of the Sabbath, confirming his divinity. But Jesus redirected his accusers to the original significance of the Sabbath — an instruction by God to early Israel that everyone should have what they need. The example he used to prove his point was their beloved ancestor, David, before he became king. At the time, David was living the life of a fighter with a group of soldiers who hid in the hills. One Sabbath, when they were hungry, they went straight into the Holy of Holies in the house of God, the place where only the High Priest was allowed, took the holy bread and ate it. It was an outrageous act. Why did they get away with it? Because they were hungry! Provision for those who are hungry took priority in the earliest teachings of Israel.

Jesus and his companions were practicing gleaning when they picked the heads of corn in the field. The instructions of God to gather only what they needed, to make sure everyone had enough, and to gather enough on the sixth day so they could still eat on the seventh was the essence of the Sabbath tradition. It was designed to provide

---

[71] Mark 2: 23 - 28

adequately for all the people, to ensure no-one went hungry, even on the day of rest. Gleaning was later instituted to ensure this basic provision once the Hebrews became farmers. However, by the first century CE this social justice tradition had been turned on its head and transformed into a list of religious laws that burdened the people, rather than freeing them to rest and enjoy the plenty of the land. Biblical scholar, Ched Myers comments on this story, "The disciples commandeering grain against Sabbath regulations must from this perspective be seen as a protest of "civil disobedience" over the politics of food in Palestine."[72] It is clear that Jesus believed in the intention and anti-poverty, social vision of Israel's gleaning laws.

Or take two little stories from Luke's Gospel — stories of two rich men. The first is not named but he's called a ruler. He comes to Jesus and asks what he needs to do to "inherit eternal life". Jesus gives the traditional answer — obey the commandments. Of course, he's done all that. But we're told he owned many properties. In the economy of the day, that may have implied fraud or possible collusion with the Romans, but it most often implied seizing land from the indebted poor. Peasant farmers took out loans against their land. When they defaulted on the loans, their creditors took the land, accumulating many properties in the hands of a few. According to the story, Jesus knew this and put his finger

---

[72] Ched Myers, *Binding the Strong Man: A Political Reading of Mark's Story of Jesus,* Orbis 1995 p.161.

on what really needed to change in the man's life. "'You lack one thing. Sell all that you own and distribute the money to the poor; and you will have treasure in heaven. Then come, follow me.' But when he heard this he became very sad, for he was very rich" (Luke 18:22 – 23).

Accustomed to wealth, the ruler assumed that eternal life, like property, was something you could inherit. But participating in what Jesus called the Kingdom of God, the vision of life as an alternative to the power of the Empire, did not come with any personal entitlement. His assumption of privilege stood in the way of his becoming part of the community that Jesus believed in. We participate in the vision of Jesus for a better world by living practically according to the values of the alternative vision. Notice it wasn't just his *attitude* to his wealth that needed to change — he was asked to liquidate his assets and redirect them to where they were needed most, to the poor. Jesus did not ask for a statement of belief, trust in God or anything religious or feel-good at all. He asked the man to alter his lifestyle according to the vision where the rights of the poor were respected and where resources circulated in the community.

The second story of a rich man is especially loved in Sunday Schools. Zacchaeus was a short man who climbed a tree to see Jesus above the crowds when he came to town. That's what we love about it. Children draw pictures of a little man up a tree. Zacchaeus was a tax collector, so of course, he was hated by his fellow Jews for colluding with the Romans. But Jesus went to his home and Zacchaeus was converted and saved, at least that's how the story is typically told. Furthermore, we turn it into a story of how Jesus loves the rich as much as the poor and God accepts anyone, even if they are unpopular. Oh, how we domesticate the stories that are the most cutting!

But if we read the story without those first-world-coloured glasses on, we discover that the only thing that really changed for Zacchaeus was a decision he made about money. He didn't say a prayer or get on his knees and give his heart to Jesus, nor offer worship at the temple. In fact, nothing is said to indicate what Jesus expected of him. The implication is that it didn't need to be said. Why? Because the public preaching of Jesus was already widely known to focus on issues of money and social justice for the poor. If Jesus talked about his vision of the Kingdom of God, then it necessarily included the economic and philosophical values of that social vision.

According to the story, Jesus doesn't ask for anything, and this is what happened. Zacchaeus simply said, "Look, half of my possessions, Lord, I will give to the poor. And if I have defrauded anyone of anything, I will pay back four times as much" (Luke 19: 8). That was it. Nothing else was asked for. That decision was the sole reason Jesus declared Zacchaeus to be restored to the family of God. We can surmise that Zacchaeus knew that following Jesus would mean tackling corruption and his own part in economic injustice. For Zacchaeus, nothing else came into the discussion — only the ungodly coexistence of affluence and poverty, exploitation and suffering, and his participation in it all.

We cannot avoid the conclusion that Jesus believed that, for rich people, repentance required making reparations to the poor. That challenge was too great for the rich young ruler, and too compelling for Zacchaeus. One turned and walked away, sad and unable to rise to the demands of the desperately poor around him. The other turned and walked towards the practical, human needs of the moment.

Countless other stories of Jesus in the New Testament confirm that after the Kingdom of God, the thing Jesus spoke about most was the use of money and social justice. When the Liberation Theologians in the 60's and 70's realised this, they asked the pressing question, "How has the church in Europe read these same scriptures, and completely ignored this central issue for so many centuries?"

The Spirituality of Economics and Christianity

It is uncomfortable for those of us in first world countries to think too long on this economic-spiritual vision. We inherit property; we believe we earn our wealth and deserve whatever we work for; we make money on investments and our companies profit from another's debt. We tend to want to hold on to what we have. First world Christians find it easy to relegate the remarkable vision of ancient Israel to the Old Testament and assume it has been replaced by faith in Jesus. Too often, we have focussed on our inner spiritual life while ignoring the divine impulse behind this alternative social vision and the need to change our lifestyle to make it a reality.

Given that since the fourth century the institutional church itself accumulated wealth in property and riches, it was left with no moral currency with which to challenge the excesses of poverty. The church sanctioned charity for the poor as an appropriate act of compassion. But it did not allow any re-examination of the economic and power structures that entrenched poverty itself. To do so would have marginalised the church from those same power structures in which it was comfortably placed.

Within the core message of the church, throughout the centuries, there has been no mention of the alternative story of abundance and sharing; no questioning of the worldview of the Empire; no recognition that the giftedness of life has social justice implications; no real vision for how we should live with one another, except a disembodied commandment to "love"; certainly, nothing that stands out as different from how people live in Empires of Power.

Instead, the church has preached a very different kind of faith. The story of Jesus was misinterpreted and co-opted to serve the agenda of power. The focus on personal salvation combined with the church's monopoly on proclaiming forgiveness, handed the church enormous spiritual and material power. But there is an awakening

Abundance, Scarcity or Enough?

happening — a re-reading of the story of Jesus without the filter of privilege and riches. It remains a minority report, but it is growing. This awakening began with the uncomfortable questioning of traditional doctrines by the Liberation theologians[73] in the Base Christian Communities of Latin America and was later picked up by Black and Feminist theologies. And, despite attempts of the church to keep these voices silenced or marginalised, the awakening has now influenced the studies of first world biblical scholars.

Mainstream Christians no longer assume that Jesus supported the philosophy of scarcity and the necessity of ruthless competition for resources. Increasingly, Jesus' convictions on social justice are becoming obvious in the reading of the Gospel stories. Unfortunately, this reading of the Gospels is still ignored by many evangelical churches who prefer to focus on personal sin and salvation. Nevertheless, although the values around abundance and sharing have not found their way into the official teaching of the church, they are increasingly understood by many at the grassroots of the mainstream Christian community.

If we live in a world of presumed scarcity, we will always fear that if others are given more, there will be less for ourselves. That self-protective impulse seems to be

---

[73] Liberation theology developed in Latin American in the 1950's and 1960's. Theologians included Gustavo Gutiérrez of Peru, Leonardo Boff of Brazil, Juan Luis Segundo of Uruguay, and Jon Sobrino of Spain, who popularized the phrase "God's Preferential option for the poor".

A Spiritual Tapestry

naturally present in all animal species, including humans. But inspiring thinkers suggest we can move beyond that narrow self-protection to a trust in the abundance of the earth. It is possible to let go our fears and embrace generosity. We know that the earth's resources are not unlimited. But with restraint, an avoidance of overconsumption and a commitment to the whole community, there could be enough for everyone.

The new spiritual perspective addresses our tendency to feel threatened by others. Why do we feel threatened? The renowned Brazilian educator, Paulo Freire[74] says,

> *It is the culture of empire, a power structure that requires two classes: a winner and a loser, an oppressed and an oppressor, a master and a slave. Both parties are necessary in this system, so that, try as we might, within a culture of empire, we cannot bring everyone up to an equal level... All these power struggles are based on perceived scarcity: we grasp for the power available to us by destroying those below us. But this locks us into a cycle where we must always fear one another."* [75]

---

[74] Paulo Freire (1921 – 1997) was a Brazilian educator, philosopher and author. He taught in Brazil and the USA. Later in Switzerland he was an education advisor to the World Council of Churches. In 1988 Freire was appointed Secretary of Education for São Paulo. He is best known for his influential work, *Pedagogy of the Oppressed*.

[75] Paulo Freire, *Pedagogy of the Oppressed*, transl. Myra Bergman Ramos, Continuum International Publishing Group 2000 p.27.

Abundance, Scarcity or Enough?

Perhaps it is only after we acknowledge this assumption of scarcity and our fear of one another that we can embrace the New Story on which to build a healthier society. Within our faith communities, we have at our fingertips stories that will help us achieve this if we have the will. Concepts of abundance, giftedness, the dignity of all, fair distribution of resources, generosity and care for the marginalised can all be found in our biblical stories if we know how to read them.

On a personal level, the presumption of scarcity is not good for our psychological or spiritual development. It means we will always fear not having enough, producing unhealthy insecurities. Fear is a destructive emotion. Despite the patterns of overconsumption in the first world, we seem driven by these fears. Cherice Bock[76] writes:

> *In American culture, we are often caught between a fear of scarcity and an awareness of overwhelming abundance. I don't know about you, but I often feel bombarded by messages encouraging me to get more, be more, have more, do more. Even as an American of modest means, I have abundant access to food and other resources. There is even an abundance of exercise equipment and regimens to help us burn off the abundance of calories we eat — and an abundance of how-to books on simplifying our*

---

[76] Cherice Bock is a Quaker from Oregon. She has a MDiv from Princeton Theological Seminary and teaches at George Fox Seminary. She blogs for the environmental studies journal *Whole Terrain*.

lives after all the stuff we buy. Abundance seems to be everywhere.[77]

In the above discussion of the ancient Hebrews in the wilderness, the idea of abundance was a positive acknowledgement of the giftedness of life. But in our present-day affluent societies, abundance has taken on the negative connotation of 'too much'. In a similar vein, renowned social work researcher, Brene Brown, says that the opposite of scarcity is not abundance but 'enough'. In his book, *Sacred Economics*, Charles Eisenstein, speaker and author on human cultural evolution, traces the history of money from ancient to modern societies. He shows how the money system has contributed to alienation, competition and necessitated endless growth. He warns that the demand for continual growth is not possible on a planet with finite resources and that it destroys natural human relationships. Speaking about the 'gift economy', Eisenstein is part of a movement to create a New Story for our society. Beyond the religious sector, prophetic thinkers like Eisenstein are recovering the perspective of giftedness. This should also be the story that people of faith are telling.

The global economy has robbed many ordinary people of a positive sense of self. Too many have been misled into thinking they are insignificant, dispensable workers at the mercy of giant companies. But that is the perspective of the Empire that we reject. We are not merely

---

[77] Cherice Bock, *Scarcity vs. Abundance: Moving Beyond Dualism to "Enough"* in *Christian Feminism Today*, https://eewc.com.

cogs in a production line. We can take time out and learn to breathe. We can confidently affirm that life goes far beyond production and profits. Our personal spiritual health and that of our society require imaginative economic and social strategies based on an alternative story of who we are our responsibility to our neighbours.

Readers take heart that there is a groundswell of voices from many disciplines including theologians, biblical scholars, economists, historians, scientists, educators, philosophers and cultural critics who are saying the same thing. We are interconnected with each other in the cosmic, creative process and everyone matters. Life, love, relationships and the abundance of the earth are all gift. Each of us is a precious individual called to community and challenged to ensure that everyone has enough. Poverty and overconsumption damage our collective health. So, let's retell that old story with its punchline, "those who gathered much had nothing over, and those who gathered little had no shortage; they gathered as much as each of them needed."

CHAPTER FIVE

Trees, Rivers, Geese, Humans, Soil, Stars: The New Story of Us

> *Earth's crammed with heaven,*
> *And every common bush afire with God;*
> *And only he who sees takes off his shoes;*
> *The rest sit round it and pluck blackberries.*
>
> Elizabeth Barrett Browning

The dominant thrust of modern culture assumes and reinforces our alienation from nature, from each other and in some sense, from ourselves. Consumerism is satisfied when we seek to fill what is missing in our lives with things or even experiences that we can buy. The new spirituality presented in this book seeks to overcome our false sense of separation from each other and the natural world. We are all a piece. Comprehending our interconnectedness is both an intellectual and spiritual experience. It is both rational and mystical.

Welcoming the Input of Scientific Discovery

Thank God for scientists! There was a time when Christians were at odds with science. Sadly, we know that is still true in some quarters of Christianity. The church once punished heretics for suggesting the earth (assumed to be flat) was not the centre of the universe. Now, some outspoken creationists argue with the scientific evidence of evolution and some deny the statistics of climate science. They regard any science that does not confirm their own views or a literal reading of the Bible as incorrect. This is a glorification of faith as ignorance. It is precisely the same stance as that taken by the church that refused to listen to Galileo and is an embarrassment in mainstream Christianity. And yet, although most churches accept the findings of science, they are unable to integrate the scientific perspective into the ancient faith. Other than the proposal that God created *through* the process of evolution, traditional Christianity still struggles with the far-reaching impact of scientific research.

Ecology is not simply about the relationship between trees and leaf matter on the forest floor. It does not apply only to the unfortunate dynamic between native frogs and introduced cane toads in Australia. Thanks to scientists, we are beginning to understand the intricate and far-reaching interconnection of *all* species, including the human species, with each other and the earth. We are learning to overcome the assumption that humans are over and above the natural world and are recognising instead that we are very much part of it. Sadly, we have become desensitised to the on-going extinction of species, even though scientists now admit that, as a species ourselves, human beings could also face extinction in the future. That very possibility goes against the grain of religious beliefs: that we are of a different order to the animals; that we have a special relationship with God, who will protect us; and that it was in fact God who gave us the natural world to use and control as we wished.

    The crisis we find ourselves in regarding the disappearance of species, the threat of climate change, the dying of the reefs, and the pollution of the air and water is producing a deep anxiety. And the anxiety is not just about how to save some of these natural beauties, nor even about the health and survival of human communities. It comes from the niggling fear that our worldview no longer makes sense. We need a new perspective, but our religious faith has none other to give us. Common sense tells us we must place limits on our use of natural resources for the sake of sustainability. But we long for a more meaningful explanation of how we, God, nature and the universe fit together. Many of us want to lose our sense of alienation from the natural world but fear that in the process we will lose the faith that taught us we are special.

Trees, Rivers, Geese, Humans, Soil, Stars: The Story of Us

If humanity is the crowning glory of God's creation, as we were taught, why have we caused so much destruction? We believed that Jesus, by dying and rising, saved for heaven those who trust in him. And so, with a limited life span here, Christianity turned the hopes of humanity towards a future spiritual home. At some point the earth may self-destruct, but Christians will be safe in heaven. There are questions that naturally flow from this belief system, but few have dared to voice them. They do not turn to their pastors, ministers or priests with their unsettling concerns, for fear that the church simply has nothing to offer that makes consistent sense. If God is going to lift us out of a decaying world and save us for eternity, does God then abandon the rest of the natural world to destruction? If so, do we still have a serious responsibility to preserve the planet if our future home is elsewhere? Beyond its temporary, practical purpose to sustain human life on earth, does nature not matter after all?

On the other hand, many Christians are learning from science and a secular community that now increasingly cares about the health of the natural world. This produces confusion in the Christian conscience, because it does not fit easily with traditional faith. If we are embedded in the natural world, should we want to be saved from it by an external God? If God is concerned with the fate of human beings, but has no serious regard for the rest of the earth and its life forms, what does that say about God? If we love nature, are we then out of step with God? Are we beginning to care too much about trees, rivers, geese, soil and stars? Are we in danger of giving too much importance to the material world and other life forms, while taking our eyes off the spiritual world of faith?

These often-unspoken concerns deserve answers. Traditional Christianity has been informed solely by biblical scholars and theologians. Even in our own time, any interest in the findings of science has been an optional, extra-curricular hobby for church members. However, a new spiritual perspective is emerging from those who take seriously both the divine presence and the realities of scientific discovery. Taking on board scientific warnings on pollution and loss of species, many preachers today stress that we are not to subdue the earth so much as be its stewards. Because of science, progressives are rethinking our relationship with the natural world.

Any tested insight or proven discovery within the cosmos can help us understand reality. There is no point in 'believing in' a God who is disconnected from the real world. Therefore, true seekers after the Real will find fellow companions in many walks of life. No-one suggests that we should simply accept the latest theories without subjecting them to proper scientific testing. Neither should we fall for the latest fads of pseudo-spirituality that are as lacking in scientific knowledge as our fourth century creeds. Neither should we put our heads in the sand and regard our faith as totally separate from our knowledge of chemistry, physics and astronomy. It is time for our theology to be formed within our own century. Therefore, some of the contributors to this discussion do not come from a Christian background. Their contributions should be weighed according to both scientific credibility and the values that we have prioritised for our lives.

Joanna Macy,[78] for example, makes significant connections between psychology, spirituality and science. Her focus is on reconnecting our seemingly separate selves with nature. She echoes and builds upon the thinking of Norwegian philosopher, Arne Naess.[79] He criticised the shallow utilitarian view of ecology that is popular with business and governments. He urged us to go deeper, to appreciate how each living thing is dependent on the existence of other creatures in a natural, complex web of interrelationships.

Australian John Seed, of the Rainforest Information Centre, also lectures on Deep Ecology and advocates worldwide for the preservation of rainforests and animal species. With Joanna Macy, Pat Fleming and Arne Naess, Seed wrote *Thinking Like a Mountain - Towards a Council of All Beings*. Seed described his activism not as protecting the forests as an outsider, but as part of them. "I am that part of the rainforest recently emerged into human thinking."[80] In other words, a spiritual vision is emerging

---

[78] Joanna Rogers Macy (1929 -) is an environmental activist, author of eight books, and an international speaker. She is a scholar of Buddhism, general systems theory, and Deep Ecology and calls her training workshops, "The Work that Reconnects".

[79] Arne Naess (1912 – 2009) coined the term "Deep Ecology". He was an activist who combined ecological thinking with the non-violence convictions of Gandhi.

[80] Quoted by Richard Rohr in *Kinship of all Life*, 2018.

that does not merely love nature but understands humanity in a far-reaching, qualitatively different way.

Eco-Spirituality

Over the centuries, some Christians have described nature as a sacrament of God. In the early thirteenth century, Francis of Assisi[81] lived a prophetic life, embracing poverty and speaking of nature itself as the mirror of God. In the nineteenth century, Jesuit priest and poet, Gerard Manley Hopkins, famously wrote, "The world is charged with the grandeur of God."[82] According to this tradition, nature is sacramentally valuable. Like the bread and the wine, it can become a visual pointer to the unseen reality of God. The idea of nature as sacrament challenges the unrestrained practice of manipulating nature for our own profit. But does it go far enough?

Two current expressions of the renewed regard for nature are the *rights* of nature and the *care* of nature. The two are closely connected, of course, with a slightly different focus.

Theologians like Sallie McFague challenge us to recognise nature itself as embodying God. Instead of adopting a utilitarian attitude towards the natural world, regarding it merely as a resource for humanity, even a

---

[81] Saint Francis of Assisi (1181 – 1226) was a Catholic Friar and preacher.
[82] Gerard Manley Hopkins (1834 – 1889), *The Grandeur of God,* first published after his death in 1918.

spiritual resource, she insists that nature has intrinsic value of its own. In earlier chapters, I suggested that we need to reimagine God, holiness and the imperfection of human nature. Continuous with this process, we also need to radically rethink our relationship with other living things and the whole earth. 'Eco-spirituality', as it is called, is a response to the narrow human-centred worldview of old-style Christianity.

Earth jurisprudence is a movement aimed at respecting the ethical and legal rights of nature — rivers, forests, animals, oceans and land — just as human rights are respected. The necessity of moving away from a human-centred ethic to a whole-earth ethic was first promoted by the Catholic priest Thomas Berry,[83] who preferred to call himself a 'Cosmologist' or 'Earth Scholar'.

Thomas Berry believed that after generations spent in self-glorification and despoiling the world, humanity is poised to embrace a new role as a vital part of a larger, interdependent 'communion of subjects' on earth. This vital role requires a transformation of our understanding of ourselves and of the cosmos. He recognised that transforming our values would not be easy. In the 1990s, after decades of research and teaching, Berry called this needed transformation the 'Great Work', which involves the political and legal order, the economic and industrial

---

[83] Thomas Berry, C.P., PhD (1914 – 2009) was a Catholic priest, author and eco-theologian. He is considered a leader in the tradition of Teilhard de Chardin. His university lecturing career has been in cultural histories, including those of China and India.

world, education and religion. The scope of his vision was grand. Berry's concept of earth jurisprudence is gaining ground and is now being taught in some university law schools.

A chapter from Berry's *The Great Work*, included in *The Emerging Christian Way*,[84] does not mention the word 'God' once, despite Berry being a Catholic priest. Although traditionalists use that to warn us off this new spirituality, there is no reason to suggest that Berry did not promote faith. Like many of us, he moved away from his church's doctrinal teaching towards a broader image of God. The faith that sustained him, although not traditionally doctrinal, was nevertheless central to his life.

While cosmologists present some frightening facts about our current environmental crisis, Thomas Berry's message was one of both challenge and hope. Embracing the 'Great Work' in our generation can be daunting and fearful. Berry understood the all-encompassing mission of altering our society's worldview. We might wonder how he avoided despair at the enormity of the challenge. His hope was clearly in God, not as an external being who would intervene to save either us or the earth, but as the One who calls and equips us to live differently on the planet. In Berry's words,

> *We are, as it were, thrown into existence with a challenge and a role that is beyond any personal*

---

[84] Michael Schwartzentruber, ed., *The Emerging Christian Way: Thoughts, stories and wisdom for a faith of transformation*, Copper House, 2006

> choice. The nobility of our lives, however, depends upon the manner in which we come to understand and fulfil our assigned role. Yet we must believe that those powers that assign our role must in that same act bestow upon us the ability to fulfil this role. We must believe that we are cared for and guided by these same powers that bring us into being.[85]

It is an act of faith to maintain hope in the midst of the continuing destruction of the planet's natural systems through disregard or in the pursuit of profit. We cannot respond to the needs of our time, to the calling of the divine, unless our hope and stamina are nurtured. Otherwise the statistics on species loss and the devastation of ecosystems will overwhelm us. Some experience of loss and grief are inevitable when we begin to care for the natural world in this way. Perhaps it is because that sense of loss would be unthinkable in its magnitude, that many prefer not to believe the scientists and statistics. And perhaps good people, who do care about nature, simply do not want to face these terrifying possibilities. Those of us, who do not turn our heads away, must cope with frustration, fear, disappointment and anguish at what is happening to the earth around us. Although faint at times, our hopes will be nurtured by the abiding presence of goodness and love. People of faith need to dig deep and find a source of hope in their divinely-inspired dreams of a better future.

---

[85] Thomas Berry, *The Great Work* as it appears in *The Emerging Christian Way*, p71.

A Spiritual Tapestry

Drawing upon scientific findings concerning our interconnectedness, the new spirituality offers a way forward. Globally renowned spiritual director and author, Richard Rohr,[86] for example, speaks about the 'greening of the self.' This spiritual movement recognises the sacredness of all life. As Rohr says, it combines "the mystical with the pragmatic, transcending separateness, alienation, and fragmentation."[87] Appreciating our deep interconnection with the material cosmos does not diminish our image of God. Rather than the distinctly separate God of traditional Christianity, it enlarges our conception of the divine. Instead of being threatened by the theory of evolution, the perspective of the 'greening of the self' sees the divine imprint within it. From within the Roman Catholic priesthood, Rohr writes,

> *By expanding our self-interest to include other beings in the body of the Earth, the ecological self also widens our window on time. It enlarges our temporal context, freeing us from identifying our goals and rewards solely in terms of our present lifetime. The life pouring through us, pumping our heart and breathing through our*

---

[86] Richard Rohr (1943 -) is an American Franciscan friar ordained to the priesthood in the Roman Catholic Church in 1970. Fr Rohr bears witness to the universal awakening within Christian mysticism. He founded the *Center for Action and Contemplation* (CAC) in Albuquerque, New Mexico. Rohr's teaching is grounded in practices of contemplation and self-emptying, expressing itself in radical compassion, particularly for the socially marginalized.

[87] Richard Rohr, Daily readings, March 2018, *Kinship of All Life*

lungs, did not begin at our birth or conception. Like every particle in every atom and molecule of our bodies, it goes back through time to the first splitting and spinning of the stars.[88]

As people of faith, we have the opportunity to tell a New Story of us. Our origins, our place in the cosmos and on this earth, the very nature of our humanity, can be placed within a new, twenty-first century narrative. Scientists are providing the story of energy, matter and evolutionary history. Learning from those exciting new discoveries, spiritual thinkers are reflecting upon the philosophical implications of that physical story.

Although deeply interwoven in a material matrix of living things, the new perspective does not depreciate humanity to the level of non-human existence. On the contrary, by recognising the sacredness of all life, we regard nature with a similar respect that we show to human beings. Could it be that it is not only humans but all living things that experience the divine impulse? That is not to deny the unique development of human brains that has allowed for reflective thinking and ethical choices. Of course, on one level we are vastly different. Through language we communicate better, think, reflect and imagine better than the other species. However, instead of relegating other living beings to the insignificant and spiritually unimportant, in the New Story we appropriately respect the distinctive, inherent value of each life.

---

[88] ibid

Other species do not need to be like us in order to have intrinsic worth and even something to teach us. The natural, instinctive life of animals and plants speaks to us of balance, beauty, healing, fragility, diversity, interdependence, persistence, resilience and acceptance of reality. Our comprehension of the scope and challenges of life can be enriched by observing and learning from these innate qualities of other living things. When we worry over what we cannot change, we should learn from the acceptance and resilience of plants and animals. According to the Gospel writers, Jesus gave a similar counsel:

> *Consider the lilies, how they grow: they neither toil nor spin; yet I tell you, even Solomon in all his glory was not clothed like one of these... And do not keep striving for what you are to eat and what you are to drink, and do not keep worrying.*[89]

Our appreciation of ourselves is deepened by contemplating the magnitude of the universe and the intricacies of other life forms. Many people of faith can attest to the spiritual benefits gained from the retreat practice of closely and silently observing trees, leaves, insects, birds, rocks and cloud formations, to name just a few. Experiencing ourselves as part of a greater natural whole, brings calmness of mind and peacefulness of spirit. This is no accident. We are, after all, interconnected with the world into which we were born.

---

[89] Luke 12: 27-29

Place-Centred Commitment to Nature and Community

The first response to nature according to the New Story, as mentioned above, is an *ethic of rights*, of 'earth jurisprudence'. The second response is an *ethic of care* associated with 'bioregionalism'.

A gentle critique of cosmologists such as Thomas Berry, has come from within progressive Christianity itself. While valuing the perspective that we are merely a part of a much larger ecosystem, thinkers like Sally McFague, Ched Myers and Wendell Berry urge us to ground our love of nature in the place where we live. Using the concept of 'bioregionalism', they suggest that cosmic theories do not change human behaviour. We need to be grounded in a specific place. By caring for the natural world that we encounter around us, our love of nature becomes real.

Think of it this way. There is no point saying you love the world if you can't stand your neighbour. Similarly, there is no point saying you love the earth and the cosmos, if you do not appreciate the plants and animals that you walk past on your way to work. Practical spirituality connects us with the land and the place in which we live — its natural contours, its trees and plant-life, its produce, its rivers, oceans and wetlands, its inhabitants both human and non-human, both indigenous and newly arrived, its history, buildings, colours and changing seasons. Caring for the planet means nothing if we fail to appreciate and care for the little piece of land on which we live. Loving the world means nothing if we fail to care for our neighbours. This spirituality means putting down roots into the earth and into the community in which we find ourselves. The 'ethic of care' emphasises our very personal connection with place.

Displacement causes trauma. Re-placement heals. Looking backwards, it is possible to trace the dis-ease of many communities to their displacement from their lands and culture. Colonisation uprooted indigenous peoples. The industrial revolution uprooted and disturbed the natural rhythms of life of many rural and village communities in Europe. Wars have uprooted the established relationship that thousands of local communities had with the land, its history and its stories. Political and military abuses of power are still displacing ethnic minority populations so that the suffering of homeless refugees around the world is now greater than ever before.

Individuals, families and communities are suffering from the traumas of alienation, disempowerment and *dis-place-ment*. The global strategies of massive profit-making companies have demanded mobility, severing the connection between employees and their communal roots. Data gatherers manipulate the consumer market by selling people's preferences for goods and services without their knowledge. Effectively taking away the control consumers have over their private information, these companies exploit billions of ordinary people, creating a sense of disempowerment and disconnection from the normal interchange of communal living. Ordinary people feel increasingly disconnected from their place, their community and control over their own lives.

We cannot turn the clock back to a pre-colonial, pre-industrial age, and most of us would not want to. But that should not stop us from naming the causes of our dis-ease or identifying what is needed for our healing. How often we hear it said, with a sigh of resignation, "That's progress." To live spiritually is to refuse to be merely a cog in the wheel of progress. It means to choose to live meaningfully, aware of our surroundings, attentive to that which nurtures the soul and builds the community. Healing for many alienated people will involve a re-placement and a reconnection with the land. It will mean establishing a relationship with a new natural environment and a new community.

Rather than exploiting, dominating, rearranging and using place solely for our own profit, driven by a consumer mentality, we can choose to live by listening and attending to and working with the natural cycles of the land under our feet. Instead of standing over and outside of the environment, the new spiritual perspective places us within our environment, observing it closely, learning from it and respecting it. This process is important for us all as human beings, whether we are native to a place or newly arrived.

Bioregionalism is a richly coloured thread in the new spiritual tapestry for our lives. Of course, the concept of rootedness needs to be broad enough to include movement in those harsh environments where migration or nomadic lifestyles are required to survive. Traditionally, this includes Australian indigenous tribes and those of the arctic circle. Yet even these nomadic tribes maintained a deep knowledge of and sense of belonging to the larger country through which they moved. The pressing question is whether a return to a bioregional lifestyle is possible in our urban, industrial world. Many claim that it is.

Prominent among these thinkers are poet, Gary Snyder,[90] and Kentucky farmer/poet, Wendell Berry.[91] Berry has inspired a movement away from large industrialised agricultural practices which displace small-holder farmers and enslaves others in debt to pay off massive machinery. Large-scale industrial farming by huge agricultural companies destroys the relationship between the farmer, the land and the local community. Instead of the impersonal cultivation of massive conglomerations of farming land, Berry advocates a return to smaller-scale farming that reduces debt and re-establishes the farming family's relationship with the land and its natural seasons. Eating is regarded as an agricultural act which has implications for us all.

At the grassroots of society, there is a groundswell of desire to re-establish a closer link between ourselves and

---

[90] Gary Snyder (1930 -) is an American Pulitzer Prize-winning poet and environmental activist. He has been described as the Poet Laureate of Deep Ecology.
[91] Wendell Berry (1934 -) is an American novelist, poet, environmental activist, cultural critic, and farmer. A prolific author, he has written many novels, short stories, poems, and essays.

the land. For decades, urban communities became increasingly distanced from the source of their food. This alienation from the production of food diminished our experience of the land itself. For many, food was only ever purchased in plastic wrapping in a supermarket. The gap of awareness and interests between city and country communities widened. But human beings are part of the natural world and felt diminished by this loss of connection.

The rise of stress-related diseases can be related to the increase in the artificial character of urban life. Studies have suggested that there is a definite psychological benefit to those suffering depression or stress from an increased connection with green spaces and gardens. Frances E Kuo, director of the *Landscape and Human Health Laboratory* in Illinois, is confident that, after isolating other social factors, it is the presence of greenery itself that improves mental health, decreasing stress and increasing resilience.[92] Other researchers suggest that this effect of the natural environment is in our genes. The acclaimed Harvard biologist E. O. Wilson[93] has suggested we are experiencing the Eremozoic age, the age of loneliness, isolated from all other living organisms. He has hypothesised that we are biologically drawn to natural

---

[92] *The Landscape and Human Health Laboratory*, of the University of Illinois, has conducted significant research into the psychological benefits of green spaces, trees and gardens in urban neighbourhoods.

[93] Edward Osborne Wilson, usually cited as E. O. Wilson (1929 -) is an American biologist, theorist and author.

landscapes. Wilson believes that nature is critical to our aesthetic, intellectual and spiritual satisfaction. Aligned with this thinking, some therapists now use gardening to assist in the healing process.[94] These researchers and practitioners are only confirming what most of us intuitively knew — that spending time in living spaces, with grass, trees, growing plants and natural water courses, calms our hearts and minds.

Therefore, it is understandable, particularly during this last decade, that we are witnessing a reaction to the trend of our alienation from nature. City-dwellers are increasingly conscious of the origin of their food. Restaurants cater to this awareness by highlighting where their ingredients are sourced. Farmers' Markets are blossoming, allowing townspeople to connect directly with those who grow their food. Street gardens are providing both a greener landscape and a place for community connection. Notice also the rise in popularity of 'paddock to plate' establishments such as the televised *Gourmet Farmer* in Tasmania and *River Cottage* (England and Australia)[95]. More and more urban community gardens provide the opportunity for people to dig their hands into

---

[94] For example, UK-based Dr Ambra Burls FRSA, who has been a mental health professional for thirty years, has a PhD in ecotherapy. She is Vice Chair of the UK UNESCO Man and Biosphere (MAB) Urban Forum.

[95] Matthew Evans, a former food critic and now farmer/restauranteur, hosts *The Gourmet Farmer* on SBS. *River Cottage* began in the UK in 1999 with Hugh Fearnley-Whittingstall and was followed by Paul West, a former chef turned farmer, who hosted *River Cottage Australia* on the Lifestyle Channel.

the soil and watch their own food grow. Even high-rise residents are gardening on their roof-tops. People are fighting back against the alienation from the land that the modern urban society had produced.

According to the new spiritual perspective, this movement to reconnect with the production of food is not simply a social trend or the popularising of a hobby. It is an expression of a spiritual need. If human beings are by nature interconnected with the earth and its living ecosystems, then we need to experience that connection for our own sense of identity and inner health. Community gardening and farmers' markets also provide the significant side-benefit of developing local relationships and a heightened sense of belonging to community. Connection to the land and connection to community are essential to spiritual health.

One of the pioneers of bioregionalism, Wendell Berry, calls us to direct the abstract notion of caring for the planet into a grounded commitment to our own specific environment and community. Berry has suggested ten commands as a kind of manifesto embodying his convictions and hopes. They include:

> *Understand that no amount of education can overcome the innate limits of human intelligence and responsibility. We are not smart enough or conscious enough or alert enough to work responsibly on a gigantic scale.*
>
> *In making things always bigger and more*

> *centralized, we make them both more vulnerable in themselves and more dangerous to everything else. Learn, therefore, to prefer small-scale elegance and generosity to large-scale greed, crudity, and glamour.*
>
> ** Make a home. Help to make a community. Be loyal to what you have made. Put the interest of the community first. Love your neighbours — not the neighbours you pick out, but the ones you have.*
>
> ** Love this miraculous world that we did not make, that is a gift to us.*
>
> ** As far as you are able, make your lives dependent upon your local place, neighbourhood, and household — which thrive by care and generosity — and independent of the industrial economy, which thrives by damage.*[96]

Because we do not all have the opportunity to live on rural land, what does it mean to love your place when you live in a city? Firstly, although we may forget it, even urban dwellers live on land. High-rise apartments are built on the land. All land has a history, a climate, the possibility of green spaces, the ability to produce a nurturing bounty and beauty if attended to. Whatever the density of our population, we all have neighbours. We can choose to buck the trend of alienation, put down roots and love the natural

---

[96] Excerpts from an address given in 1989 by Wendell Berry at the College of the Atlantic in Maine. It was later published by Harper as *The Futility of Global Thinking*.

place with its inhabitants, where we live. It begins with recognising the natural rhythms that surround us and our interdependence with each other.

Another advocate of this grounded love of place is author, activist and biblical scholar Ched Myers, renowned for his commentaries on the Gospel of Mark.[97] In his book on first-world discipleship, Myers makes a strong case for digging down deep — body, soul and spirit — into the place that is home. For him that is California. The following excerpts from Myers' own personal reflections give us a glimpse of how an all-encompassing love of country is embodied by an urban Christian.

> *Since returning to Los Angeles, I have, with increasing intentionality, re-placed myself in this soil. Over the past six years I have worked on excavating the buried layers of culture and history in this land and in myself, to understand my connection to, and severance from, Aztlan*[98]*... California. Here is where my own deepest bioregional loyalties lie... [T]his is a diverse place, hosting all ten of the world's major soils, hundreds of natural communities and thousands of flora types, and more plant diversity than all of the central and northeastern parts of the U.S. and Canada combined... The*

---

[97] See *Binding the Strongman: A Political Reading of Mark's Story of Jesus*, Orbis 1988 and *Say to this Mountain: Mark's Story of Discipleship*, Orbis 1996.
[98] Aztlan is the ancestral home of the Aztec peoples.

assaults upon her songlines and insults to her spirits are too numerous to catalog...

In my teenage years I loved to walk among the coastal canyons of this area and surf in front of its gentle bluffs. These peaceful rolling foothills were first the southernmost habitat of the Gabrielino peoples, then the domain of the old San Joaquin and Niguel land grants, and finally of the Irvine Ranch. Now they are buried beneath endless rows of high-priced homes and condominiums... Thanks to the ruthless alchemy of real estate profiteers their golden beauty has been transformed into the obscene, gated suburban ghetto of... greater Laguna... that provoke in me particular sadness, rage and shame... Yet my work around the state has woven me into the fabric of friendship among the 'refugios' of hope... Above all, the land itself offers refuge and renewal, ever offering its love, waiting for us to return it... My deepest desire is to relearn the forgotten songlines of this place and to defend what is left.

Los Angeles. Finally, a word about the city in which I live and work... There are few oak trees left along the avenue, and the once-wild Arroyo Seco it parallels is now fully paved over. Yet each day on my way to work I pass Eagle Rock, a sacred site to the Gabrielino... And I see in my neighbourhood the multicultural promise of 'nuestra America'. I am grateful to be able to share the promise and pain of this city with sisters and brothers at 'refugios' such as the Catholic Worker, Dolores Mission and United University Church, and many other unheralded communities of faith committed to discipleship in this place. I am equally grateful for all those of diverse conviction in Los Angeles with whom I have had the privilege of collaborating with in the work of resistance, humanization, advocacy and reconstruction.[99]

The spirituality of love of place is not naïve or fanciful. It is an eyes-wide-open commitment to real communities and the real earth. Myers' commitment to social justice in his own neighbourhood and his love of place are grounded in the history of its communities, the diversity of its natural features, its tragic spoiling by industrial developers, and his solidarity with neighbours who share a passion to protect the majesty and welcome of the land. Like many residents of our cities, Myers himself does not work with the soil or even garden. And yet he draws spiritual nourishment from biblical, indigenous and other communal traditions, while taking time out under the grandmother oak tree beside the cascading water of the San Gabriel River.[100] I have quoted at length from Myers because he demonstrates so well how a genuine love of place courageously faces the pain of modern urban living and affirms the healing power of God's gift of the land.

---

[99] Ched Myers, *Who Will Roll Away the Stone? Discipleship Queries for First World Christians*, Orbis 1994, pp.372 – 376.
[100] Ibid p.418.

Interconnectedness and Faith

The book weaves a new spiritual tapestry from the frayed threads of traditional Christianity. But do any of the threads of cosmic and natural interconnection described in this chapter come from Christian traditions? The simple answer is 'no'. Traditional Christianity offers virtually nothing that equates to this particular insight.

Jesus had nothing to say about our connection with nature or bioregionalism. Yes, he used some rural images in his storytelling, but that's about it. In truth, Jesus and his friends would not have been able to imagine a world in which waterways, forests, climate and numerous species were threatened. Prior to the industrial revolution, even in the cities one was never far from the land or the source of one's food. Jesus and all his contemporaries would have taken their natural, direct connection to the land for granted. Therefore, we should not expect that the New Testament would have anything to say on these issues that confront us in the twenty-first century. Although Jesus' spiritual wisdom is still relevant for us, on these matters it is significantly limited. We need to draw on other resources, insights and scientific wisdom for a broader grasp of what faces us today.

The Old Testament provides a theology of the land in relation to Israel's possession of it, but no theology of the innate human connection with the earth and its life forms. Unfortunately, God's promise of the land to Israel, according to the narrative, was given in the context of conquest, dis-placing the communities that already were connected to that land. Possessing and owning the 'promised land' meant reaping the benefits of its cultivation — "a land flowing with milk and honey." The land's value was in its service of the chosen people. This attitude has permeated our Judaeo-Christian culture ever since.

The majesty of nature is given a passing mention in a few Old Testament passages, perhaps the best-known being, "The heavens declare the glory of God; the skies proclaim the work of his hands" (Psalm 19:1). But although the beauty of nature witnesses to the glory of God, the thrust of the old tradition is that we human beings are intended to dominate and "subdue the earth"[101]. The current realisation that this attitude of dominance has been destructive, perhaps irreversibly, has forced us to question the old values.

When asked if the perspective of our interconnection with nature is 'Christian', Sally MacFague draws upon the teaching of Jesus to "love your enemies." We are urged to regard our enemies, not merely as the object of our personal fears, anger and political agenda, but as legitimate human subjects in their own right. McFague suggests that extending that concept to our relationship with non-human life fits well with the ethic of Jesus. "If enemies are to be shown respect and care, should not other lifeforms also, as well as the habitats that support

---

[101] Genesis 1: 28

them?"[102] While there is some logic in this suggestion, it draws a long bow and demonstrates that if we are looking for a direct reference to our relationship with nature, we will not find it in the Bible.

Christians who attempt to fit this new perspective into traditional beliefs sometimes refer to incarnational theology — if God is present in the flesh in Jesus, God can also be present in other forms of the material world. Again, it draws a long bow and fails to make the connection between humans and their natural environment. Referring to a few brief images of nature in the scriptures, love of enemies or incarnational theology does not establish the idea within traditional Christianity. We need to admit that the attempt to integrate interconnectedness with Christian teaching is grasping at straws. These philosophical and scientific ideas were simply not on Jesus' radar.

The new spiritual perspective proposes that all life forms have an intrinsic worth and that we are ourselves embedded both physically and spiritually in the natural order of the cosmos. Human beings belong to the earth from which we came, and our souls are naturally drawn to nature for refreshment, calm and perspective. Christian doctrine does not include this idea, even though numerous Christian mystics throughout the ages have believed it. We must look beyond creedal faith to affirm the truth that

---

[102] Sally McFague, *Consider the Lilies of the Field*, in *The Emerging Christian Way: Thoughts, Stories and Wisdom for a Faith of Transformation*, Copper House 2006, p 94.

overcoming our sense of separation from the world and others is important for our spiritual health.

Church members may worry that we are beginning to care too much about trees, rivers, geese, soil and the stars. They may wonder if we are in danger of attributing too much significance to the material world while taking our eyes off the spiritual world of faith. Traditional colleges that train ministers for the church do so by teaching from the writings of theologians and biblical scholars and preachers tend to shape their sermons from the insights of specifically Christian authors. Church life has long reflected this narrow pool of resources and thinking.

People of faith may enjoy the intricate details of animal society revealed by David Attenborough[103] and be awed by the findings of astronomy presented by physicist, Brian Cox.[104] However, when it comes to what they believe about humanity, nature and God, Christians tend to revert to a theology that has no real place for these insights. Yet surely, if we hold a conviction about our connectedness with the natural world, it should be consistent with our spiritual or religious beliefs. If we must compartmentalise our faith away from these other convictions because they do not easily fit together, it suggests that our faith is too narrow and does not encompass the whole of life.

---

[103] Sir David Attenborough (1926 -) is a world-renowned English broadcaster and naturalist.
[104] Brian Cox OBE (1968 -) is an English physicist who serves as professor of particle physics in the School of Physics and Astronomy at the University of Manchester. He is well known as a television science presenter.

Does it really matter that God is not mentioned in scientists' writings? The divine presence does not need protection from probing human questions. The impulse of God in the universe will make itself known to us in ways that are both real and consistent. In our small-mindedness, we should not attempt to use every insight from science as proof of God's existence or the correctness of our beliefs. Under the guise of 'defending God and Jesus', Christians have protected themselves in their own comfort zone from anything that does not confirm their belief system. That stance of closed thinking does not lead to personal growth or faith development.

Charles Eisenstein, cultural critic, author and public presenter, is another fellow traveller on this journey. Although Eisenstein does not speak of God in the traditional manner, in many ways he does indeed speak the language of faith. Eisenstein draws upon the findings of quantum physics that suggest a connection between the observed and the observer. Although these findings are not yet fully explained, they have ushered in a new perspective in scientific thinking. The idea that we are all distinctly separate selves has been challenged. The view that humans and human society are somehow materially and spiritually distanced from the natural world in which we live is fading, even in the scientific community. These new insights make a positive contribution to the spirituality of interconnection. Eisenstein points out that philosophically we are in a time of transition towards the reunion of matter and spirit.

Trees, Rivers, Geese, Humans, Soil, Stars: The Story of Us

We're learning that matter has all the properties that we once ascribed to spirit. We are revaluing materiality and working with our hands. That dematerialising has been part of separating ourselves from nature, of transcending nature. We became its lords and masters. The scientific dimension of this separation can be seen in the development of robots and synthesising food, independent of nature. The spiritual dimension of the separation can be seen in the holy person who has nothing to do with the flesh or the world. Seeing the world as unspiritual has led us to treat it as such, as something not sacred. We are healing from that right now. We've been looking for sacredness everywhere but where it is. We can't sustain that any longer. We need a New Story.[105]

Reflecting on the life force of trees, rivers, geese, soil and stars inspires the soul and calms our anxieties. We learn from nature if we *attend* to nature. 'Attending' is an important practice in spiritual life. It means to observe closely what is in front of us: the trunk of a tree, a hidden flower, or the force of a flowing river. Attending means to allow ourselves to see what life is like for the object of our gaze — to consider the growth and intricate beauty of that life, its stamina and fragility, its ways of coping with stress and what nurtures it. It means to comprehend this tiny part of nature as a valid life with its own inherent dignity

---

[105] Charles Eisenstein, excerpt from a TED Talk at Whitechapel, *A New Story of the People*, 2013

and worth. No longer do we value it merely for how we can use it, wood for a house or fire, flowers for the table, the river for water sports. We now value nature on its own terms — not only for its beauty but for its life lived in its own way.

It is true that when we do this we appreciate our own smallness. We comprehend that we are only a tiny part of a magnificent whole that is beautiful, fierce, vulnerable, creative and irrepressible all at once. And being just a tiny part of that mysterious reality is more than wondrous. It means we participate in the divine life force that is both within us and far beyond us. The conception that the heartbeat of the universe, that throbs within every microexpression of the cosmos, also pulsates through human beings confers upon us significance beyond measure. There is healing for the soul in this realisation.

Traditional Christians may fear that this emphasis upon nature is a move towards a secular worldview. From the experience of progressive faith, that fear is ungrounded. Our image of God is not reduced to nature. Rather, it is our perception of nature that is altered — not equating nature with God but bringing it into the realm of the divine presence and care. This faith is a way of seeing that produces gratitude and awe.

The depth of what we experience through a connection to nature is best communicated through art, images, music or poetry. After all, a satisfying spiritual life will not be discovered through intellectual debate. In the end, God is experienced only in the spirit. To that end, I recommend the evocative poems of Wendell Berry.

> *The Peace of Wild Things*
>
> *When despair for the world grows in me*
> *and I wake in the night at the least sound*
> *in fear of what my life*
> *and my children's lives may be,*
> *I go and lie down where the wood drake*
> *rests in his beauty on the water,*
> *and the great heron feeds.*
> *I come into the peace of wild things*
> *who do not tax their lives with forethought*
> *of grief. I come into the presence of still water.*
> *And I feel above me the day-blind stars*
> *waiting with their light. For a time*
> *I rest in the grace of the world, and am free.*[106]

One pathway towards a heightened awareness of God's presence and lure is through an observant, loving encounter with the natural living world. The very earth beneath our feet is holy ground. 'Take off your shoes.' Be still and unhurried. Simply observe what is before you without assessing or categorising it. Allow nature its place, for we are all a piece. This is the New Story of us.

---

[106] Wendell Berry, *The Peace of Wild Things* from *The Selected Poems of Wendell Berry*, Counterpoint *1999l* and available online. On a number of online sites, it is possible to hear Berry himself recite *The Peace of Wild Things*.

CHAPTER SIX

Dismantling the Barriers that Separate Us

> *He drew a circle that shut me out –*
> *Rebel, heretic, thing to flout;*
> *But love and I had the wit to win*
> *We drew a circle that took him in.*
>
> Edwin Markham

Imagining that we can create a peaceful, thriving, global village through restraints on violence alone would be foolish. It is not enough for individuals and nations merely to refrain from killing each other. We must work intentionally to develop respectful relationships with those who are different from ourselves. The vision of "a more beautiful world we all know is possible"[107] only becomes

---

[107] This is the phrase used by cultural commentator, Charles Eisenstein, to describe our motivating vision of the future.

practical when we take seriously the need to dismantle the humanly constructed barriers that separate us. The new spiritual tapestry includes the conviction that we are called to dismantle whatever causes division and hatred. Although Christian doctrines do not refer to this need or teach these skills, this chapter will draw upon two biblical stories that have wisdom to inform and help us.

Forgiveness has always been central to Christian faith. Apparently, the radical Jesus said we should forgive our enemies. According to tradition, while he was dying in excruciating pain, Jesus asked God to forgive those who crucified him — practising forgiveness beyond what most of us can imagine doing. And central to traditional Christianity is the idea that God has forgiven us. Therefore, it is not that communities influenced by Christianity don't value forgiveness as a compassionate and godly act. The trouble is, it's so very hard to do.

Forgiveness, like friendship, is a treasure that grows slowly through deliberate reflection and conscious choice. There are stages in the forgiveness process and we cannot demand it happen quickly. There is a delicate balance to be reached between practising forgiveness and fighting injustice when we have been wrongfully harmed. Forgiveness is not based on pretending no harm has been done. At some point on the journey of reconciliation forgiveness and/or apology may become the key to the healing process. Unfortunately, there is no simple formula to teach us how to forgive. But there are two ingredients that cannot be left out of the mix. The first is truth-telling and the second is engaging with the other person or group on the level of our shared humanity. These cannot happen unless we choose to cross the barriers that separate us and open a dialogue.

Developing cross-cultural links and respect between people that are currently divided contributes to a positive peace. This chapter is not about eliminating natural differences in language and culture. We can establish links across such natural divides through education and cultural exchanges. At the same time, it is immensely valuable to maintain and cherish differences of language, history and folklore that give a community its unique identity. Human beings, including those with a mixed heritage, need cultural roots. Diversity is a treasure. For instance, it would not be a step forward for everyone on earth to speak the same language. But it would be a step forward if everyone learned one of the languages of their neighbours. Learning to live together does not mean we all become the same. Whenever that is expected, it usually means that those of the dominant culture insist that minorities 'fit in' and become 'like us'. That is not the path to respectful relationships.

It is the humanly constructed, artificial barriers that separate us that should be dismantled. These include the destructive divisions of wealth/poverty, military or economic power / dependency, the long-term effects of oppression / submission, and opposing claims of religious / ideological truth. Entrenched divisions caused by economic inequality, use of violence and other forms of coercive power or injustice are all spiritual issues. These divisions will not be healed without addressing their root causes. The fight for social justice is justified on its own merits and also because it aids the peace-building effort. This issue is addressed in chapter four, *Abundance, Scarcity or Enough?* This chapter will deal primarily with the fourth barrier, that created by religious and communal ideologies. Added to them are two natural differences that society develops into artificial barriers — race and gender. We can celebrate our ethnic and gender differences while recognising the destructive power of racism and sexism — attitudes fed by arrogance, ignorance and social power.

Encountering and welcoming the 'other' is a spiritual act. This may be experienced as we openheartedly share our stories with someone of a different cultural tradition. It may happen as we take steps to see what life is like for those who are poor in our neighbourhood or engage in advocacy work. It may happen as we lobby in the political arena for the needs of indigenous or other marginalised groups and for their voices to be heard. It may happen when we refuse to fear or judge an asylum seeker or refugee, choosing instead to listen to their personal story. It may happen when we share a meal with a Muslim, Jew, Buddhist or Hindu and discover the needs, hopes and dreams that we have in common. And it happens when we glimpse the otherness and wonder of the divine impulse from far beyond ourselves.

In other words, being open to the 'other' in a different person, community, religious or cultural group is 'of one piece' with being open to the 'Other' whom we call God. Each experience requires us to let go the fearful, judgemental and protective habits of thought that keep us separate from whatever lies beyond our knowledge. It means suspending our tendency to assume that we know best how the world works, that our experience of it is normal and healthy and that whatever differs from this is suspect. This tendency is within us all. And perhaps, in the early stages of our evolution, it was necessary for our species to survive in a dangerous world. But if we want the world to be less dangerous, as a human species we need to grow beyond this tendency and create a new normal — the normal of open listening, respect and seeing from the other's perspective.

These may read like 'motherhood' statements. But if our society gives such widespread affirmation to cross-cultural respect, why are there such deep divisions in our community? Firstly, we need to acknowledge that even giving intellectual assent to equality and respect for those who are different is not as widespread in the world now as it was even thirty years ago. What is referred to as a populist political movement across Australia, USA, United Kingdom, France and many other nations is fed by just the opposite. Increasingly, it is acceptable to publicly denigrate minorities of race, religion and culture. Social media forums have made it easy for sentiments of hatred and racism to be shared.

Ugly, hurtful, racist remarks are one thing. Most of us still find them abhorrent. But there is a softer version of the populist movement evident now in mainstream politics and culture. Leaders who would never say overtly horrid things about other cultures, nevertheless express their fears that racial and religious differences are causing problems in our community. In the public discussion of threats to our dominant, white, Christian or secular way of life, outspoken leaders barely disguise racist attitudes in slightly more acceptable language. These politicians clearly know that rhetoric of this nature strikes a chord within sections of the population and wins votes.

The groups that are scapegoated now tend to be Muslims, indigenous groups, immigrants, asylum seekers, undocumented workers, and in some sections of society, women. The debate taps into our primal fears of protecting our territory against 'others'. These are the irrational fears, the self-protective tendency that we must overcome. But our fears are not being overcome, they are being fuelled by negativity and the lack of a strong, compelling, alternative vision.

There is another reason that widely-held values of equality and respect are not evident to the extent that might be expected. It has to do with power. Not only do we fear losing our sense of identity if another culture is given too much air-time in our space, we also fear losing our positions of privilege. The claims of indigenous people, women or minorities to be included meaningfully in decision-making are a threat to those whose power has been fast-tracked by historical privilege. White male privilege has dominated our society for centuries. During the twentieth century, liberation and social justice movements achieved significant changes in that pattern of domination. In 1966 women were finally allowed to work after marriage in the Australian Public Service. Australian indigenous people were made legal citizens in 1967. A few decades later the need for child care gained acceptance. From 1973, the 'White Australia Policy' was changed and migrants from beyond Europe were welcomed. But now there is a backlash against these social changes and the concept of equality needs to be championed afresh.

What does the traditional Christianity have to offer this deeply spiritual challenge? There are varied Christian responses, as one might expect. Some Christian congregations are at the forefront of offering the hand of friendship to those who are marginalised because of race or religion. Some have forged new paths of understanding with indigenous, ethnic minority or Muslim communities. But other Christians are engulfed in fear in the same way as many other sectors of society. They erect even stronger barriers against Muslim and other religious groups than existed in earlier decades. Within scripture we also find a mixed bag. Those who look for it can certainly find passages in both the Old and New Testaments supporting the idea of the superiority of the Judaeo-Christian culture. But there are also stories suggesting that God's way is freely open to those who are different. I will draw upon two of these stories shortly.

The irony of some religions is that while they purport to teach love, compassion and holiness, they end up producing self-righteousness and judgement of outsiders. The flaw of religious dogma is that it presents only one path to holy or spiritual living. By definition then, others must be wrong. If there is nothing within a belief system itself that makes space for alternative views, barriers are inevitably erected. For example, an inconsistency is created within Christianity. While encouraging humility in one's own relationship with God, the teaching that other religions are both wrong and ungodly encourages a superior attitude towards the non-Christian world. Humility is not consistently encouraged.

Unfortunately, within Christian faith, the assumption of superiority towards others is not easy to dismantle. The church has not found a way to teach its doctrine of the Trinity as valid for itself without also having to be the ultimate and only truth. The church is founded on a belief system that its members must confess. A confessional system does not have the flexibility that is offered by a movement or convictions concerning a way of life. Even moderate Christians who want to establish friendly relationships with people of other faiths, rarely dismiss the hope that these outsiders will one day acknowledge Jesus as uniquely the Son of God. Although compassion for those who do not believe is encouraged within the Christian community, it also harbours the niggling assumption that the spiritual experience of Muslims, Hindus, Jews and others is invalid. Suppressing or hiding these assumptions, in order to engage respectfully in inter-faith dialogue, is not the same as questioning them.

People of different faiths in Australia now find themselves as workmates, neighbours, even political allies, but rarely friends. The kind of friendship that values, affirms and defends the other through all joys and sorrows is a treasure. But deep friendships that cross over religious divides are rare. Religion is experienced as a barrier to friendship because differences in belief cannot be easily ignored or overcome. Our current cultural climate of fear and practice of scapegoating minorities in Australia has heightened these divisions.

I am aware of a church community who refused to share its carpark with people planning a local mosque on a day when the carpark would otherwise have been empty. Although the church leadership had originally agreed to the request, there was such a furore within the congregation that the offer was withdrawn. Was this because of fear? Christians reflect the fears held widely in the general public when it comes to mosques and the rise of Islam within our society. There is abroad an irrational fear that Muslims are taking over the country and that Christianity will have to fight for survival. Perhaps the fear goes even deeper. Perhaps even subconsciously in this case, these good Christian people feared that the church grounds, dedicated to the service of God, might somehow be compromised, even defiled, by those who worship another God altogether — that is, by those who worship wrongly. As a result, an opportunity to engage with one another as human beings with much in common has been missed.

Jesus and the Woman

Must religious divisions always be this way? Sometimes the ancient writings contain wisdom that is overlooked. I bring two ancient stories to our attention. The first, a New Testament legend concerning Jesus, dates from the late first or early second century.

> *So he [Jesus] came to a Samaritan city called Sychar, near the plot of ground that Jacob had given to his son Joseph. Jacob's well was there, and Jesus, tired out by his journey, was sitting by the well. It was about noon. A Samaritan woman came to draw water, and Jesus said to her, "Give me a drink." (His disciples had gone to the city to buy food.) The Samaritan woman said to him, "How is it that you, a Jew, ask a drink of me, a woman of Samaria?" (Jews do not share things in common with Samaritans.) Jesus answered her, "If you knew the gift of God, and who it is that is saying to you, 'Give me a drink,' you would have asked him, and he would have*

given you living water." The woman said to him, "Sir, you have no bucket, and the well is deep. Where do you get that living water? Are you greater than our ancestor Jacob, who gave us the well, and with his sons and his flocks drank from it?" Jesus said to her, "Everyone who drinks of this water will be thirsty again, but those who drink of the water that I will give them will never be thirsty. The water that I will give will become in them a spring of water gushing up to eternal life." The woman said to him, "Sir, give me this water, so that I may never be thirsty or have to keep coming here to draw water." Jesus said to her, "Go, call your husband, and come back." The woman answered him, "I have no husband." Jesus said to her, "You are right in saying, 'I have no husband'; for you have had five husbands, and the one you have now is not your husband. What you have said is true!"

The woman said to him, "Sir, I see that you are a prophet. Our ancestors worshiped on this mountain, but you say that the place where people must worship is in Jerusalem."

Jesus said to her, "Woman, believe me, the hour is coming when you will worship the Father neither on this mountain nor in Jerusalem. You worship what you do not know; we worship what we know, for salvation is from the Jews. But the hour is coming, and is now here, when the true worshipers will worship the Father in spirit and truth, for the Father seeks such as these to worship him. God is spirit, and those who worship him must worship in spirit and truth."

John 4: 5 – 24

Did this really happen? Who really knows? Probably not, given that it is not recorded in any other accounts of Jesus' life and is clearly intended to convey a theological conviction that Jesus had superpowers of knowledge and was recognised as the Messiah even by non-Jews. This story tends to be a favourite with Christians and has given rise to numerous comforting sermons over the years. The romantic notion is that the man, Jesus, was able to look inside people and know all about them.

The beautiful image of living water that quenches our thirst forever is usually taken to refer to our relationship with Jesus himself. But it can also speak to us of a spiritual connection that satisfies the soul, the kind of spiritual connection that Jesus himself taught and practised through times of prayer and quiet reflection. Who among us does not long to be loved, at peace and at rest in the core of our souls? It may be articulated variously as 'having a relationship with God', tapping into the divine presence, or experiencing love and purpose. In a world of superficiality, this picture of living, refreshing water draws us towards true depth of spirit and resonates within us.

Breaking Barriers of Gender, Ethnicity and Religion

Beyond the comforting sermons, there is a strong barrier-breaking story here that also needs to be told. Let's take the story at face value, putting aside the issue of historical accuracy. Something remarkable happened at that well that should not have happened. Jesus stepped across the three barriers of gender, ethnicity and religion.

Instead of focussing on the questionable morals of the woman, as most preachers do, notice that Jesus chose to open the conversation. He asked for a drink. She had a bucket. She could have delayed her task and helped him. But then we discover the request for a drink was primarily a way of making a connection. The very act of inviting a conversation with a woman on her own broke the custom of the day. It's not that men couldn't speak to women at all but doing so without male companions was not the accepted social norm. And the kind of conversation that ensued was a theological debate usually reserved for men. We discover that this woman was living with the sixth man in her life and they were not married. The moral struggles, tragedies, or abuses in her life had not weakened her intellect or her wit. She was a person who could engage in debate over important matters.

Although Jesus had suggested she bring her husband out for the discussion, she persisted alone and launched into the religious arguments that divided them. Fortunately, Jesus rose to the challenge and continued engaging with her on her own. It later becomes clear that the disciples wouldn't have given her the time of day. But this woman was not to be written off by judgemental or discriminatory males. And she wasn't. In the end, both Jesus and the woman teased each other into an important human encounter. *Gender — the first barrier dismantled.*

The setting was Samaria and she was Samaritan. Church-goers will be familiar with the history of bad-blood between Jews and Samaritans. Each of their leaders taught that it was wrong to have any contact with the opposite group, and neither was to enter each other's territories or even to speak to one another. These tensions were exploited by the Romans as they had done between rival tribal factions in other territories. The historian, Josephus, reports numerous violent confrontations between Jews and Samaritans throughout the first half of the first century. Despite much shared heritage, Jews regarded Samaritans as enemies. The seemingly harmless sentence, "Jesus came to a Samaritan city", describes a radical departure from custom. Jesus crossed the geographical boundary, inviting an encounter that could not happen in normal circumstances. In order to break down barriers, we must enter the home ground of those we consider different, enemies, or other than us. *Ethnic conflict — the second barrier dismantled.*

The division between these enemies was very deep by the first century. The split had developed over identity and belief, following the time of the exile. The place for worship was central to their fierce disputes. The Samaritans worshipped at Mount Gerizim where they had built a temple and the Jews worshipped in their temple in Jerusalem. This woman, who came to the well in the middle of the day, met Jesus, and rather than defer to the men for controversial debate, went straight to the heart of what stood between them. "Our ancestors worshiped on this mountain, but you say that the place where people must worship is in Jerusalem." There was no way to compromise. So here they were, having an inspiring encounter as human beings concerned for what nourishes the spirit, and yet their ethnicity and religion divided them. This is the perennial reality in the human community, that religion more often divides than unites. We can almost hear the sadness in her as she laments in effect, "We are on opposite sides of a chasm that is far bigger than either of us, and it will ever be so."

At first Jesus gives the typically religious, Jewish response. He insists that his religion is better than hers. Jews are right. Samaritans are wrong. Disappointing to hear such words of racial and religious superiority on the lips of Jesus. But he was a man of his time and along with all his countrymen, this expresses his indoctrination. The tragedy of this divisive teaching stands in stark contrast to the conversation they have just shared. And it seems the frustrating sadness of that is not lost on Jesus either. He is forced to face the limitations of his own religion. Having engaged with her on the common ground of their humanity about living water, a more satisfying spirituality, the inadequacy of his own answer confronts him. Despite saying that salvation is from the Jews, Jesus himself is moved to admit that the structures of Judaism will one day fall away. In effect he says, "The hour is coming when ... the religious structures of both our faiths will be gone." Could it be that religious organisations, with all their grandeur and limitations, are not permanent in the big scheme of things?

We know that this ancient text was written after the Romans destroyed the temple in Jerusalem in 70CE. The story aimed to comfort Christian Jews with the idea that worship of God is not tied to the temple but to Jesus himself. The idea supported the trend adopted at the end of the first century and the early second century by Christian Jews who refocused their worship in just this way. This transition eventually became the basis of creedal Christianity. At the same time, non-Christian Jews were also refocusing their faith practices. Following 70CE, with the Temple gone, the Jews transitioned their faith towards keeping the law through what became Rabbinic Judaism. Like the transition we find ourselves in today, religion itself was changing.

And yet, according to this story, Jesus did not lament this change and loss. Remarkably, it becomes a life-enhancing release. Although not historically accurate, the story expresses the hope that when the religious structures disappear, human beings will be able to experience a deeper spirituality and "worship in spirit and in truth." When religion no longer dictates externally how or where people should relate to God, people of faith will be freed to explore a more authentic, integrated spirituality. There is no suggestion here that this development of a more mature religious spirit will be automatic or easy. Many people depend upon the church, synagogue or mosque to organise their spiritual life. Without those structures, we are responsible for our own spiritual practices and communal experience. Many people find that difficult and prefer to depend upon organised religion to shape their spiritual lives. This is exactly the situation that many former church members find themselves in today.

When a religion focusses its communal worship in specific buildings, it sets the scene for conflict with outside communities who make a special claim to that same place. It also sets up the likelihood of conflict within the religion itself between groups who are attached to different centres of worship. This is exactly what happened in ancient times between Jews and Samaritans. Where should one worship? At the Jerusalem temple or on Mount Gerizim? If such disputes divide us, how can we find common ground? Can I open my heart to you, if my religion teaches me that the way you honour God is wrong? How can we build a relationship of mutual respect and trust if I have no respect for your cultural heritage? Must I honour God by refusing to recognise your desire to worship God differently in the manner of your upbringing?

Is it possible to let go of who is right and who is wrong? The way the story is told, this was not Jesus' first response. He insisted that his religion was right and hers was wrong. "Salvation is from the Jews." But then the conversation took that remarkable turn. We're told the impossibility of that stock-standard answer was obvious, even to Jesus. The typical religious answer is unsatisfying. And so it is for us. The traditional explanation of what divides us is found to be inadequate when we discover our common ground with others — when we dare to become friends. There can be no shared humanity or positive peace between different cultural groups if we hold so tightly to, "Ours is the only way."

Remarkably, in our story, a third way opened up. Perhaps the place of worship doesn't matter so much after all. If the beloved, central temple is gone, the sacred place for worship can no longer be essential to spiritual life. According to this ancient legend, Jesus himself realised that the solution was not to focus on buildings, place, the law, tradition or communal authorities. All these religious norms are external human constructions and cause division. They can be set aside as secondary to humanity and shared spirituality. The need was, and is, to go deeper, to focus on that which only God sees fully — the human spirit. "God is spirit, and those who worship him must worship in spirit and truth." Jesus and the Samaritan woman at the well met, connected, faced the hate-filled barriers between them and found common ground in spirituality. In effect, this realisation brought their conversation back to its beginning, to the *living water.* *Religion — the third barrier dismantled.*

Separating the Sacred from the Secular

Religions hold certain places as sacred. They are elevated by consecration for worship or a legendary event such as the birth or death of a religious character, the place of miracles or the relics of holy people. For Jews, for instance, the Western Wall, the remnant of the temple wall closest to the temple Mount in Jerusalem, is the holiest place to pray. And many Christians, for instance, stream to the 'Holy Land' to see for themselves where Jesus is believed to have been born, walked or died. Around the world, cathedrals and churches are blessed and set apart from ordinary use for worship. Some Christians make pilgrimage to Lourdes and Fatima as sites of visions and healings. Muslims regard the mosques in Mecca, Medina and Jerusalem as the holiest sites to which they make pilgrimage. Buddhists make a pilgrimage to the birthplace of Buddha and the Mahabodhi Temple that houses what is believed to be the Bodhi Tree where the Buddha realised enlightenment. Hindus regard various temples as holy as well as the Ganges River. In China, traditionalists regard the Temple and Cemetery of Confucius as holy places. It is a natural human tendency to mark as sacred any place where holiness was experienced or evident.

It is important to differentiate between places that are merely special because they remind us of loved ones or significant events and those places that are called 'sacred'. The latter implies that there is a peculiar connection between God and humanity facilitated within that space.

We are taught to regard a holy place as qualitatively different from other places. The sacredness often derives from a vision or revelation or from a religious ceremony that creates a spiritual demarcation around a site. Many believe there is a kind of power associated with sacred places that can touch the spirit in ways that ordinary places cannot. Positively, these places can facilitate an awareness of the divine presence, partly through the spiritual wisdom associated with their history and partly through the heightened expectations of the pilgrim.

There is, however, a serious downside to regarding certain places, people or times as sacred and different from all other places, people and times. This religious outlook discourages us from recognising the presence of the divine in the everyday. Ordinary places are devalued. Our homes, landscapes, cities and wild-places are overlooked as the location of God. Formal religious creeds and rituals do not affirm the experience of the divine in a magnificent waterfall or a beautiful flower, nor in the meeting of friends, nor in the everyday chores of feeding babies or preparing a meal. We forget that everything is infused with the holiness and wonder of divine beauty if only we open our inner eyes to appreciate it.

Instead, the religiously minded seek the presence of God in gatherings within church buildings, synagogues, temples, mosques and other dedicated sites. The stage is thus set for religious disputes over sacred sites, the kind of vehement disputes that divide communities to this day. Similarly, ceremonies deemed to be sacred because they invoke the presence of God can become barriers even between members of the same religion. Religious communities should be reassured that worship is not essentially linked to specific ceremonies, words or liturgies. It is not about whether we kneel, stand, or prostrate ourselves. It is not about whether we prefer choral, organ or modern music. It is not about whether we pray facing a certain direction, cross ourselves or finish every prayer with the words, "In Jesus' name." These ceremonial forms of religion may or may not reflect an inner spiritual attitude. We should aim to worship "in spirit and in truth." In the end, it is the intention and longing of the soul that opens a connection between a human being and the divine presence. It is within the spirit that love takes root. It is within the spirit that compassion and beauty arise and our interaction with others originates. Outward forms of religious practice are helpful only if they encourage these inner realities.

A time is coming when faithful worshippers will not worship God in Jerusalem or on Mt Gerizim — did Jesus himself really predict the death of religious forms and structures? As a faithful Jew living prior to 70CE, that is highly doubtful. Nevertheless, his teaching throughout the gospel stories suggests that a person's inner spiritual disposition mattered more than outward religious observance. Social justice for the poor and marginalised mattered more than worship traditions. Jesus made it clear that people who purported to serve God but valued power over compassion lacked spiritual integrity. Holding on to 'correct' religious beliefs mattered less than what was in the heart. Overall, we have enough from the Jesus tradition encouraging us to dismantle these divisive barriers between the sacred and the secular.

The Early Church Was Forced to Rethink its Beliefs

There is another biblical story worth revisiting regarding the crossing and dismantling of barriers between people. It comes not from the stories of Jesus, but from the legends of the early Christian community. It is found in Acts 10 and Acts 11:1-18 — the delightful story of the conversion of the Italian centurion, Cornelius. Even for Acts, a romanticised account on the whole, this story stands out as non-historical. It reads like the script of a play. At the least, it is a stylised legend to mark the spread of the new Christian movement into the gentile population. It deserves to be told for the sheer beauty of its irony and balance. There is space only for excerpts here, but the whole story is worth reading if a Bible is at hand.

> *In Caesarea there was a man named Cornelius, a centurion of the Italian Cohort, as it was called... One afternoon at about three o'clock he had a vision in which he clearly saw an angel of God coming in and saying to him, "Cornelius. ... Now send men to Joppa for a certain Simon who is called Peter."... He called two of his slaves and*

a devout soldier from the ranks of those who served him, and after telling them everything, he sent them to Joppa.

About noon the next day, as they were on their journey and approaching the city, Peter went up on the roof to pray. He became hungry and wanted something to eat; and while it was being prepared, he fell into a trance. He saw the heaven opened and something like a large sheet coming down, being lowered to the ground by its four corners. In it were all kinds of four-footed creatures and reptiles and birds of the air. Then he heard a voice saying, "Get up, Peter; kill and eat." But Peter said, "By no means, Lord; for I have never eaten anything that is profane or unclean." The voice said to him again, a second time, "What God has made clean, you must not call profane." ... Now while Peter was greatly puzzled about what to make of the vision that he had seen, suddenly the men sent by Cornelius appeared. ... So Peter invited them in and gave them lodging. The next day he got up and went with them, and some of the believers from Joppa accompanied him. The following day they came to Caesarea. Cornelius was expecting them and had called together his relatives and close friends. ... Then Peter began to speak to them: "I truly understand that God shows no partiality, but in every nation anyone who fears him and does what is right is acceptable to him..." While Peter was still speaking, the Holy

Spirit fell upon all who heard the word. Then Peter said, "Can anyone withhold the water for baptizing these people who have received the Holy Spirit just as we have?" ... Then they invited him to stay for several days.

Acts 10: 1-17a, 23-24, 34-36, 44-48

Although Cornelius is the one who is formally received into the Christian community, it is in fact Peter who undergoes the greatest change. His ingrained prejudices were deeply challenged, resulting in an immense heart-type transformation. Jews shunned gentiles on the grounds of ethnicity and religion. But their military oppressors, the Romans, were hated most of all. Although Cornelius is described as a man who feared the Jewish God, he still represented those on the other side of that social / psychological chasm. Peter, the devout Jew, was about to be shocked to his core.

Peter learned through a strange vision that the impurity label, concerning animals, food or people, is an artificial human creation. God never considers anyone impure, whatever their race, religious upbringing, occupation, gender or role in the social order. Better than any other in the New Testament, this story captures the radical insight that all human beings are equal in the sight of God — an idea that was unheard of in the ancient world.

The travel motif is beautifully balanced. The first journey by Cornelius' men is from Caesarea, a Roman stronghold, to Joppa, a thoroughly Jewish town. The second journey is the one back from Joppa to Caesarea by Peter and his attendants. This geographical crossing of boundaries is symbolic of crossing over the deeper divisions between them. Days of walking across the miles from one territory to the other required time. The effort of walking became a physical act of commitment, allowing the walkers slowly to exit their comfort zone and enter the unknown territory of the 'other', not sure of where it all might lead.

And every step of the way, the story tells us, it was God who took the initiative. The new boundary-breaking experience wasn't a thought-out strategic plan on the part of the early church. An unexpected revelation broke into the consciousness of these men through visions. After Peter arrived in Caesarea, he didn't even get a chance to finish his preaching when the hearers become ecstatic with praise. There is no record of Cornelius and his household repenting or making a statement of belief, or even Peter performing the laying-on-of-hands. The whole spiritual event bypassed the religious protocols that were standard, both for those first Christians and for many throughout the centuries since.

Peter was a leader of the fledgling Christian community. He had travelled with Jesus in person and committed himself to the Way of Jesus after his death. But according to this story, everything he assumed about how God connected with people was thrown into question. It seems an experience of the divine presence doesn't require the rituals that the church attaches to it after all. How often people of faith assume that their ceremonies are essential for spiritual health. Apparently not, according to this little narrative gem.

When Theology Conflicts with Our Experience of God

Perhaps the most overlooked but essential message of this story is that our experience of the divine presence and our theology or understanding of it can be way out of step with each other. Remember that this narrative is found in Acts 10. But eight chapters earlier, in Acts 2 is an idealistic, romanticised account of the wonder and power of the earliest Christian community. We are told the disciples were filled with the Spirit, performed healing miracles, were effective in outreach and radical in caring for the needy. They were astonishing times! When church people today say they want to be 'a New Testament church' they usually mean that they wish they could return to the wonder-filled days of the church in Acts 2-9. Nothing seemed to be lacking in the first followers' faith or experience of God in those very early days. It is usually assumed, therefore, that their understanding of God, Jesus and the faith was sound at that point. But not so.

Indeed, in Acts 10 we are shocked to discover huge gaps in their understanding of God's presence and action in the world. Their theology was inadequate even though their experience of God's presence was breath-taking. The account of Cornelius and his dramatic experience of God reveals that the belief system of the earliest church was actually so narrow as to be in urgent need of correction, which was later recorded in Acts 10 and 11. In other words, it is quite possible to be strong in faith, feel empowered by God, and even to see lives changed as a result, while being quite blinkered in theological understanding.

Embedded in the psyche of these first Christians was the notion that they pleased God by keeping themselves uncontaminated by anyone or anything 'unclean'. Until the positive, personal encounter with gentiles recounted in the story in Acts 10, they hadn't recognised this 'shadow side' of their beliefs. In facing this, they were about to move through to another stage of faith. *Sometimes Christians imagine that being faithful to God means holding tightly to what they have been taught and never admitting new ideas that might compromise their beliefs. But if we take our cue from this story in Acts, we will realise that spiritual growth involves adjusting our beliefs following new experiences that introduce us to new insights. That process is not compromise but faith development.*

It is important to keep this in mind when the church uses stories of dramatic conversions, healings and changed lives that are presumed to validate traditional Christian teaching. Spiritual experiences can be real for human beings across the globe irrespective of their belief systems or lack thereof. Experiences of change and of God's presence may be real but prove nothing in relation to doctrine or theology. Like the earliest followers of Jesus, our inner awareness of the divine presence can be truly at odds with our beliefs about God and others. For instance, we can be grateful when new Christian converts find renewed hope and sense of purpose from God's presence, without agreeing with the fundamentalist doctrines that they promote. We do not need to belittle a person's inner experiences because we do not accept their theological views. Others will understand God differently from ourselves because we and they have had different experiences and been nurtured within different religious communities. If only we can remember this, it will help us to regard others with humility and respect. Likewise, we can ask for the same respect in return.

Breaking Barriers of Custom and Culture

It is not without significance that at the end of this unexpected experience, the story says, "Peter stayed a few days" in the house of Cornelius. This wasn't a case of travel to a new place, do some missionary preaching, then travel safely home again. Ever shared a home with different people? Sharing a meal together is itself a barrier-breaker. Jews did not share table fellowship with gentiles. The dietary and purity laws made that impossible. To say that Peter stayed in the home of Cornelius — eating with the household, participating in the family intimacy involved in sharing space day and night — is loaded with significance. He was breaking all sorts of rules and expectations.

Perhaps one of the most transforming experiences any of us can have is to live with those who are vastly different from ourselves. I know this from personal experience of living for some years in a multi-cultural, multi-faith residential community. As human beings, we all face the same character challenges, whatever our faith. It becomes more difficult to hold on to prejudices when sharing our stories, our hopes and dreams and the ordinary tasks of everyday life with others. The imagined impregnable barriers of custom and culture dissolve when people become friends. Moving into the realm of the other person physically assists the journey of the heart and spirit. In the biblical story, Peter and Cornelius broke through the barriers of narrow-mindedness that had stood between them. They achieved this breakthrough by going beyond their comfort zones, travelling across geographical barriers and sharing personal space. *Custom and culture – the fourth barrier dismantled.*

Sometimes, when we imagine that we are ourselves in control of our social / political world, something inexplicable happens when new initiatives are taken by unlikely people in unfamiliar ways. We are surprised by the imaginative contribution made by someone or some group that we had dismissed or underestimated. Because they don't do things our way, we find our own minds and hearts stretched. Those people we had put in a box and

Dismantling the Barriers that Separate Us

ignored have gifts to share with us that we had not understood.

In Australia, we have experienced this with waves of refugees and immigrants. Since the Second World War, Italians, Greeks, Vietnamese, Cambodians, Iranians, Rwandans and Sudanese, just to name a few, have been welcomed to Australia with hesitation and wariness because none of them shared white Australians' British heritage. In each case we have been enriched by their unique gifts and culture. Most of all, we white Aussies have been taken on a journey that has stretched our imagination beyond ourselves and what we thought we knew.

In our story, after Peter's destabilising experience in the home of Cornelius, he returned to the Christians in Jerusalem to share with them what had happened. (This continuation of the story is found in Acts 11.) Peter could no longer regard gentiles, even Romans, as 'less than', impure, or in any way inferior as spiritual human beings. It would have been unnerving for the early Christians to discover that what they had assumed about the exclusive claims of their faith was quite inadequate to explain the new situation. The ground had shifted under their feet and they were having to catch up with this new reality and adjust their belief system to accommodate it. Finally, after much heart-searching and arguments, they named the challenging new reality that God had included even the gentiles in the spiritually renewed life. It was a groundbreaking insight that forced the early Christian community to change.

A Spiritual Tapestry

Over the centuries, the church has had to rethink its theology in relation to issues such as slavery, the inequality of women, colonialism, racism, the harsh treatment of children, homosexuality and what it means to be church. Christians often debate whether the church will have any place in a future society when they themselves no longer consider its doctrines credible nor its institutional framework worthy of respect. We simply don't know the answer yet. But we do know two things. The church only has a future if, like the Christians in this story from Acts, it is prepared to rethink its basic beliefs and exclusive assumptions. The Christian community must expand its thinking and incorporate new wisdom for a new world. Secondly, we know that the impulse and presence of the divine will always be experienced by human beings well beyond the confines of the church's theology, structures and ceremonies.

We don't need to belittle or criticise others in the process of defining our own identity and our own faith. We should define ourselves, not by whom we exclude, but by whom we include. The challenge for people of faith in our current pluralist society is to embrace diversity with the humility to learn from what we do not understand. Bruce Sanguin[108] comments thus on the story of the three Magi who travelled from the East to see the baby Jesus:

---

[108] Bruce Sanguin, Psychotherapist, Marriage Therapist and Minister of the United Church of Canada, author in the field of evolutionary spirituality.

They have the wisdom to realise that the Holy One is not restricted to revealing Herself to only their people. They've taken their heads out of their own Bibles long enough to gaze up and out at what is the source of our fundamental unity, rather than at what divides us. The wise ones intuited what science has now confirmed, that the basis of the unity of all peoples of faith is biospiritual. We have come from the same place and are made of the same stuff. We are stardust, reconfigured in human form, inspired by the Creator. They gaze up at the stars and realise that a very special human being is about to be born, a child who is meant to transcend cultures, transcend religious differences, and point us all in the direction of a compassionate Father, the love which fired it all into being.[109]

Adjusting our thinking and confronting our prejudices alone will not bring an end to conflict. It would be naïve to pretend that merely making friends with people of other cultures and faiths will put an end to wars. The processes of truth-telling, forgiveness, reparations and treaty agreements are all critical where there has been civil violence, theft of territory or war. There are some notable examples of where a Truth, Justice and Reconciliation Commission or similar body has formalised truth-telling and aided healing. But irrespective of whether these formal

---

[109] Bruce Sanguin, *Paying Homage: Being Christian in a World of Many Faiths* in *The Emerging Christian Way*, Copperhouse 2006 p.138.

processes are in place, the basics remain the same. Encountering each other at the level of our shared humanity is the first step towards understanding and forgiveness. The focus of this chapter has been on taking the first step in that direction.

We have a choice. We can remain in our segregated corners, entrenched in our legitimising theologies and national ideologies or we can move beyond them, into the territory 'in between' where anything could happen. There is no third choice. Practising forgiveness and all the steps that lead towards healing are central in the spiritual life. Whatever happens politically, it is at the level of communal and individual prejudice and hatred that the on-going task of breaking down barriers is needed. We all have neighbours, so we all have a part to play in the process. The question is, will our faith tradition help or hinder us?

So often in the past two thousand years, Christianity has contributed to the cycle of hatred and the hurts of history. But hidden in plain sight, within scriptural narratives such as those above, is the key to dismantling the seemingly insurmountable barriers that divide the human family. Drawn from the biblical tradition, a commitment to dismantle those barriers has become part of the new spiritual tapestry. As a first step towards addressing our ugly divisions, we must refuse to dismiss whole communities as wrong or inferior based purely on differences in race, gender, culture or religion.

CHAPTER SEVEN

Our Beautiful Messy Lives

> *Who looks outside, dreams.*
> *Who looks inside, awakes.*
>
> Carl Jung

How are we to understand ourselves? Is there a relationship between spiritual and psychological dynamics and if so, does it matter which language we use to speak about the personal aspect of faith? These days, spiritual growth is sometimes described as 'becoming more fully human' — but what does that mean? Theological colleges have traditionally offered courses on 'Humanity, Sin and Grace'. Does the new spiritual perspective discard these doctrines, or are there some threads of insight worth retaining? This chapter seeks to unpack the psychological effects of the interrelated issues of judgement, morality, shadow self, true self, false self, spiritual awareness, perfection, imperfection and the creative transformation of the heart and mind.

In the 21st century we have a much better grasp of psychological development than we had in earlier times. The currently popular phrase, 'becoming more fully human' suggests an increase in our self-awareness, the development of healthy relationships, acceptance of our mortality and our role within the interconnected life-system on this planet, maturity in selflessness and compassion, and fulfilment of our life-giving potential. It is almost unheard of in this modern discussion to speak of 'sin and grace', as though to do so introduces old-fashioned religious jargon that was always unhelpful and is now totally out of place. Perhaps that is true, and yet, many Christians seek to be reassured that they have not 'thrown out the baby with the bathwater'. Is it possible to construct a meaningful, faith-oriented concept of humanity to replace the negative doctrines we may reject?

Sin, Judgement and Shame

The concept of spiritual growth in traditional Christianity emphasises firm, trusting belief in God the Father and Son, moral excellence, and evidence of the 'fruit of the Holy Spirit'. Contrasting with the 'gifts of the spirit' that refer to sporadic, perhaps supernatural gifts from God, the 'fruit' of the spirit were described by Paul in his letter to the Galatians as "love, joy, peace, patience, kindness, generosity, faithfulness, gentleness, and self-control."[110] These character qualities and ideals of spiritual maturity are valued by most of us whose faith has been formed in the church. However, they were not always valued within church culture.

By the second century, the church's concerns shifted focus from faith in Christ and the development of a Christ-like character to the consequences of sin and the nature of the second person of the Trinity. By the third and fourth centuries, the fear of judgement and hell had become a prominent theme in Christian debates. At that time, it was thought that 'serious' sins committed after baptism would not be forgiven. Hence, the Emperor Constantine was not baptised until he was on his deathbed in 337CE (having been converted in 312CE) for fear that he might sin after baptism and not enter heaven.

This practice of deathbed baptism was not uncommon while debate raged over the possibility of a 'second repentance'. Regarded by many at the time as having the authority of scripture,[111] in relation to baptism,

---

[110] Galatians 5:22-23 Although the earliest reasonably complete manuscript of Galatians dates to approximately 200CE, the original letter would have been composed around 50-60CE.

[111] This was long before the Council of the Church decided which books should be accepted as part of a second scripture or the New Testament. *The Shepherd of Hermas* was written in the late first or early second century. The New Testament canon of today was not accepted until the Council of Bishops at Carthage in 397CE. Even after this date, church leaders debated the inclusion of certain books. This was especially so during the Protestant Reformation of the church in the 16th century.

The Shepherd of Hermas states, "Indeed, all the saints who have sinned up to this day will be forgiven, if they repent with all their heart and drive away double-mindedness from their heart" (Vision II, 6.4). Notice the phrase, "up to this day". Early believers were deeply troubled by the fear of not being forgiven by God at their time of judgement. That fear of God's eternal punishment persisted, so that visions of heaven and hell fell like a shadow over the lives of Christian believers in ancient and medieval times.

This all begs the question, "What is sin?" A number of specific sins are mentioned in the New Testament and give an indication of what the early Christians considered serious offences against our relationship with God. "For it is from within, from the human heart, that evil intentions come: fornication, theft, murder, adultery, avarice, wickedness, deceit, licentiousness, envy, slander, pride, folly. All these evil things come from within, and they defile a person."[112] In time, lists of sins considered particularly serious were drawn up and, by the Middle Ages, seven 'deadly' sins had been identified: pride, envy, anger, avarice or covetousness, sloth, gluttony and lust. In the medieval Church, sermons, poems and wall paintings presented the sins vividly as a warning of the possibility of being sent to hell. It is not an exaggeration to characterise medieval Christianity as a religion of fear and repression.

Sin was to be avoided at all costs, so church members were urged to purge themselves of any thoughts

---

[112] Mark 7: 21-23. A slightly different list is given in Galatians 5: 19-21

considered sinful. At the same time, the sign of salvation was that the Christian grew into 'the likeness of Christ'. Thus, the church created an unrealistic expectation of moral perfection. The burden of moral demands was psychologically damaging because it placed a weight of unavoidable shame and guilt on ordinary people. Others resisted the sense of shame by projecting false affectations of their own righteousness, which was equally damaging to themselves and the Christian community. Christians were hindered in their personal development because the assumption of guilt and shame that they absorbed from the church's teaching worked against healthy self-acceptance.

The theology of eternal punishment was developed in a pre-scientific society whose view of the structure of the universe was far removed from our own. Heaven was 'up there' where God sat on the judgement throne and hell was 'down there' below the flat earth.[113] In the Jewish and Christian imagination, their God was the only unseen, living God, creator and ruler of the world. Yet still, this unseen God in the heavens, like many other gods of the ancient world, reflected human tendencies towards

---

[113] Ancient Mesopotamian societies believed that there were seven levels of heaven and that the earth also had seven levels below. This belief is mirrored in Islam, Hinduism and Jainism. Early Christianity, and Jesus himself, inherited this belief. In 2 Corinthians 12:2-4 Paul assumes this layering of heaven, saying that he had been caught up into the "third heaven" where he had a vision. It possibly reflects the ancient observation, without the benefit of telescopes or science, that there were seven heavenly bodies that moved in patterns across the sky — the sun, the moon, Mercury, Venus, Mars Jupiter and Saturn — the "classical planets".

revenge, punishment and protection of the tribe. In the spatial worldview of the time, the God who ruled heaven and earth was far removed from our lives, which only served to underscore human unworthiness.

A perfect God and imperfect humanity could not coexist in heaven without some effective purification of human souls. In the minds of early Christians, believers achieved this acceptability to God through two spiritual processes. One process was described as enduring a 'refining fire' — all impurities within our souls being burned up.[114] The other, somewhat contradictory idea was that purity of soul depended upon the 'imputed holiness' of Christ. According to this idea, Christ ascribed or imputed his own holiness onto the believer who was thus made acceptable for the presence of God. The clear message of this doctrine of humanity is that there is no choice we can make outwardly or spiritually to make ourselves acceptable to God. The unworthiness that is deep within our souls can only be cleansed by the action of God from without or the spiritual covering of God the Son. Nothing within our own human nature was affirmed as holy, valuable or acceptable to God. The church cultivated a sense of personal unworthiness, shame and fear that could cripple the spirit.

Although the concepts of judgement and punishment do not appear to have been central in the

---

[114] Malachi 3:2 "But who can endure the day of his coming, and who can stand when he appears? For he is like a refiner's fire and like fullers' soap."

thinking of the historical Jesus, they formed the basis of church doctrines. Without the fear of hell, the doctrine of 'salvation' had little meaning. Without the fear of hell, there was no need for a blood sacrifice and that particular interpretation of Jesus' death. Through the doctrines of heaven and hell, the institutional church was able to make life and death pronouncements concerning the destiny of ordinary people based on what the church deemed as sinful behaviour. This centuries-long grip on spiritual and social power by the religious elite has been waning only in our own lifetimes.

Each of the doctrines of humanity, sin, judgement, heaven, hell, forgiveness through Christ's death and salvation is founded upon the presumption and exercise of ultimate power — the presumed power of God and the power of those who operate in the name of God. We may not wish to recognise it, but an uncritical admiration of coercive power fuels these beliefs. Such power-based assumptions are a far cry from the alternative concept of a divine presence that infuses and energises all life. Religious thought emerges from two very different perspectives concerning divinity, heaven and hell, and humanity. In order to develop a cohesive, alternative spirituality, we must ask more probing questions concerning human nature.

Following a reassessment of the notion that divine power is coercive power and that God pronounced death as the penalty for human sin (see chapters one and two), we should question the themes of punishment and fear that undergird the traditional view of humanity. But if we reject the Christian teaching on the consequences of sin, are we in danger of losing all sense of morality? What do we need to learn and experience to become more fully human? Could we be called to 'holiness' by God without the disempowering concept of imputed holiness? Could we value creative personal transformation without framing it in terms of sin and conversion? Can we embrace wholeness, fulfilment and even 'Christlikeness' without an unreal notion of perfection? Is it straying too far to suggest that there might be a beauty in our imperfection? What stories or insights within the old tradition might be worth preserving to inform a new perspective on our own nature?

Who is Really Blind?

Let's turn to one of the biblical stories that is only found in John's Gospel. It originated within a fierce intra-communal conflict between traditional Jews and Christian Jews. The immediate target of the story was the Jewish religious hierarchy who opposed the disruptive presence of fellow Jews who followed Jesus. We need to look beyond the propaganda of the original story to hear its enduring spiritual challenge. The witty tale of the man born blind is beautifully crafted — full of humour, artistry, irony and profound insight into human nature.

> As he walked along, he saw a man blind from birth. His disciples asked him, "Rabbi, who

sinned, this man or his parents, that he was born blind?" Jesus answered, "Neither this man nor his parents sinned; he was born blind so that God's works might be revealed in him. We must work the works of him who sent me while it is day; night is coming when no one can work. As long as I am in the world, I am the light of the world." When he had said this, he spat on the ground and made mud with the saliva and spread the mud on the man's eyes, saying to him, "Go, wash in the pool of Siloam" (which means Sent). Then he went and washed and came back able to see.

The neighbours and those who had seen him before as a beggar began to ask, "Is this not the man who used to sit and beg?" Some were saying, "It is he." Others were saying, "No, but it is someone like him." He kept saying, "I am the man." ...

They brought to the Pharisees the man who had formerly been blind. Now it was a sabbath day when Jesus made the mud and opened his eyes. Then the Pharisees also began to ask him how he had received his sight. He said to them, "He put mud on my eyes. Then I washed, and now I see."

Some of the Pharisees said, "This man is not from God, for he does not observe the sabbath." But others said, "How can a man who is a sinner perform such signs?" And they were divided. So they said again to the blind man, "What do you say about him? It was your eyes he opened." He said, *"He is a prophet."*

The Jews did not believe that he had been blind and had received his sight until they called the parents of the man who had received his sight and asked them, "Is this your son, who you say was born blind? How then does he now see?" His parents answered, "We know that this is our son, and that he was born blind; but we do not know how it is that now he sees, nor do we know who opened his eyes. Ask him; he is of age. He will speak for himself." His parents said this because they were afraid of the Jews; for the Jews had already agreed that anyone who confessed Jesus to be the Messiah would be put out of the synagogue. Therefore his parents said, "He is of age; ask him."

So for the second time they called the man who had been blind, and they said to him, "Give glory to God! We know that this man is a sinner." He answered, "I do not know whether he is a sinner. One thing I do know, that though I was blind, now I see." They said to him, "What did he do to you? How did he open your eyes?" He answered them, "I have told you already, and you would not listen. Why do you want to hear it again? Do you also want to become his disciples?" ... They answered him, "You were born entirely in sins, and are you trying to teach us?" And they drove him out. ...

Jesus said, "I came into this world for judgment so that those who do not see may see, and those who do see may become blind." Some of the Pharisees near him heard this and said to him, "Surely we are not blind, are we?" Jesus said to them, "If you were blind, you would not have sin. But now that you say, 'We see,' your sin remains.

Excerpts from John 9: 1 – 41

The story becomes a cautionary tale for those who assume moral or religious authority in communities and nations. The one who is considered physically defective, socially outcast and morally or spiritually lacking is found to be the one who has the more legitimate grasp on truth and reality. Those who presume to know what is good and able to make pronouncements upon another's moral or spiritual state are found to be living in a false world of their own making. Being deceived by their own self-righteousness, they are blind.

The Shadow Self and the False Self

The renowned psychologist, Carl Jung,[115] spoke of the 'shadow' in the human psyche. Spiritual writer, Richard Rohr,[116] emphasises the 'true self' and the 'false

---

[115] Carl Gustav Jung (1875 - 1961) was a Swiss psychiatrist who founded analytical psychology.
[116] Richard Rohr (1943 -) is an American Franciscan friar, a Roman Catholic ordained priest, spiritual writer and founder of the *Center for Action and Contemplation* (CAC) in Albuquerque, New Mexico.

self. And psychotherapist, Thomas Moore,[117] speaks of the 'soulful person' who has given up all 'pretence of innocence'. This story from John's Gospel is about the unacknowledged shadow, the projected false self and the pretence of innocence. Those who resist any awareness of their own failings and imperfections by presenting an image of moral excellence or godliness, who see sin only in others, pretend to be something they are not. Because they claim to be the ones who see the world correctly, they make themselves blind to what is real.

Natural human qualities and feelings, that we deny exist within ourselves, become part of our shadow self. Family and religious values and cultural mores determine which aspects of ourselves are destined to become part of our shadow. It is a mistake to make value judgements concerning the shadow in our own souls. The desire for power, sexual urges, ambitions, anger, affection, even talents, laughter and a sense of fun can all be denied if our family or cultural surroundings are disapproving. It is true that repressed life forces, consigned to our shadow self, can erupt in uncontrolled, destructive behaviour. But those life forces are not evil in themselves. They are dimensions of our humanity that need understanding, sensitivity and, sometimes, careful management. If acknowledged and

---

[117] Thomas Moore (1940 -) is an American psychotherapist, former monk and spiritual writer who was influenced by the work of Carl Jung. He has degrees in theology, musicology and philosophy. His book, *Care of the Soul: A Guide for Cultivating Depth and Sacredness in Everyday Life*, was on the New York Times bestseller list for almost a year.

allowed appropriate and creative expression, these aspects of our nature will enrich our personality.

Notice, for instance, how some cultures accept and encourage loud displays of grief when a loved one dies, while in other cultures mourners enter a quiet, private corner to shed a tear. Notice how some cultures celebrate the joys of physical movement in enthusiastic and rhythmic dancing. Yet other cultures tightly control physical movement and teach approved steps, removing the spontaneity and sensuality of dance. Those raised within the Christian church have inherited an anti-body set of values ever since the time of Augustine.[118] Hence the joke told against moralistic Methodism of the 20th century: Question: "Why are Methodists opposed to sex?" Answer: "Because it might lead to dancing." Because sexual desires were considered sinful in church communities, they were often denied. Whatever is denied cannot be adequately understood and integrated. We cannot set appropriate boundaries on the expression of inner drives that we deny exist.

Although not deriving from the historical Jesus, the association of sin with sex has, until recently, wreaked havoc upon the healthy development of generations of pious Christians. Church leaders were expected to be asexual and hence these natural desires were pushed into

---

[118] Augustine (354 CE - 430 CE) was Bishop of Hippo in north Africa. He developed the idea of original sin as the sin of Adam (disobedience to God) inherited by all human beings through concupiscence (strong desire and lust). It could only be cleansed through baptism.

the shadow self of priests and other prominent Christian leaders. Instead of acknowledging the appropriate, positive life force of the sexual drive, insistence upon celibacy resulted in some clergy projecting a false self to the world. The world has been shocked and dismayed at the extent to which this unhealthy process of repression has contributed to the widespread sexual abuse by clergy of vulnerable people and children in their care. Priests pretending to be something they were not and the church pretending to be the innocent, trustworthy institution that it was not has done enormous damage to everyone concerned. The shadow self is never destroyed. Instead of an acknowledged life force finding healthy expression, it too often erupts from the shadow self in uncontrolled, destructive behaviour. In effect, narrow church doctrines on sin and humanity, uninformed by the insights of modern psychology, have failed the whole community.

In political 'hotspots' around the world, some communities have been immersed in violence for decades. Their children learn that violent opposition to the hated enemy is a virtue. Individuals in these societies have pushed the longing for harmony and transparency into the shadow self. Forced to adopt both an aggressive and constantly protective stance, those raised within generational hatred and violence regard any urge to forgive or create harmony as a weakness. A culture of hatred distorts healthy human development because the natural longings for tenderness and openness with others are denied expression. Maintaining a constant high level of hate cripples the personality. Prevented from becoming well-rounded human beings, people are unable to move past the immature obsession with *my* needs, *my* family, *my* tribe. Life-long combatants miss out on the significant experience of inclusive community.

Like the Pharisees in our story, when we project an image of ourselves as righteous, moral and equipped to judge others, we live in an imaginary world of our own making. The self we present to the world is undeveloped and we draw others into this false, shallow world by convincing them of our moral convictions. This is a common temptation within religious communities. The tendency to equate holiness with perfection makes it particularly difficult for religious men and women to recognize and integrate their shadow self. The cost of denying our shadow self is that our soul withers and our personality becomes rigid and harsh. Our laughter becomes forced and, unable to simply 'be ourselves', we do not free others to 'be themselves' either. Instead, we insist others live within the constraints of our preferred moral codes. We are not good company and feel threatened by the creative power of others, whom we strive to control.

When such judgemental, brittle personalities assume positions of leadership they can do much harm. They tend to become bullies in the workplace, believing their behaviour is wise and good for the group. Yet they remain quite unaware of the desires and motives that are hidden beyond their conscious self. When the shadow self is so totally denied, people are unable to recognise what is driving them. Unless we acknowledge, accept and integrate our shadow self, we will become dangerous to our group. The image and convictions that we project outwardly will lack integrity. Therefore, the culture of the community we influence can become toxic for others. We suspect that we are not what we pretend to be but fear looking too closely at hidden aspects of our personality that threaten our self-esteem. To protect the hidden self from exposure to others, we erect barriers in our relationships. Like those who condemned the simple, open-hearted, blind man in the story, our self-righteousness is a delusion. We pretend to have insight, but we are blind.

Our Imperfect, Messy Lives

A spiritual life is not a perfect life. There is no such thing. Therefore, rather than pretending innocence, if we acknowledge that within our own soul there is a mixture of love, selfish ambition, lust, fear, generosity, greed, jealousy and compassion, we have the possibility of embracing our own power creatively. If we understand our complex desires, we can choose our actions more wisely. It becomes possible to reflect on what we really want. We can choose not to let the destructive elements of our personality dictate our behaviour. Instead, we can integrate the elements of our shadow into our lives creatively and manage and control their expression appropriately. Because we recognise lesser motives within ourselves, we are less judgemental when we observe those same drives in others. We can recognise our imperfection and be OK with it. More than OK, we can practice patience with ourselves and appreciate the beauty within our imperfect, messy humanity. We are 'at home in our own skin' and do not have to expend energy projecting a false image for the approval of others. Being able to relax and simply 'be ourselves', we become pleasant company and enjoy the creativity of others.

Thomas Moore likens the life force within to the Greek god of Mars.

> *In the presence of deep power, life becomes robust and passionate, signs that the soul is engaged and being given expression. Mars, when he is honored, gives a deep red hue to everything we do, quickening our lives with intensity, passion, forcefulness, and courage. When he is neglected, we suffer the onslaughts of uncontained violence. It is important, then, to revere the Marsian spirit and to let the soul burst into life — in creativity, individuality, iconoclasm, and imagination.* [119]

It is time people of faith put aside the imaginary concept of perfection. At this point, readers brought up in the church will probably be hearing in the back of their minds the verse from the Gospel of Matthew, "Be perfect as

---

[119] Thomas Moore, *Care of the Soul: A Guide for Cultivating Depth and Sacredness in Everyday Life*, Harper Collins 1992 p. 136.

your heavenly Father is perfect." Coming at the end of the Sermon on the Mount, this verse has sometimes been used as evidence that all the exhortations prior to it are unattainable. We know we cannot be perfect, so Jesus' ideas on moral thought and action can only be an ideal, a dream to aspire to, but not actually achieve. The argument has been, "We can't be perfect, so obviously Jesus didn't expect us to really live that way — to love our enemies or be pure in heart, to turn the other cheek or become peacemakers." But that too easily dismisses the challenge of Jesus' vision for the world.

It is better to read the verse the other way around. Jesus dreamed of a real world where non-violence could be a way of life; where people not only refrain from murder and rape, but go the next step and treat their enemies and women with respect; where there is no need for oaths because honesty is the default standard in the community; where people show mercy and work for peace and harmony; where those who suffer or are grieving are supported; and where those in humble positions are valued as much as the materially rich. This is the breadth and depth of Jesus' vision as laid out in the whole of Matthew 5 — 'the Sermon on the Mount'. Although this teaching is not in the creeds of the church, it remains in the Gospels as a witness to the values of the historical Jesus. In the Western world, it is not that most of us, our institutions and our governments, haven't heard of the Sermon on the Mount, or that we don't understand it. Its moral vision is ignored simply because it is too challenging.

Jesus' vision was a call to go far beyond the usual expectations of religion and the moral codes of the community. He urged his listeners to allow the desire for peace, respect, compassion and justice to become the longing of their inner selves, not an external behavioural code imposed by religion or society. After casting his vision, he concluded by saying that those who live this way, who allow these values to penetrate their desires, would reflect the very nature of God. Peacemaking, respect, humility, honesty, and compassion for the poor and vulnerable all express the impulse of the divine Presence in our lives. When we choose this way of life, when we let it go deep into our hearts and minds so that it motivates us in all our relationships, we mirror the nature of God. We become 'more fully human', more complete, more 'perfect' as God is complete and 'perfect'.

New Testament scholar, Lorraine Parkinson, remarks in similar vein concerning this verse in Matthew 5:48:

> Here I turn the reader's attention to the word *tamam* in Jesus' language, Aramaic. It has been filtered through the Greek word *teleioi* in Matthew's gospel and finally into English as 'perfect'. Both *tamam* and *teleioi* have the meaning of something which is whole or complete. This does not concern moral fulfilment, but is most closely related to the idea

> *of human integrity in a personality which contains no corrupting or divisive elements.*[120]

We can dismiss the artificial, humanly constructed concept of 'perfection' associated with moral purity. Rather than attempt to squeeze ourselves into someone else's idea of the pure human being, it is far better to accept our imperfections, our messiness, and be inspired instead by a vision of the good. Sensing the prompting of the divine presence to move towards expressions of compassion, justice, beauty and respect for the 'other', we will move towards holiness. Holiness is not an abstract notion of purity, a cardboard cut-out of a perfect personality, which simply does not exist. Holiness is real as a reflection of the longings of God. It is not based on ancient, medieval or Victorian assumptions of morality and immorality. Holiness derives from our wholeness, human integrity and the choices we make for the good.

Instead of experiencing our failings and weaknesses as a recurring source of shame and guilt, we need a more nuanced view of our humanity. Brene Brown, acclaimed social worker and author, remarked that we should not be trying to keep our children 'perfect' but, in effect, say to them, "You're imperfect and you're wired for struggle. But you are worthy of love and belonging."[121] Her research shows that the 'wholehearted' are those who accept their

---

[120] Lorraine Parkinson, *The World According to Jesus... his blueprint for the best possible world*, Spectrum 2011 pp 19-20.
[121] Brene Brown, *The Power of Vulnerability*, TED Talk, 2010.

own vulnerability. This echoes the understanding that our imperfections do not prevent us from embracing wholeness or holiness.

This spiritual perspective is not some easy or soft way of moral compromise aimed at avoiding our sinfulness, as some traditionalists would argue. On the contrary, being real about the shadow parts of our psyche is essential to becoming integrated, mature human beings. Being honest about our whole selves will increase our awareness of those habits and tendencies that do not reflect the good that we admire. In fact, facing those aspects of ourselves is essential for our creative transformation. We should not pretend we have no 'sin', to use the religious word. Neither should we give in to those who want to control our lives by telling us what our 'sins' are. We do not need to live with a constant sense of shame in order to become responsible, moral adults. The messiness of our lives is not necessarily ungodly. It is simply a sign of the beauty and natural complexity of being human.

Morality

Morality has an important place within the new spirituality. However, it is not exactly the same as morality in traditional Christianity. As we have seen, moral living was once described according to lists of sins that must be avoided and qualities of character that must be expressed. Are these then rejected? Not exactly. Prohibitions against murder, dishonesty and theft, and personal qualities of patience, gentleness and self-control are still valued. The 'fruit of the Spirit' will develop within the personality of a person who learns to integrate their shadow self. These traditional values of character formation do not conflict in any way with the insights of modern psychology. Nor does the new spirituality deny the existence and possibility of sin in our lives. But rather than creating lists of sins that condemn individuals and generate a sense of shame, the new perspective focusses upon the positive, creative power of love. According to Matthew's Gospel, Jesus was asked to comment on this very issue.

> *[O]ne of them, a lawyer, asked him a question to test him. "Teacher, which commandment in the law is the greatest?"*
>
> *He said to him, "'You shall love the Lord your God with all your heart, and with all your soul, and with all your mind.' This is the greatest and first commandment. And a second is like it: 'You shall love your neighbour as yourself.' On these two commandments hang all the law and the prophets."*
>
> Matthew 22: 35 - 40

The imperative to love God, self and neighbour suggests that if we hear that divine lure towards goodness, generosity and justice, and move towards it, we will naturally find ourselves avoiding those things that harm others. Consider the church's classic list of 'mortal sins' in the context of the person that integrates their shadow self and experiences the lure of God towards love. The sins are pride, envy, anger, avarice, sloth, gluttony, lust. Avarice, or greed, is the unbridled expression of the necessary desire to provide for our needs and the needs of our loved ones. The alternative to greed is not the embrace of poverty or asceticism, as was once assumed. Rather, the positive alternative to greed is the responsible assessment of when enough is enough. When governed by love and respect for our neighbours, the spiritually alert person will want to share generously with those who do not have enough. It is not that we must deny our desire to acquire material goods, but recognising that we may be tempted to accumulate more than we need, we can manage this desire and not allow greed to run riot in our lives.

Similarly with lust, sloth, pride, anger and gluttony — each one, apart from envy perhaps, expresses some quality that, in moderation, is essential to being fully human. Corresponding to this list, note that it is healthy to incorporate respectful sexual relationships, relaxation and rest, confidence and a positive self-image, indignation at and a refusal to accept injustice, and the enjoyment of food into our lives. When any of these drives and experiences are out of control, their dark side becomes damaging to ourselves or others. The religious term for the dark, destructive expression of these natural human impulses is 'sin'. Understandably, we may prefer not to use the word 'sin' because it carries the connotations of the moralising, judgemental, shame-producing culture of traditional

Christianity. In other words, within a new, love-focussed spirituality, destructive 'sins' are still acknowledged, but the preference is for different, less judgemental language. We should be real about these possibilities in our lives and respond by seeking greater self-awareness while focusing on the life-enhancing alternatives.

Yes, there are times when we need to acknowledge that we have been selfish, dishonest or lacking in compassion. Yes, there are times when we need to apologise or put right some wrong for which we are responsible. Yes, there are times when we need to 'do the time' because we have 'done the crime.' But our lives need the balance of love. We need to accept that we 'screw up' sometimes, we misjudge and at times disappoint ourselves. But we are still learning to love others as well as ourselves. We need to recognise that sometimes our sense of shame derives from our social training and our own unreal expectations rather than the conviction of God. In other words, we need to combine courageous honesty about our uncontrolled drives or behaviour with a gentle and forgiving acceptance of our need to grow and change. Because God is still present to us with an invitation to love, justice and beauty, it is that invitation that should focus our attention rather than attitudes of blame, self-recrimination and shame.

When we let go of a dualistic, black and white view of the world, we begin to accept the messiness of our lives. Embracing imperfection, we are less likely to assume that we are always right and those who disagree with us are wrong. We tend not to pronounce that others are 'blind' because we know that we are all simply finding our way in a complex world with many shades and shadows. We will be less sure of the 'right answer' and more aware of the layers of questions. Combining a non-dualistic worldview with an openness to the lure of God, we are able to integrate our shadow self, let go of the false self we once presented to the world, abandon the pretence of innocence, and become 'more fully human'. Despite not having the certainty of answers to so many of life's complex questions, we find we are more at peace within ourselves. The desire of our hearts becomes more attuned to goodness and beauty and less drawn towards doctrine and institutional or political propaganda. Rather than demand answers, we delight in the rich mysteries of life.

Thomas Merton, spiritual director and contemplative, found an exciting wisdom in ignorance acknowledged. When he felt himself in the 'dark', with a disturbing sense of uncertainty, he used it as an invitation to seek the 'thin places', the places where he would glimpse the presence of God. He expressed it so well in this well-known prayer.

> *My Lord God, I have no idea where I am going. I do not see the road ahead of me. I cannot know for certain where it will end. Nor do I really know myself, and the fact that I think I am following Your will does not mean that I am actually doing so. But I believe that the desire to please You does in fact please You. And I hope I have that*

> *desire in all that I am doing. I hope that I will never do anything apart from that desire.*
>
> *And I know that, if I do this, You will lead me by the right road, though I may know nothing about it. Therefore, I will trust You always though I may seem to be lost and in the shadow of death. I will not fear, for You are ever with me, and You will never leave me to face my perils alone.*[122]

On this journey in which we desire to become more loving, just, patient, kind, self-controlled and generous, we need to be gentle with ourselves and others. To 'love our neighbours as ourselves', as Jesus urged, requires patience and compassion for both.

Creative Transformation

Can we experience personal transformation without reference to the traditional concepts of sin and conversion? It may be obvious from the discussion above that the move from the false self to the real self through on-going honest and fearless reflection is an important experience in our personal transformation. But it is unnecessary to think in terms of 'sin' to address the dark side of our personality and behaviours. And it is preferable to speak of 'transformation'

---

[122] Thomas Merton, *Thoughts in Solitude*, 1956. Merton (1915 – 1968) was an adult convert to Christianity, a Trappist monk, a poet, social activist and student of comparative religion.

rather than 'conversion'.

What is needed for this journey towards wholeness? The spiritual mystics and radical thinkers speak of an inner awakening. It is not simply facing our own shadow and letting go of our preferred image, our false self. This is essential. But spiritual awakening also requires a transformed view of the world, embracing new communal values of equality, diversity, fairness, kindness, generosity and love. Process theologians call it *creative transformation*.

The traditional term for this transformation was being 'born again'. Unfortunately, this phrase now conjures up images of evangelical rallies where it means 'accepting Jesus as your Lord and Saviour', sometimes ignoring the need to turn away from corrupt social practices. The decision to 'accept Jesus' does not reflect the transformation in lifestyle and perspective that the phrase 'be born again' originally intended. Of course, within the evangelical tradition there are inspiring stories of transformed lives that must be respected. However, the most common use of the phrase produced a stunted 'conversion', concerned with religious beliefs only rather than transformed values.

An alternative to 'born again' might be the apostle Paul's words in Romans, "Do not be conformed to this world but be transformed by the renewing of your minds, so that you may discern what is the will of God — what is good and acceptable and perfect."[123] The spiritual life is not just about me, it is about everything. It is not about what happens to me after death — ideas of judgement, heaven and hell. It is about the process of orienting my inner life to the greater Reality around me. Spiritual director, Richard Rohr, says,

> *You are objectively in communion with God from the moment of your conception, and there is really nothing you can do about this, except choose to enjoy it and draw life from this Endless Spring or to let it lie idle, which is the only real meaning of sin.*[124]

It would be a mistake to focus on a specific instant when this awakening happens. While we may be able to point to milestones on the journey, spiritual growth is an on-going process and there will no doubt be many 'conversions' along the way. The personal dimension of this spiritual awakening is liberating because we no longer feel we must strive to be what we are not. And if it is real, the personal will also become the communal.

The spiritual life requires us to recognise the addictions and lies that are central to our dominant culture so that we can resist being sucked mindlessly into them. It is about seeing clearly the pretentions and deadening

---

[123] Romans 12: 2
[124] Fr Richard Rohr, OFM, *The Ticking Life Bomb*, adapted *from The Great Chain of Being: Simplifying Our Lives*, quoted on the Centre for Action and Contemplation website, Feb 2015.

values that seduce our society. Some might object that they do not have the gifts of social analysis to do this and fear this spirituality is only for academics. Not so. Many who are not drawn to intellectual analysis, are more than able to intuitively critique the dominant values of their community. We do not have to analyse the abuse of power in society (manipulation, extortion, exclusion and political self-interest) to reject it. People, who primarily do not engage with life intellectually, can still *know* when something is wrong — they sense it. Although we should not disengage our intellect, the perception of what is real, good, just and compassionate takes place in the spirit.

Fortunately, there are some gifted prophets who can articulate the conflict of values for us. They prod our conscience and help us to think through what really matters. Throughout history, the prophets have always 'spoken the truth to power', challenged the mighty ones and called for an alternative way of living. Some of these prophetic voices are directly inspired by the teachings of Jesus, while others echo the same values without any connection to the Christian tradition. All of them highlight the ethical and spiritual choices before us.

Prophets tend to be attacked by those whose power is threatened by their ideas. Too many have been assassinated or suffered for their cause. In former years prophets of the spiritual struggle have included Francis of Assisi, William Wilberforce, Elizabeth Fry, Sojourner Truth, Mahatma Gandhi, Martin Luther King Jr, Rosa Parks, Rachel Carson, Nelson Mandela, Desmond Tutu,

Daniel Berrigan and political dissidents in oppressive regimes. Today's prophets include imaginative thinkers such as Wendel Berry, Arundhati Roy, Ched Myers, Gillian Triggs and Charles Eisenstein, to name just a few of those who have inspired me. Thank God for the prophets!

But we must not think that only a certain class of thinker is called to take a stand. It takes courage to speak out. It takes courage to refuse to participate in the judgemental, selfish choices of our nation and community. And whatever our circumstance, that courage is required of us all. Those who awaken to the spiritual realities around them, who comprehend the destructive values of the powerful, who welcome truth-telling, who look inside and cease pretensions of innocence, will not be satisfied with anything less than movement towards that which Jesus called the Kingdom of God.

Spiritual growth brings with it a heightened awareness of the pain of others. We anguish over suffering in the world and act with compassion wherever we can. Being open to the presence of God entails openness to our neighbours and their insecurities. It becomes increasingly difficult to distance ourselves from those who are discriminated against and exploited. We cannot connect with a God who is intimately involved in the pain of the world without feeling some of that pain ourselves. We cannot turn a blind eye to horrific crimes of injustice simply because our own life is comfortable. Involving ourselves in social or political advocacy and the promotion of alternative values will most likely bring a harsh reaction from some.

Our Beautiful Messy Lives

Alongside the rewards of meaningful engagement with the world, will be stress, failures, disappointments and sadness. That is par for the course. The personal growth we seek within our own spirits is based upon the same creative transformation that we long to see in our community. Slowly, this creative transformation helps us find the courage to be fully alive. Being fully alive means feeling, accepting and participating in whatever is real — the beauty and the horror. And because this connection with the real is so invigorating and enlivening, we would not want to return to our comfort zone or the self-delusion of worldly pretensions of innocence.

New Testament scholar, Ched Myers, in discussing a similar story of a blind man in the Gospel of Mark, talks about the struggle of 'defection'. "And if your right hand causes you to sin, cut it off and throw it away; it is better for you to lose one of your members than for your whole body to go into hell."[125] If our involvement in a project, group action or public message threatens to collapse our values and prevent us hearing the lure of the divine, we need to remove ourselves from it. We must extricate ourselves from the corruption of the world and refuse to participate in it as we turn towards the impulse of God. Myers says these metaphors of amputation "accurately describe the painful practices of severance that must characterize a genuine community of discontinuity."[126] A

---

[125] Matthew 5: 30
[126] Ched Myers, *Who Will Roll Away the Stone: Discipleship Queries for First World Christians*, Orbis, 1994, p.176.

'community of discontinuity' does not refer to a total withdrawal from the world or having nothing to do with those who think differently from ourselves. It simply means not contributing to the promotion or activities of hurtful and divisive ideas.

Rejecting the destructive and addictive values of our society means engaging respectfully in the conversation by offering alternative perspectives. Because we know that the world does not divide into the 'right' and 'wrong', the 'spiritual' and the 'sinful', the 'good' and the 'evil', we know that it makes no sense to separate ourselves completely from those with whom we disagree. Because all our lives are a messy mix of motives and habits, there is no fear of being 'contaminated' by unspiritual people. It is important to respect and care for our neighbours as people, while reflecting independently on their point of view. There may be times when our neighbours will reject us because they do not agree with our convictions. Speaking out against injustice, domestic violence, theft by large corporations or the degradation of the environment will not always win us friends. However, we should not moralistically condemn those who do not see the world the same way. A 'community of discontinuity' offers a new vision by living according to alternative, compelling, spiritual values.

When our dominant culture is practicing exclusion of the vulnerable, entitlement for the rich and the abuse of power, there will be ways we can challenge it. We make a stand, not because we are different as human beings, morally better, or more righteous, but because we recognise the destructiveness of these forces and how easily we can become complicit in them. Our own transformation involves awakening to the ways we have participated in the ungodly, power-based values of our dominant culture and choosing another path. Myers quotes a verse from another prophet, Dan Berrigan, that is apt for our story of the man born blind.

> *In the house where all cry out "I see!" and continue to do the works of darkness there is only one classic action open to the wise: strike yourself blind and explore that kingdom.*[127]

Creative transformation helps us see the bigger picture of the struggle between two competing visions of life and society. In our story, the Pharisees represent one perspective — that of judgement, self-delusion, power and the assumption of entitlement. Jesus' gave his life in the work of co-creating, with God and his friends, an alternative society that he called the Kingdom of God. In the social reality created by this alternative vision, outsiders are honoured, the unassuming are invited to the top of the table, the poor become our teachers and strength is experienced in vulnerability. It is not those who oppress the powerless who demonstrate the wisdom of God, but the little ones, the ones who are usually overlooked.

---

[127] Ibid. Daniel Berrigan (1921 – 2016) was an American Jesuit priest, anti-war activist and poet.

A Spiritual Tapestry

Everything is turned upside-down in Jesus' dream of a different world.

By honestly examining our motives and behaviour, integrating our shadow self, realigning our values with the values of God, focussing our morality on the demands of love and respect for the other, and refusing to participate in the destructive forces of society, we engage in a life-long process of creative transformation. This expansive vision will energise our beautiful, messy lives.

CHAPTER EIGHT

Let Me Tell You a Story

> *Sometimes reality is too complex.*
> *Stories give it form.*
>
> Jean-Luc Godard

Once upon a time there was a man who told stories to change the world. I think perhaps he hoped that one day, when he was long-forgotten, people would remember his stories. Those were dangerous times and he was killed for wanting to change the world. The times are still dangerous, and we owe it to him to keep telling life-enhancing stories.

Stories have intriguing power. Although philosophy and theology can help us understand what we believe, complex theories can become too cerebral for the spirit. Nurturing the spiritual life is more appropriately achieved by taking in the living world around us, contemplating art and listening to music and storytelling rather than to creeds and books about God. The spiritual life is not grounded on certitudes, but on glimpses of possibilities. When we gather together, we should not spend so much time concentrating on explanations but on listening to stories, music and silence. Stories can turn the world upside down. Stories tease our imagination, invite us into new dimensions of what is real, enchant us with unexpected endings and challenge us to live in new ways.

Stories help us to understand truth bit by bit. Each time we re-listen to a story, we hear something new. We may find ourselves reflected in a character that had seemed distant to us before. Some disturbing trend in our world may emerge in an ancient narrative plot. We may see the pattern of our lives reflected in the unfolding of the story and find ourselves observing it from the outside. Stories, like poetry and art, can be subversive, revealing the shadow-side of our community and ourselves. They can challenge the false narratives that cripple our society. Stories give us the courage to act, to address trauma or shape a new future. They allow us to live through another's experience and discover another's truth. Good stories should be revisited because they will have changed since we last read them.

Let me tell you a story — well, seven stories actually. The Christian scriptures are full of inspiring tales and the collection in this chapter is merely a taste — a sample from this rich resource — which I hope encourages readers to revisit the stories they may have left behind.

Irrespective of whether they purport to recount real-life events or fictional parables, each story has something to tell us that should not be ignored. They speak to us about our humanity, our neighbours, our enemies, morality, the important and trivial, about who we are and how our lives can have meaning. These stories have been taken from the old scriptures and are in danger of being forgotten. Some have been smothered by tradition and theology and their power to change the world almost lost.

Stories are for all ages. Although some appeal to children, none of them was intended as a 'children's story'. Increasingly, people do not have a memory bank of the ancient legends to reflect upon when life becomes challenging. This chapter reflects my desire to preserve some unique tales for the next generation and, also, to uncover their power for adults who have not heard them, except as fairy-tales. That has been the mistake of the Christian tradition — reducing the most subversive stories to harmless, fanciful, entertaining tales for Sunday School children. In reality, it takes the wit and courage of adults to absorb their warnings, instructions and spiritual impact.

Each of the stories in this chapter will be followed by a short reflection. However, my comments are definitely not intended to exhaust the meaning of each story, only to tease out some possibilities. Ideally, they should be workshopped by a group so that each person's interpretation can add to the insights gleaned by the others. Some are taken from the Old Testament, from thousands of years ago. Others a little later, from the legends and parables of Jesus in the first century. Those from a church culture will recognise these stories, but I urge the reader to read them afresh. Jesus told stories to change the world. If we are open to change in ourselves and in our community, we need to listen carefully to wise stories, appreciate the characters, the ethical challenge, the dangers and fears, consider the unexpected twists and turns. Ask yourself, "Who changed during these events?" Ask yourself, "Where am I in this story and who else is with me?"

1. The God Who Attempted to Destroy Evil

Based on a pre-historic, mythical legend, this magnificent epic tale is rich in meaning. Although it is brimming with truth, the story should not be taken literally. Remember that this narrative reflects the world of the Ancient Near East at a time when divine characters were described in very human terms. Although this version can be set beside similar and earlier flood narratives from other cultures of the time, we will take it at face value as it appears in the Christian scriptures.

> *Now the earth was corrupt in God's sight, and the earth was filled with violence. And God saw that the earth was corrupt; for all flesh had corrupted its ways upon the earth. And God said to Noah, "I have determined to make an end of all flesh, for the earth is filled with violence*

because of them; now I am going to destroy them along with the earth. Make yourself an ark of cypress wood... For my part, I am going to bring a flood of waters on the earth, to destroy from under heaven all flesh in which is the breath of life; everything that is on the earth shall die.

In the six hundredth year of Noah's life... all the fountains of the great deep burst forth, and the windows of the heavens were opened. The rain fell on the earth forty days and forty nights. The waters swelled and increased greatly on the earth; and the ark floated on the face of the waters... [God] blotted out every living thing that was on the face of the ground, human beings and animals and creeping things and birds of the air; they were blotted out from the earth...

At the end of forty days Noah opened the window of the ark... Then God said to Noah, "Go out of the ark, you and your wife, and your sons and your sons' wives with you"... Then Noah built an altar to the Lord, and took of every clean animal and of every clean bird, and offered burnt offerings on the altar. And when the Lord smelled the pleasing odour, the Lord said in his heart, "I will never again curse the ground because of humankind, for the inclination of the human heart is evil from youth; nor will I ever again destroy every living creature as I have done.

As long as the earth endures, seedtime and harvest, cold and heat, summer and winter, day

> *and night, shall not cease"... Then God said to Noah and to his sons with him, "As for me, I am establishing my covenant with you and your descendants after you, and with every living creature that is with you... I establish my covenant with you, that never again shall all flesh be cut off by the waters of a flood, and never again shall there be a flood to destroy the earth." God said... "I have set my bow in the clouds, and it shall be a sign of the covenant between me and the earth."*
>
> Excerpts from Genesis 7 - 9

Who changed in this story and who learned the most? Noah and his family had a gruesome adventure, but they emerged the same from the ark as before (still righteous). The violent ones died — they were denied the chance to change or learn. It was God who changed and learned. God attempted to destroy evil by destroying those who do evil. But it failed. For all the death and human suffering and heartless destruction of innocent animal life, the whole endeavour failed.

Where are you in this story? Are you judged for your immorality or tendency to violence or aggression? Would you have drowned? Or, like Noah, do you please God? Would you have been singled out for a place on the ark? And your friends? Would your community or nation have been blotted out by this God intent on destroying evil? Or would God's assessment of the evil ones correspond to the 'axis of evil'[128] that we have ourselves attempted to blot out from the face of the earth? Have we learned what God learned from the failure of the flood?

How did God fail and what did God learn? Could it be as obvious as it seems? That it is not possible to eliminate evil by killing those who do evil? Why not? What did God misunderstand? That it is not possible to divide the world into those who are evil and those who are righteous? God had assumed it was. But the world is not like that. It is not black and white. We are all a mixture of good and evil inclinations. We are, in fact, a messy mixture of shame and glory, greatness and ugly possibilities. This is a story of a ruthless God who did not understand human nature.

Thank goodness this legend is not real. There may well have been a massive flood in the Ancient Near East, and the various accounts of that flood demonstrate how differently the cultures in the area interpreted it. But these religious interpretations are not historical. Nevertheless, we might wonder how a tale of genocide and the senseless killing of living things became a favourite subject for children's colouring-in books and costume plays! The church has an incredible knack of domesticating the horrific. I presume the only way children are taught to

---

[128] The phrase 'axis of evil' was first used by U.S. President George W. Bush in his State of the Union address in 2002. Following the 9/11 attacks in 2001, he often used it to describe foreign governments that sponsored terrorism and sought weapons of mass destruction. The idea of linking nations such as Iran, Iraq and North Korea in an axis of evil was used to gain the support of the US people in the 'War on Terror'.

enjoy this story of death is by assuming these two things: that God cannot abide wrongdoers, and that we ourselves are good people like Noah. We see ourselves on the side of Noah and are drawn into God's desire to punish the wicked. This sense of safety is reinforced by focussing on God's promise not to destroy the earth by flood in the future. Just focus on the rainbow and all is well.

If this ancient story deserves to be preserved it must be because it still has relevance for us. God's conclusion was that, "I will never again curse the ground because of humankind, for the inclination of the human heart is evil from youth." Is this an overly grim view of human nature, or does it express a truth? It may mean that God accepts the inevitability of sinful actions by all people who are simply that way inclined. Or it may mean that God realised that no-one is totally 'righteous', that people cannot be divided so easily into two groups. Every human being has the potential for violence, given the right circumstances. Certainly, as young people we tend to be focussed on ourselves. Selfless action and unselfish choices only come with personal development and even then, we are never totally devoid of self-interest. If God had wanted to eliminate any potential evil in the world, God would need to have killed Noah too. The sobering reality is that while humanity exists, the potential for evil exists.

Centuries later, Jesus tells us that, "[God] causes his sun to rise on the evil and the good and sends rain on the righteous and the unrighteous" (Matthew 5:45). Although it sounds a little as though there are still two distinct sets of people, the stronger meaning is that God does not distinguish or judge. We are all in this endeavour of life together and God, who now understands the complexity of human nature, provides for the whole of humanity alike. According to the biblical story, God learned in the earliest days of humanity that it is naïve to separate humanity into 'righteous' and 'wicked', or 'good' and 'bad'.

Every generation needs to learn the same lesson. Unfortunately, the attitude of so many is not grounded in modern science and psychology. Even today, a common tendency is to think in terms of the 'good' and the 'bad'. Sometimes we make our judgements according to behaviour and sometimes according to race, religion, culture or class. Taking that next step of attempting to eliminate the perceived evil through war or genocide is almost unthinkable. Yet we know it has happened and still happens today. Following World War II, when the horrors of the Nazi concentration camps were revealed in full, the world was so shocked we prayed it could never happen again. Yet it has, more than once. Currently, the attempted genocide of the Rohingya people is shocking the world again. The United Nations has described the military offensive against Rohingya villages in Myanmar's Rakhine State, which has provoked an exodus of refugees, as a "textbook example of ethnic cleansing".

No nation sends its military to destroy villages, rape women and kill as many of the men, women and children in a communal group as it can, if it considers them "good people". The Rohingya people are scapegoated because they belong to a Muslim religious minority in a Buddhist country, because their ethnic lineage and language is different from the majority population and because they are an easy target. They are non-people to the majority in Myanmar and it is easy to demonise non-people. Likewise, the Nazis demonised the Jews before and during World War II. They spread the ideology of racial superiority, pretending that humanity would benefit if it was rid of the evil presence of the Jewish people. And now, in the West, we are in danger of going down a similar ideological path.

Following the 2001 terrorist attack on the USA, many nations joined forces with the USA to fight in Afghanistan and Iraq. And on home soil, whole populations have felt conscripted into an unofficial civil war against would-be terrorists. We are all told to be alert for suspicious, possibly terrorist behaviour. To maintain the ideological impetus for this war mentality, the rhetoric of leaders on all sides of politics has sown the seeds of distrust of all Muslims. Sections of the Christian community have joined forces with this ideology because of their fear that Islam threatens the expansion of Christianity.

We are well aware that extremist Muslims have carried out evil acts of violence against those who do not bow to their ideology and power. This has provided ample raw material for the demonising process. Popular scapegoating of the whole Muslim community worldwide has been strengthened by the ideology of hatred that separates the world into 'us and them'. How is it that in

2016 the United States elected a president who campaigned on a platform of scapegoating Muslims and Mexicans for the difficulties facing their nation? Why would the evangelical community support this campaign if not because it perceives Islam as a threat to its own religious status? How is it that certain Australian politicians attempt to win votes by campaigning to stop Muslim migration? If, in our perception, these were 'good' people, we would find such campaigning distasteful. The reason these politicians win seats is that a significant number in our community has begun to believe that Muslims are 'bad' people.

These are complex times and fear motivates many of us — fear of losing our culture, fear of challenges to our religious beliefs, fear of violence towards us, fear of being 'overtaken' by foreigners and minorities. Some fear is understandable, given the horrific, ideological killing of innocent civilians by terrorists. These televised scenes of slaughter, that are broadcast into our living rooms, are evil in anyone's books. But there are no easy answers, given that the popular responses to terrorism include an escalation of violence, war and the loss of communal freedoms, which are all evil to some extent. According to the story of Noah and the flood, it was violence itself that God originally called evil. However, we need to listen carefully to this story. God was wrong. It was not possible to wipe out evil by destroying those who do evil. Attempting to eliminate the evil of violence by using greater violence only leads to further death. It will not work, because *any* of us is capable of evil.

God promised not to destroy humanity, but to have patience with us — to send sun to shine on us and rain to fall on us, all of us. Demonising whole sections of humanity is not a way forward. If, as God discovered in this story, all human beings are essentially alike, there must be another way. Certainly, violent acts need to be dealt with under the law in order to protect the community. But labelling people 'evil' is dangerous. The first step in finding a way that does not lead to more violence is to learn what God learned. There is no such thing as an 'axis of evil' except in our own false ideology. All of us have the potential for making good and evil choices. Because of our complex humanity, our strategies for responding to historical hurt, discrimination, and hatred needs to be multi-faceted and imaginative. With all our shades of morality and immorality, we must enrich the global community by respecting the humanity of all.

2. How Should We Judge?

People tend to judge others according to exterior attributes and not the qualities of the soul. What values are in play when a person gains social status? Judgements are made around wealth, success, connection with people of influence, a strong physique, sporting or military prowess, gifts of rhetoric, charisma and good looks. Those who excel in a few of these areas are headed for celebrity status. Looking back three thousand years to ancient times, it seems things were just the same.

The following is a much-loved, legendary story about a real-life character. Set during the early history of Israel, the first king, Saul, had developed a mental health disorder, becoming unpredictable and unstable. Israel needed someone to succeed him. This is where we pick up the epic tale of David.

> *The Lord said to Samuel, "How long will you grieve over Saul? I have rejected him from being king over Israel. Fill your horn with oil and set out; I will send you to Jesse the Bethlehemite, for I have provided for myself a king among his sons." Samuel said, "How can I go? If Saul hears of it, he will kill me." And the Lord said, "Take a heifer with you, and say, 'I have come to sacrifice to the Lord.' Invite Jesse to the sacrifice, and I will show you what you shall do; and you shall anoint for me the one whom I name to you." Samuel did what the Lord commanded and came to Bethlehem. The elders of the city came to meet him trembling, and said, "Do you come peaceably?" He said, "Peaceably; I have come to sacrifice to the Lord; sanctify yourselves and come with me to the sacrifice." And he sanctified Jesse and his sons and invited them to the sacrifice.*
>
> *When they came, he looked on Eliab and thought, "Surely the Lord's anointed is now*

A Spiritual Tapestry

before the Lord." But the Lord said to Samuel, "Do not look on his appearance or on the height of his stature, because I have rejected him; for the Lord does not see as mortals see; they look on the outward appearance, but the Lord looks on the heart." Then Jesse called Abinadab, and made him pass before Samuel. He said, "Neither has the Lord chosen this one." Then Jesse made Shammah pass by. And he said, "Neither has the Lord chosen this one." Jesse made seven of his sons pass before Samuel, and Samuel said to Jesse, "The Lord has not chosen any of these."

Samuel said to Jesse, "Are all your sons here?" And he said, "There remains yet the youngest, but he is keeping the sheep." And Samuel said to Jesse, "Send and bring him; for we will not sit down until he comes here." He sent and brought him in. Now he was ruddy, and had beautiful eyes, and was handsome. The Lord said, "Rise and anoint him; for this is the one." Then Samuel took the horn of oil and anointed him in the presence of his brothers; and the spirit of the Lord came mightily upon David from that day forward. Samuel then set out and went to Ramah.

1 Samuel 16: 1 - 13

David, the most famous king of Israel, had become a legend by the time of Jesus approximately one thousand years later. Fortunately, we do not read these stories to learn history. We read them to learn about life and to absorb spiritual wisdom. David's morals as king were not exemplary, and yet he retains a place of honour in the mythology of Israel. But for now, the focus is not actually on the young David.

Who changed and who learned the most in this story? Little David doesn't utter a word, he merely receives the blessing from the prophet. We're told, 'the spirit of the Lord' was strong in David from that time of blessing. However, there is no indication that the young David actually changed during this story.

Samuel and Jesse, the human characters with the most to say, represent the values of society. They are not against God, they merely take for granted that their assessments of people are the same as God's. Until recent times, even in our own society, the oldest son in a family enjoyed the highest status and inherited the most property. The youngest son in a large family was of little account and the girls were not mentioned. That kind of success and status has nothing to do with ability, inner qualities of spirit or even intellect, but with the accident of birth. However, as events unfold in the story, each son of Jesse from the oldest downwards parades before the prophet. Samuel expected the oldest to be chosen as Israel's future king. But with the appearance of each one, Samuel, the most influential prophet in Israel, does not 'feel right'. There is no recognition of God's "yes" in Samuel's spirit. The tension in the narrative builds after all the sons have come forward and Samuel still feels uneasy. He suspects there must be another son. David, the youngest, the one of no account, the one left out in the field looking after the sheep while everyone else is invited to the sacrificial ceremony with the great prophet, is finally brought in and recognised as the one God chooses.

Who changes or learns the most? Samuel is surprised. His expectations are countered by his sense of being led by God. He learns not to accept blindly his assumptions about people. He learns that society's values are sometimes different from God's values. Jesse and his other sons are shocked. What must they have felt about their decision to leave little David out in the field when he was brought in and anointed by the prophet? No-one valued the youngest. They had only complied with accepted social values and done what would have seemed normal. But they were wrong.

We don't really know if Jesse learned from this shock event. We do know that David's brothers did not. Despite the decision of the prophet, they still did not respect their youngest brother. Later in the epic tale, when David comes forward to fight Goliath, the giant of a man from Israel's enemy, his brother ridicules him for thinking that he had any place in this fight.[129] They would learn the hard way that being older and stronger did not fit them for leadership. David's brothers represent social conventions that valued strength, age and status.

It is a stylised story and quite beautiful. In fiction and sometimes in real life, we love to 'go for the underdog'.

---

[129] 1 Samuel 17

Here we are given a romantic story of the reversal of fortunes — the forgotten boy who became a great king. Perhaps that is what we love about it. The story appeals to Australians because traditionally we have seen ourselves as the forgotten, smaller nation in the global arena, the underdog. However, in all honesty, we only barrack for the underdog when we don't have another stake in the fight. When we ourselves have the strength and power, we want to win. Do we value equality and fair opportunity for the younger and smaller participants in the global arena? Or do we, like the rest of the world, value power and might?

In military terms, we Australians have allied ourselves with the strongest power on earth, the USA. In sport, we have celebrated our mastery in the pool, in rugby league field and on the cricket pitch. When it comes to international competitions, we lose sight of the underdog and celebrate being top of the ladder. In resources and finance, we Australians were willing to use our technological advantage to attempt to take ownership of the $65 billion oil and gas fields in the Timor Sea. In this fight against impoverished East Timor, Australia was Goliath. Soon after the agreement between these two nations was signed in 2018, we discovered that the Australian intelligence service had been ordered to 'bug' the offices of East Timor illegally to gain the advantage in negotiations. You see, we only 'go for the underdog' when *we* are the underdog or when we are removed from the issue. Whenever we can, like people the world over, we take advantage of whatever power and strength we can wield over others. Perhaps our values do not always align with the way God looks at the world.

Have we absorbed the wisdom upon which this beloved biblical story is built? So often we do not look past the superficial trappings of a person and make assumptions of importance based on things that do not matter. It is true that David is described as a beautiful boy. But that is incidental to the story. God's choice of David rested on the quality of his spirit. Or, as God tells Samuel in the story, "[T]he Lord does not see as mortals see; they look on the outward appearance, but the Lord looks on the heart."[130] According to divine values, leadership is a gift related to the uncorrupted motives of the heart or spirit before any other talents. What personal qualities are we swayed by when we choose our leaders?

The responsibility of representing God to the nation would eventually fall to David. In all of David's exploits that follow this story, he is clearly clever, strong and able to outwit Israel's enemies. And yet, at every turn the epic tale of David underscores the point that he trusted God. This sense of trust, rather than arrogance and a sense of entitlement, is what made him a legendary king. (The next story will deal with the notable exception when David did not act in trust or with honour.) Significantly, at the beginning of his career, David is the one everyone overlooked. If it were not for Samuel, who listened to the divine leading within his spirit, no-one would have given

---

[130] 1 Samuel 16: 7

David a second thought. He was at the bottom rung of the ladder in this family. He had no outstanding physical stature, no status, no wealth, no track record of success, only boyish good looks, and that didn't count for much in a world of strong men. By society's criteria, no-one would have seen leadership potential in David. But God sees differently.

How often in social conversations do we ask, "What do you do?" Our society makes judgements about a person's worth, intellect, income and importance according to their profession, trade or job. That is one of the struggles facing stay-at-home mums, particularly if they have previously worked in high-status positions. There is no status or income attached to mothering. In our current global obsession with celebrities, the attributes of good looks and wealth seem to be enough to attract fame. Being too quick to judge, how many people do we foolishly overlook when it comes to investing in relationships or employment potential? How often do we ignore the inexperienced youth, the one without income or social position? We must learn to look beyond superficial appearances and, instead, value the integrity and greatness of a person's heart.

A thousand years after the story of David is set, Jesus famously warned his disciples,

> *Do not judge, and you will not be judged; do not condemn, and you will not be condemned. Forgive, and you will be forgiven; give, and it will be given to you. A good measure, pressed down, shaken together, running over, will be put into*

> *your lap; for the measure you give will be the measure you get back... Why do you see the speck in your neighbour's eye, but do not notice the log in your own eye? Or how can you say to your neighbour, 'Friend, let me take out the speck in your eye,' when you yourself do not see the log in your own eye? You hypocrite, first take the log out of your own eye, and then you will see clearly to take the speck out of your neighbour's eye.*
>
> Excerpts from Luke 6: 37 – 42

Jesus addressed our common tendency to make negative judgements of others, not just on their outward appearance, but on everything about them. How easy it is to be critical of others while judging ourselves more leniently. In doing so we separate ourselves from them, placing ourselves on a different plane. In a similar vein to those who condemned the blind man, in the last chapter's story, we are blinkered by our own false image of ourselves.

Reality television has encouraged an attitude of judgement. Everyone's a critic — we vote by phone on the worth of other people's talents; we lodge our assessment of who should survive or be eliminated in a competition; we write internet reviews about everywhere we go; we go online to add our comments to those of official judges. The cyber and television world has encouraged our society to approach individuals, businesses and places with a judgemental eye.

The danger is that we may lose the habit of entering a café, a home, a motel or even another country with the eyes of appreciation. We lose something in our spirit when we are always judging. "I like writing reviews. I'm fair but honest," is a comment I have heard so often. Yes, but do you live into someone else's reality and appreciate life from their perspective? Do you walk into someone else's world to appreciate it or to judge it? Have you developed the art of seeing the world through someone else's eyes? Or are your own criteria of success and worth all that matters?

Making some assessments of the character and potential of others is unavoidable. In fact, in a democracy it is essential if we are to vote with discernment. Arguably, we cannot live successfully without making wise judgements about who can be trusted with what. However, the act of judging becomes damaging to our own spirits and to others both when we overlook someone, judging them to be insignificant, and when we approach everyone and everything with a judgmental, critical eye.

So, how should we understand and assess the worth of a person for leadership, employment or influence in communal relationships? In line with the story of David, Jesus affirms that the quality of goodness in a person's heart or spirit is what really matters. "[F]or it is out of the abundance of the heart that the mouth speaks," he says.[131] If we are going to make judgements of others, as we inevitably will, we should not only assess their skills, but

---

[131] Luke 6: 45

the values that drive them — the selfless or self-serving motives behind their actions, their commitment to honesty or willingness to deceive, the intention of the heart that lies behind their words.

The values of our celebrity-drenched society are so superficial, they can draw us into a false world. It is important to take a step back and critique the judgements that we are making. Popularity, wealth, good looks, charisma, and influence are fickle and untrustworthy criteria compared with integrity of the heart.

3. Holding the Abuse of Power to Account

No-one is above the law. Although that is believed in modern Western nations, it is being tested everywhere. The concept is relatively recent, coinciding with the development of democracies. For much of history the king, emperor, feudal lord or army general controlled the law and how it was applied within their domain. Peasants of a society were not protected by law from exploitation, violence or abuse. Ideas of morality did exist but dealing with injustices was in the hands of the local ruler and how he did so could alter with his mood. In some situations, for example the Roman Empire, a rule of law did exist but only for official citizens of the Empire. The citizens of many nations today still do not have the protection of the law, making it unsafe for them to challenge the president, ruling party or military leader.

Let Me Tell You a Story

Before the Babylonian captivity in 587 BCE, ancient Israel was a kingdom. When the kingdom was created, the moral law of Israel's God was built into the nation's identity and mythology. Although the king was powerful, it was always believed that he would uphold the values of God. But how would the king himself be held accountable for the abuse of power or corruption? The following story stands out in the scriptural tradition because it urges us to 'speak the truth to power'. We will pick up the narrative quite a bit further along from the previous section in the epic of David.

> *It happened, late one afternoon, when David rose from his couch and was walking about on the roof of the king's house, that he saw from the roof a woman bathing; the woman was very beautiful. David sent someone to inquire about the woman. It was reported, "This is Bathsheba daughter of Eliam, the wife of Uriah the Hittite." So David sent messengers to get her, and she came to him, and he lay with her. (Now she was purifying herself after her period.) Then she returned to her house. The woman conceived; and she sent and told David, "I am pregnant"...*
>
> *In the morning, David wrote a letter to Joab, and sent it by the hand of Uriah. In the letter he wrote, "Set Uriah in the forefront of the hardest fighting, and then draw back from him, so that he may be struck down and die"... When the wife of Uriah heard that her husband was dead, she made lamentation for him. When the mourning*

was over, David sent and brought her to his house, and she became his wife, and bore him a son. But the thing that David had done displeased the Lord, and the Lord sent Nathan to David.

[Nathan] came to [David], and said to him, "There were two men in a certain city, the one rich and the other poor. The rich man had very many flocks and herds; but the poor man had nothing but one little ewe lamb, which he had bought. He brought it up, and it grew up with him and with his children; it used to eat of his meagre fare, and drink from his cup, and lie in his bosom, and it was like a daughter to him. Now there came a traveller to the rich man, and he was loath to take one of his own flock or herd to prepare for the wayfarer who had come to him, but he took the poor man's lamb, and prepared that for the guest who had come to him."

Then David's anger was greatly kindled against the man. He said to Nathan, "As the Lord lives, the man who has done this deserves to die; he shall restore the lamb fourfold, because he did this thing, and because he had no pity."

Nathan said to David, "You are the man! Thus says the Lord, the God of Israel: I anointed you king over Israel, and I rescued you from the hand of Saul; I gave you your master's house, and your master's wives into your bosom, and gave you the house of Israel and of Judah; and if that had *been too little, I would have added as much more. Why have you despised the word of the Lord, to do what is evil in his sight? You have struck down Uriah the Hittite with the sword, and have taken his wife to be your wife, and have killed him with the sword of the Ammonites"...*

David said to Nathan, "I have sinned against the Lord." Nathan said to David, "Now the Lord has put away your sin; you shall not die. Nevertheless, because by this deed you have utterly scorned the Lord, the child that is born to you shall die." Then Nathan went to his house.

Excerpts from 2 Samuel: 11 – 12

This story is an outstanding demonstration of the abuse of position, speaking the truth to power and personal change. By the time David was king, the court prophet was Nathan whose task it was to speak for God. It seems strange to our idea of national governance, but all ancient societies feared gods or some version of a God. The court prophets in the history of Israel were sometimes 'yes men', telling the kings what they wanted to hear. But Nathan was a man of integrity who dared to confront David with his immorality and crime. Nathan remained constant. The king could have had him killed or exiled. If David had not listened, had not faced his own crimes and changed, he would have taken Israel down a murky path of deceit and corruption. Nathan took a huge risk and it paid off. David changed.

There are two facets of this story that are particularly relevant to our own spiritual journeys. The first is that no-one is beyond doing something immoral if such attractive circumstances present themselves. The stories of David are rich with courage, humility, daring and whole-hearted living. But here we are disappointed to read that our beloved hero, the ridiculed young boy who became king, the courageous youth who defeated the threatening Goliath, could give in to his passion and commit such a crime. Do we presume that we would never do such a thing? Perhaps until we realise that we also could be driven by passion and act immorally, we have not learned enough about ourselves. And then, despite our disappointment, we find we identify with David's regret, his anguished cry, "I have sinned against the Lord." If David could be forgiven by God, we take heart that the awful things we have thought or done can also be forgiven. That David could face his dark side, his horrific actions and turn away from them, gives us hope for ourselves and our own leaders.

The more pointed relevance of this story is Nathan's demonstration of courage and conviction. He was not willing to compromise. Nathan is our model. When witnessing the abuse of power against vulnerable people, we are called to speak up, even at the risk of our own safety, job or reputation. Even in our democracies, the rule of law has its limitations and does not always protect the powerless. The law has sometimes been difficult to apply because of power imbalances and while this is slowly changing in some sections of our society, in other quarters we seem to be going backwards.

Because of the gender power imbalance, women have not always been protected by the law. In this ancient tale of King David, the woman, Bathsheba, is treated as property. The fact that David used his power as king to take her for his own suggests rape. Although there is no suggestion of physical violence, the power imbalance meant that she had no choice. Even Nathan did not focus on the sin against Bathsheba. Instead, like a beloved lamb owned by a poor farmer, she was thought of as no more than the treasured property of Uriah, the Hittite. David had many wives, but he desired and took Uriah's wife and his sexual possession of Bathsheba is presented as a sin against Uriah. David's sins are described only as theft and murder. Systemic sexual abuse against women is poignantly present in the story through the absence of comment. The silence concerning the rape of Bathsheba is deafening.

In our day, naming sexual abuse takes courage. It is well known that many rapes go unreported to the police because the legal process does not protect women from further violation. Until quite recently, rape within marriage was not recognised by the law. During the last twelve months, women who were vulnerable to losing their jobs or reputation if they named sexual exploitation in their workplace, have courageously put up their hands and said, "Me too." Actors and staff members sexually harassed or raped by a former Hollywood film producer and tycoon have led the way in this fight for justice. This is not only about gender but the broader issue of power. When the person that is abusing or harassing others is in a position to employ, dismiss or reduce their victim's opportunities for work, a power imbalance is being exploited. Since these women have spoken out, both women and men in other workplaces also have found the courage to name similar situations.

In a good democracy, the law should ultimately uphold the fight against the abuse of power in those cases where enough evidence can be provided. It won't end well in all cases because the truth of a matter cannot always be proven. Some victims of abuse, as well as some alleged perpetrators, will feel unsupported by society and will not receive justice. Those who have suffered from exploitation, abuse or bullying need to speak the truth with courage. They also must be careful not to misuse the power of public shaming without proper cause so that others are not unfairly demonised. We all need to recognise what power we have in each sphere of our lives so that we can act with care and respect in the workplace, the church, the family and the community. The important thing in this discussion is that no-one in a position of authority should assume they are free to use their power however they please.

As mentioned above, in some quarters of society it is becoming more difficult to address power imbalances. Our leaders model a set of ethics to the nation and influence the thinking of society. When the President of the USA speaks disparagingly of women, brags about sexual harassment of women and scapegoats people from minority communities, he subtly gives permission for others to voice similar views. The internet is awash with some of the most horrid racist and sexist comments that would have disgusted the general population just twenty years ago. Sadly, it is easier to embrace hateful speech than to do the hard work of learning to see life through the eyes those who do not belong to the dominant culture. In Australia also, some leaders misuse their positions of political power to belittle people without social standing. Holding influential leaders to account for dishonesty and unethical behaviour requires great courage.

Despite the popularity of this prophetic story of Nathan and David in the Christian scriptures, many religious leaders have not heeded its warning. Although the conviction of some church leaders for child sexual abuse has awakened clergy to their duty of care, others still refuse to hear the outrage of the nation. Beyond the extensive reports of child abuse, some religious leaders have misused their positions in other ways, such as bullying and using the church for financial gain. Many of these cases have still not been brought to light. Similarly, in secular workplaces, wherever there is a power imbalance, the potential for abuse exists. Whether it is the misuse of finances, actual violence or the harsh treatment of staff, the principle is the same — human beings deserve respect and fair treatment whatever their place in society. Whether king, president, producer, politician, doctor, clergy or CEO, we all must be accountable for the way we use our power over others.

A Spiritual Tapestry

Two issues converge in this discussion — that which is illegal and that which is unethical or immoral. When the prophet Nathan called David to account for his actions, he was demanding that the values of God be acknowledged by observing the rights of the powerless. Although in our society, respect for the values of God is contentious, in a secular sense, the majority of decent people value fairness and respect the rights of the vulnerable. However, in the market economy, the temptation for corporations is to place profits above the rights of ordinary people. Individuals' values do not always influence workplace practices. Institutions, professions, churches and businesses each have their own culture according to which personnel often act with lesser respect for others than they would in the private arena. But there is no reason why we should not aim to create workplace cultures based on spiritual values, which may be of a higher standard than that which can be enforced by the law.

As people of faith, we need to hold ourselves to the highest standard of respect for others and support leaders who demonstrate those same values. When we break our own ethical standards, the responsibility is upon us to recognise our failure, apologise and put right what we can. Even when we are not brought to account legally, we are brought to account by the still, small voice of God. The purpose of this spiritual process is not to punish or load us with guilt, but, like King David, to lead us towards self-awareness, change and personal growth.

4. Assumptions of Entitlement

Within the storytelling legacy of Jesus is this much-loved parable in Luke's Gospel. Let's hope we can keep this story in the public domain long after church-going is a thing of the past. Not only is it a beautiful and moving tale, it contributes wisdom on important themes in human community.

> *Then Jesus said, "There was a man who had two sons. The younger of them said to his father, 'Father, give me the share of the property that will belong to me.' So he divided his property between them. A few days later the younger son gathered all he had and travelled to a distant country, and there he squandered his property in dissolute living.*
>
> *When he had spent everything, a severe famine took place throughout that country, and he began to be in need. So he went and hired himself out to one of the citizens of that country, who sent him to his fields to feed the pigs. He would gladly have filled himself with the pods that the pigs were eating; and no one gave him anything. But when he came to himself he said, 'How many of my father's hired hands have bread enough and to spare, but here I am dying of hunger! I will get up and go to my father, and I will say to him, "Father, I have sinned against heaven and before you; I am no longer worthy to*

A Spiritual Tapestry

be called your son; treat me like one of your hired hands.'" So he set off and went to his father.

"But while he was still far off, his father saw him and was filled with compassion; he ran and put his arms around him and kissed him. Then the son said to him, 'Father, I have sinned against heaven and before you; I am no longer worthy to be called your son.' But the father said to his slaves, 'Quickly, bring out a robe — the best one — and put it on him; put a ring on his finger and sandals on his feet. And get the fatted calf and kill it, and let us eat and celebrate; for this son of mine was dead and is alive again; he was lost and is found!' And they began to celebrate.

"Now his elder son was in the field; and when he came and approached the house, he heard music and dancing. He called one of the slaves and asked what was going on. He replied, 'Your brother has come, and your father has killed the fatted calf, because he has got him back safe and sound.' Then he became angry and refused to go in. His father came out and began to plead with him. But he answered his father, 'Listen! For all these years I have been working like a slave for you, and I have never disobeyed your command; yet you have never given me even a young goat so that I might celebrate with my friends. But when this son of yours came back, who has devoured your property with prostitutes, you killed the fatted calf for him!' Then the father said to him, 'Son, you are always with me, and

all that is mine is yours. But we had to celebrate and rejoice, because this brother of yours was dead and has come to life; he was lost and has been found.'

Luke 15:11-32

Who do you identify with in this story? Who changed and who learned the most? We tend to hear the parable from the perspective of the prodigal, the one who rudely demanded his birthright even before his father was dead. He squandered it all and finally, when he was starving, turned to his father for help once again. Even those of us who think we have led moral lives tend to identify with the prodigal, perhaps because deep down we have a sense of guilt about something or because we all want to be swept up in that wholehearted embrace of the loving father. It touches us with a message of forgiveness. And so it should. As American Christian author, Philip Yancey, commented so poignantly many years ago, "There is nothing we can do to make God love us more. There is nothing we can do to make God love us less."[132] When we feel undeserving, this parable speaks to our deepest need and tells us that we are still loved.

However, like most of Jesus' parables, there is more to it than that. Who changed? The father remained constant and loved both his sons throughout the story. The elder son went through a range of emotions but didn't change. The rebellious son changed direction, but did he

---

[132] Philip Yancey, *What's So Amazing About Grace*, Zondervan 1997.

change in himself? One could argue that he used his father's wealth for his own comfort and survival both before and following his misadventures. However, one thing did change — his sense of entitlement.

In the beginning, the prodigal son presumed to claim his future inheritance. His sense of entitlement was far greater than his sense of responsibility. When he reached the end of his inheritance and "came to himself", he realised that the money he had spent was not all his father had to give. There was something more that he had not valued before. His father loved him. Living with the pigs in utter squalor, where no-one cared whether he lived or died, brought back memories of the life that he had once taken for granted. He belonged to a family and that family was a place where he was loved, where he could find forgiveness, mercy and help, even if he didn't deserve it. He learned that love, care and compassion are not exhausted in the same way money can be. This younger son dared hope that the love and acceptance of family might survive the offence he had given. What a sad way to discover the treasure of love.

When the prodigal son returned home, he had lost his sense of entitlement and faced his own selfishness. He did not ask for anything except the bare minimum that he could work for. He only hoped for what might be given out of compassion, not duty. The world did not owe him anything. All that could save him now was love, forgiveness and generosity. These he had not earned and could not earn. The humility of the younger son's approach to his father's home suggests that he had learned the difference between entitlement and relationship. The money would have been his entitlement eventually. But money is such a temporary, fragile blessing. Once it is gone, it is gone. A relationship of love, on the other hand, is a strong, enduring, precious gift.

There are those amongst us who have been brought low, made mistakes, or lost everything. Those who feel responsible for their own losses, through poor choices, unwise business decisions or failed relationships, carry a burden of guilt as well as the material hardship of starting all over again. The ones who survive these crises are usually those who have at least one person who stays by them, who still loves them. Others have lost everything through no fault of their own, as survivors of natural catastrophes, violent conflicts or crime. In the most heartbreaking cases, these survivors have also lost their loved ones. Without even emotional support, they find themselves at the mercy of total strangers.

It is no coincidence that many who have experienced profound loss have developed strong values of relationship, service towards others and compassion. Experiencing complete powerlessness and facing the possibility of death sends human beings to a place of appreciation for what really matters — kindness, safety, generosity, belonging and love. In real life, unlike the parable, there is no wealthy, loving, generous father running out to welcome home those who are in desperate need. If the father represents God, then the message is clear. God offers the unconditional love that changes lives. Forgiveness doesn't really get a mention in the story, although it is implied. Before the son's apology is even voiced, the father's welcome puts all regrets in the past. All sense of unworthiness is swept aside in the joy of relationship restored.

We who name God in our lives are called to welcome those who come to us in humility, need and trust with as much joy as this father offered his prodigal son. The parable enacts a model of welcome. It also enacts the alternative model of judgement and hard-hearted entitlement. The elder son, who was sensible, responsible and dutiful, felt he'd earned his inheritance and could not cope with the apparent injustice of the father's generosity to his undeserving younger brother. The prodigal did not deserve any generosity, let alone a party where he was the guest of honour. If this story was teaching the value of cold justice, the younger son would have been sent packing. It is certainly not a story about justice.

The elder son had not yet learned the difference between entitlement and relationship. Neither son had *earned* the father's love and generosity and neither *deserved* to be treated like royalty. None of us earns the riches of family, unconditional acceptance, patience or being special in someone's eyes. These things are the spiritual gifts of human relationships. They are treasures beyond measure. In a sense, they are our birthright but not because we earn them or have some special entitlement or privilege of status. The gifts of acceptance and enduring love are intended for each of us simply because we are born into a human family and community. We are meant to discover these priceless treasures, value them and, as adults, give them to others. And when the misfortunes of life rob a person of these gifts, it is our role, as members of the human community, to offer them to those in desperate need.

What does the world owe us? Growing up in an affluent society, we tend to develop a sense of entitlement. Perhaps you are like me — we grew up with the common comforts of shelter, clothes, food and entertainment; we live in a society with resources and lifestyle expectations; we have universities and expect an education; we have hospitals and social security safety nets; we were born into a modern, safe, resource-rich nation where we belong to the dominant, white culture. Yes, we call ourselves 'lucky' to be Australian, and yet we still feel a sense of entitlement to all those resources. Those who try to emigrate to our country or come here as refugees or asylum seekers are not entitled in our view. We admit no relationship with these people. They can only share in our riches if we choose to 'let them in' and we will only let them in if we judge them to be deserving. We are deserving because we were born here. We are the elder son. We desperately need to learn the difference between entitlement and relationship.

The spiritual perspective on life is not concerned with who deserves what. The parable is consistent with our new perspective on God. The divine presence that always lures us towards the good and beautiful, that always seeks our happiness, is like the father. Whatever our achievements or errors of judgement, we will not force God's presence and lure away from us. If we choose a destructive path of life, the most we can do is deafen our spiritual senses so that we do not hear the longings of the divine. But the invitation to life, goodness and love is always there. To experience that surge of hope and overwhelming acceptance, all we need do is 'turn towards home'.

And when others find some fresh hope and direction in their lives, we can rejoice with them, knowing that their discoveries do not detract from our own sense of belonging and identity or limit our own wonderful experiences. We are related in one way or another to all other human beings — they are our brothers and sisters. And when they approach us in profound need it is *we* who need to run out in welcome, to meet them with open arms, generosity and rejoicing that we are bound together in the human family.

5. The Healing Touch

Her name can't go down in history because she was unnamed. We can't be sure she was even a real person, or if she simply represented everyone who has ever been desperate for healing from chronic ill-health. There is a rawness in this story that is so real, it doesn't matter if it never happened.

Then one of the leaders of the synagogue named Jairus came and, when he saw [Jesus], fell at his feet and begged him repeatedly, "My little daughter is at the point of death. Come and lay your hands on her, so that she may be made well, and live." So he went with him. And a large crowd followed him and pressed in on him.

Now there was a woman who had been suffering from haemorrhages for twelve years. She had endured much under many physicians, and had spent all that she had; and she was no better, but rather grew worse. She had heard about Jesus, and came up behind him in the crowd and touched his cloak, for she said, "If I but touch his clothes, I will be made well." Immediately her haemorrhage stopped; and she felt in her body that she was healed of her disease.

Immediately aware that power had gone forth from him, Jesus turned about in the crowd and said, "Who touched my clothes?" And his disciples said to him, "You see the crowd pressing in on you; how can you say, 'Who touched me?'" He looked all around to see who had done it. But the woman, knowing what had happened to her, came in fear and trembling, fell down before him, and told him the whole truth. He said to her, "Daughter, your faith has made you well; go in peace, and be healed of your disease."

> *While he was still speaking, some people came from the leader's house to say, "Your daughter is dead... When they came to the house of the leader of the synagogue, he saw a commotion, people weeping and wailing loudly. When [Jesus] had entered, he said to them, "Why do you make a commotion and weep? The child is not dead but sleeping"... He took her by the hand and said... "Little girl, get up!" And immediately the girl got up and began to walk about (she was twelve years of age).*
>
> Excerpts from Mark 5: 22-42

Traditionally we have imagined God as somewhat distant, unchangeable, untouchable. Without implying that Jesus was God in the traditional sense, we can certainly read this story as a powerful connection between two human beings through which the divine spirit is experienced. It affirms what we have always wondered — yes, we do have an impact on God.

Mark has wrapped the story of the woman's healing inside the story of the healing of Jairus' daughter, so that we are compelled to notice the contrasting characters. They all moved on from that day forever altered — Jairus, Jesus, the woman and the girl. Everyone changed because of the divine power of human touch.

The temptation for those who want to change the world is to consign specific people or groups to the opponent's corner. They are 'the problem', the ones who must be defeated. They are the corrupt ones, the powerful 'movers and shakers', the builders of coal mines, the developers of the concrete jungle, the big business CEO's, the self-serving politicians or the owners of multi-media giants. In the other corner are the 'greenies', the poor and the social justice activists. While it is fine to choose between different sets of values, it is not fine to stereotype or judge individuals who have different opinions to our own. As a leader of the synagogue, a powerful man in the community, Jairus, came from the opponents' corner. Yet in this story we discover he is human like the rest of us.

The purity codes were part of the fabric of Jewish life and were presided over by the religious elite of whom Jairus was one. Jesus defied the codes deliberately to break open new possibilities for human community — possibilities that gave dignity and honour to all and excluded no-one. By challenging the purity codes, Jesus threatened the system that worked well for those who had privilege — like Jairus. So, what prompted this Jewish aristocrat to ask Jesus for help? The fear of losing our loved ones is a great leveller. When his little girl was so ill, when her life hung in the balance, personal pride and status suddenly seemed so trivial. Jairus found himself experiencing need as desperately as many in the crowd that day. Something flipped inside Jairus. His priorities, his values changed, and he swapped his power of superiority for humility.

When Jesus pauses in his journey of healing to attend to a nameless outcast woman in the crowd, Jairus doesn't speak up and insist Jesus keep moving. He doesn't stand on his privileged position. He says nothing. Yet we can imagine his fear rising as he stands there helpless, feeling the minutes pass by. How dangerous it is for Jesus to delay! His daughter might die. And yet, Jairus silently waits and watches as Jesus first attends to an unclean peasant woman. In coming for help, Jairus was acknowledging that Jesus' view of the world held truth; that Jesus' concern for the needs of the poor was legitimate. It meant accepting that healing was not just a physical act — it was a spiritual realignment, away from self-interest and towards the things of God. In experiencing a crushing fear for his daughter, Jairus found the courage to refocus on what really matters.

It is worth noting the contrasts between Jairus and the woman. He is a man; she a woman. He is a leader; she an outcast. He is Jairus; she unnamed. He advocates for his daughter; she has no one to speak or seek help for her. He has the confidence to seek help openly; she reaches out anonymously. He is rich; she poor and exploited by physicians. He makes a legitimate request; ritually 'unclean', she cannot ask Jesus to touch her without becoming 'unclean' himself.

A privileged little girl and a poor, ritually unclean woman. The narrative insists we see them side by side. Until this illness struck, the little girl had enjoyed twelve years of comfort and attention. The woman had suffered twelve years of shame, dysfunctional relationships and pain. "Unclean! Unclean!" That's what people called out when someone like her passed by. No-one cared. Few of us know what it is like to be at the bottom of the bottom.

Men were not supposed to speak to women in the street. The social context highlights Jesus' radically inclusive values as he ignores the relative importance of the aristocrat's daughter compared to the outcast woman. He refused to play off one against the other. He refused to say that for someone to win there must be a loser. He refused to court the favour of the religious elite by giving priority to Jairus when another's desperate need was so palpable.

The females in this story are equals as human beings, even though their experience was remarkably different. It is implied that the little girl was brought back to life from death, and yet it is not her story that moves us. Her healing became a story about her healer rather than herself. She passively receives a healing touch then goes about her life as normal. We are not allowed into her inner life or emotions. Perhaps the innocence of her young age protects her from scrutiny. Her only change is her physical healing.

By contrast, the unnamed woman actively participates in her own healing. She and Jesus exchange something profound that changes them both equally. Given her hopeless status, we might wonder why she even dared to turn up that day. She planned to be anonymous in the crowd. But she acted on the one hope she had left — that perhaps in the eyes of a good and loving God, her life was still worth living. It is a testament to this woman's inner strength that, despite all her suffering, that spark of identity as a worthy human being was not yet extinguished. And so she dares to reach out, not to touch Jesus, only the hem of his cloak. Instinctively perhaps, she knew that we do not need to experience the divine fullness, to 'see the face of God', as it were. To experience meaningful living, all we need as human beings is to have a tiny glimpse of the goodness and beauty of the divine presence. That is enough — to touch the hem of the cloak.

Touch is that essential connection we all need to grow as human beings. In this instance, Jesus did not heal — he was passive. She, not he, was the one who produced the healing touch. He felt something happen but did not make it happen. Her reaching out, her touch gave expression to the surviving hope in her spirit. Jesus was right — it was her faith that had made her whole. She was changed in every way — physically, emotionally and socially. Touch expresses a spiritual connection linking need, faith, desire, love and power. And along this spiritual pathway there is a flowing back and forth.

The healing touch stopped Jesus in his tracks. He needed to know the person who had connected with him in this deepest way. He would have none of her plans for anonymity. It didn't matter who or what she was — male or female, rich or poor, clean or unclean. She had made a claim on him that God had honoured. She caused him to become aware of the flow of the power of God, and that doesn't happen every day. He was changed. He wanted to look into the eyes of this woman who had become his equal.

"Daughter," he called her. On his way to heal an aristocrat's daughter, Jesus had a life-changing meeting with a daughter of Israel.

6. Every Little Thing Matters

The following account from Matthew's Gospel may seem a strange choice for stories to preserve for future generations. Unfortunately, it assumes a future judgement by God where some people are eternally rewarded and some eternally punished. We will be able to focus on the story's real wisdom if we keep in mind two things: 1. Scholars do not attribute this passage to the historical Jesus. 2. The focus of the story is not the concept of judgement. The judgement is simply the setting for the real story. It is not necessary to buy into the doctrine of a judging God to discover the story's relevance for today. The real story centres on the criteria for acceptance by God. We can simply reframe the question from, "By what shall we be judged?" to, "What matters the most to God?"

Our priorities, values and actions, as seen through the eyes of God, are brought into focus here. What carries the most significance in the bigger scheme of things — is it obedience to religious law, worship at the temple or synagogue, moral purity or worship of Jesus as Lord? Or is it something different altogether? The compelling conclusion of the story can be disturbing for traditional Jews and Christians alike.

> *Then the king will say to those at his right hand, "Come, you that are blessed by my Father, inherit the kingdom prepared for you from the foundation of the world; for I was hungry and you gave me food, I was thirsty and you gave me something to drink, I was a stranger and you welcomed me, I was naked and you gave me clothing, I was sick and you took care of me, I was in prison and you visited me." Then the righteous will answer him, "Lord, when was it that we saw you hungry and gave you food, or thirsty and gave you something to drink? And when was it that we saw you a stranger and welcomed you, or naked and gave you clothing? And when was it that we saw you sick or in prison and visited you?" And the king will answer them, "Truly I tell you, just as you did it to one of the least of these who are members of my family, you did it to me."*
>
> Matthew 25: 34-40

When the world is in crisis and so many important causes vie for our attention, we might wonder if the little things in our lives still matter. When we take time out of a busy schedule to play with our children or visit a sick friend, who notices or cares? From the perspective of spirituality, the question is irrelevant. It simply doesn't matter if anyone knows or cares when we engage in acts of kindness. In the realm of God, every little thing matters whether noticed by others or not.

Although we may feel insignificant, we cannot exempt ourselves from the global challenges of our time. Those challenges are not merely environmental or political, but spiritual too. Do we want a safe, sustainable, inclusive and peaceful global community? If so, we are the ones who will create it, not God or politicians or 'important' people. We cannot opt out. Our lives and all we do have significance. We are creating the future, whether or not we recognise it.

A comprehensive spiritual vision will incorporate both our inner, individual experience and our outer, communal engagement. The relationship between our daily lives and our involvement in world events should not be weak or contrived. There must be a seamless connection between the personal and the global. For instance, our advocacy to reduce the pollution of land and waterways derives from the same conviction that dictates how we shop, source our food and dispose of household waste. Walking or cycling to work is a personal dimension of our care for the health of the atmosphere. We may wonder if our small efforts will change the global reality, but our personal choices should not be based upon this calculation. Our actions are based upon the values we hold dear.

If we show care for a person in our neighbourhood we are contributing to a compassionate world, even if no-one else knows about it. If we share our resources with those who have less, we are contributing to a more just society, even if no-one else knows. If we listen with respect to the pain of someone aggrieved, and respond with as much care as we can, we are contributing to a more peaceful society. If we submit an appreciative comment to a website where others are raging with criticism or abuse, we are contributing to respectful public conversation. Every single person contributes to the culture of the world in which we live. Every word and act contribute to the whole and have significance.

A person who demonstrates this seamless connection between the local and the global in their life is said to have 'integrity'. Having integrity means we cannot espouse a communal or global value without applying it to ourselves. According to the story above, religious beliefs and public statements are worthless if not enacted in our own lives. A person who wants to contribute to peacemaking in the world will examine their own relationships for estrangements that need to be healed. Preaching the principle of compassion is worthless if we are overly harsh or demeaning in our own relationships. Talking about selfless love is meaningless if we use others in the community to further our own interests.

Being a strong supporter of the doctrine of the incarnation or the Trinity is not what enriches our relationship with God. Believing firmly in God, Jesus, Moses, Buddha, Mohammed or the virgin Mary means nothing if we fail to love and care for the 'little ones' in the family of God. This warning is given again two chapters later when Jesus is reported to have said, "Not everyone who says to me, 'Lord, Lord,' will enter the kingdom of heaven, but only the one who does the will of my Father in heaven" (Matthew 7:21). In the end, what matters is not how we worship or how fiercely we believe in Jesus or anyone else, but how we reflect the values of God which are tied directly to the treatment of vulnerable people.

The story singles out those who are most disadvantaged as the 'little ones' in God's family. The conventional wisdom these days is to put ourselves and our own family first. Our society needs to hear the alternative wisdom of compassion that was embedded in the stories of Jesus. Not only do the little things we do matter, but the 'little people' we care for also matter. In the end, it is not about us, it is about them. They may be hidden away or ignored by society, but they matter to God. As Dave Andrews points out,

> *It is not easy to begin to relate to those in society whom most consider least, when we ourselves are numbered among the 'most' who 'consider them least'... Where we are concerned for weak, ignorant, boring, ugly, poor and insignificant people, we tend to put the ones that we feel hopeful about first and the ones that we feel hopeless about last... So we never get around to investing meaningfully in the lives of those whom most of us consider least. They are the last people we have in mind.[133]*

The crises facing the world are daunting and many people struggle to understand them, let alone know how to

---

[133] Dave Andrews, *Not Religion But Love: Practising a radical spirituality of compassion,* Tafina Press 1999 p.43.

become change-makers. But there is no need for anyone to feel disconnected or powerless. Developing the habits of care and compassion, even in small, unnoticed acts of kindness, carries more significance in the universe than we might think. According to the story, giving a cup of water to someone who is thirsty, or clothes to those who have none, or offering a caring relationship to someone shut away from the world, matters to God. In a society where the income-earning power of every endeavour is weighed up, taking time off to care for an elderly dying friend or sit with someone in grief has value in the world of the spirit that cannot be measured by economics. We need to reaffirm that small kindnesses are important.

Taking this one step further, process theologians speak of the impact that all events have upon God. In other words, not only are our actions valued by God but all that happens is absorbed into the life of God. According to this understanding of reality, God cares what happens in the world and responds to every living thing, including ourselves, in every moment of life. Therefore, because God is present to every creature, no moment of its life is unimportant. As John Cobb writes,

> *God everlastingly enriches the divine life through inclusion of all that happens. God everlastingly responds perfectly to the ever-changing situation of creatures. This is the meaning of divine love.*[134]

---

[134] John Cobb, *Is God Incomplete?* 2002, https://processandfaith.org

Perhaps glimpsing something of this deeper truth, the ancient Gospel writer put it this way — "[J]ust as you did it to one of the least of these who are members of my family, you did it to me" (Matthew 25: 40). It stretches our imagination to comprehend that God identifies not only with us, but with those who are more vulnerable than us. The 'least' in the human community are family to God and any small act of kindness to a 'little one' is received by God and leaves God changed. Every little thing matters.

7. Step Out in Faith

The spiritual life is an adventure, full of surprises, challenges, sacrifices, unexpected encounters and rewards. One of the most inspiring themes in the Christian tradition is that of stepping out in faith to follow the leading of God.

This last story, spanning three years from the life of Jesus, is compiled from snippets of Matthew's Gospel. It takes a glimpse at the adventures of Jesus' first followers. The life of Jesus certainly reads like the greatest story ever told and the following excerpts can only express a little of the excitement. Although these accounts are not historical as such, they speak to the realities of living in faith. We understand the miracles and legends concerning Jesus as fulfilling a late-first-century agenda, yet no-one would wish this story to be lost to the contemporary world. Children of every culture deserve to hear it, not to be converted, but to be excited by the spectacular life of Jesus and the very human failures, daring and dreams of his followers.

> As [Jesus] walked by the Sea of Galilee, he saw two brothers, Simon, who is called Peter, and Andrew his brother, casting a net into the sea — for they were fishermen. And he said to them, "Follow me, and I will make you fish for people." Immediately they left their nets and followed him... A windstorm arose on the sea, so great that the boat was being swamped by the waves; but he was asleep. And they went and woke him up, saying, "Lord, save us! We are perishing!" And he said to them, "Why are you afraid, you of little faith?" Then he got up and rebuked the winds and the sea; and there was a dead calm...
>
> Then Jesus went about all the cities and villages, teaching in their synagogues, and proclaiming the good news of the kingdom, and curing every disease and every sickness... These twelve Jesus sent out with the following instructions: "As you go, proclaim the good news, 'The kingdom of heaven has come near.' Cure the sick, raise the dead, cleanse the lepers, cast out demons. You received without payment; give without payment. Take no gold, or silver, or copper in your belts, no bag for your journey, or two tunics, or sandals, or a staff; for laborers deserve their food. Whatever town or village you enter, find out who in it is worthy, and stay there until you leave... Those who find their life will lose it, and

those who lose their life for my sake will find it..."

When evening came, he was there alone, but by this time the boat, battered by the waves, was far from the land, for the wind was against them. And early in the morning he came walking toward them on the sea. But when the disciples saw him walking on the sea, they were terrified, saying, "It is a ghost!" And they cried out in fear. But immediately Jesus spoke to them and said, "Take heart, it is I; do not be afraid." Peter answered him, "Lord, if it is you, command me to come to you on the water." He said, "Come." So Peter got out of the boat, started walking on the water, and came toward Jesus. But when he noticed the strong wind, he became frightened, and beginning to sink, he cried out, "Lord, save me!" Jesus immediately reached out his hand and caught him, saying to him, "You of little faith, why did you doubt?" When they got into the boat, the wind ceased...

At that time the disciples came to Jesus and asked, "Who is the greatest in the kingdom of heaven?" He called a child, whom he put among them, and said, "Truly I tell you, unless you change and become like children, you will never enter the kingdom of heaven. Whoever becomes humble like this child is the greatest in the kingdom of heaven... Then Peter said... "Look, we have left everything and followed you. What then will we have?" Jesus said to them"...

[E]veryone who has left houses or brothers or sisters or father or mother or children or fields, for my name's sake, will receive a hundredfold, and will inherit eternal life. But many who are first will be last, and the last will be first"...

Then one of the twelve, who was called Judas Iscariot, went to the chief priests and said, "What will you give me if I betray him to you?" They paid him thirty pieces of silver... Then they came and laid hands on Jesus and arrested him... Now Peter was sitting outside in the courtyard. A servant-girl came to him and said, "You also were with Jesus the Galilean." But he denied it before all of them, saying, "I do not know what you are talking about"... Then Peter remembered what Jesus had said: "Before the cock crows, you will deny me three times." And he went out and wept bitterly... Then they led [Jesus] away to crucify him...

But the angel said to the women, "Do not be afraid; I know that you are looking for Jesus who was crucified. He is not here; for he has been raised, as he said... When they saw [Jesus], they worshiped him; but some doubted. And Jesus came and said to them, "[R]emember, I am with you always, to the end of the age."
                                              Excerpts from Matthew's Gospel

If it is possible, read a whole Gospel in one sitting as that really is the best way to take in the grandeur of

Jesus' life. Space does not permit a more comprehensive coverage of the story, but these short snippets point to the possible meaning of 'living by faith'.

We can live our lives by simply doing what is in front of us or expected of us. That is not wrong or bad as such. For some, that is the gentlest way to discover the joys of human life. But for some who are called to be daring, who want to go to the edge of their humanity and intentionally contribute to the unfolding destiny of the world, it will not be enough. Some pursue excellence in sport, in music and the arts, in philanthropy and humanitarian work or in geographical or scientific exploration of one sort or another. Whichever field of endeavour we choose, we will only make a meaningful contribution if we take ourselves to the limits of our knowledge and courage. Perhaps this is what faith is — setting out to achieve our hopes and longings, knowing that we cannot without a dream that is bigger than ourselves.

The first followers of Jesus would have had no idea of what they were in for when they first accepted his invitation to leave their jobs and families behind and go on the road. They were captivated by his vision of a different future that he described as the 'Kingdom of God'. Sounding part religious, part adventure and part political, Jesus' call was an invitation to make a difference in the world.

Nothing of worth is won easily and rarely without opposition. The 'storms' that threaten our progress can seem overwhelming. Just because we have the courage to step out on a new path, doesn't mean we won't be fearful at times. But, like the disciples in the boat, centering ourselves in the divine presence brings us back to what is real, what matters and a sense of perspective that calms our panic.

We cannot plan ahead for every possible situation. Sometimes we will find our resources are too limited. We may have to tighten our belts and be patient. But there is no point trying to provide for every foreseeable circumstance. If we wait until we have all we need for the adventure that beckons us, we may never set out. Jesus told his team to move out without extra provisions, no extra shoes, food, clothes or money. They would learn to take each day as it came. Along the road, they would find support from generous people and at other times there would be little or no support. But they had not joined his mission to gain wealth or popularity. They would learn to be grateful for the material support they received, not only because they were fed, but because it confirmed that others shared their convictions and wanted to share their commitment.

Sometimes we respond to a sense of call to a new path, feeling that it is 'right' for us, maybe even 'God's will'. But later, we are afraid we have made a huge mistake. We lose focus and forget to go back to that core relationship of love for our courage. We may even become unsure of the existence of the divine presence and feel quite alone. We identify with Peter in his daring step into the unknown, 'onto the water' as it were, and only breathe again when we hear the rebuke and reassurance of God. *But when [Peter] noticed the strong wind, he became frightened, and beginning to sink, he cried out, "Lord, save me!" Jesus immediately reached out his hand and caught him, saying to him, "You of little faith, why did you doubt?"*

Undertaking the challenge to shape a better world will inevitably engage us in teamwork with like-minded people. In these relationships we will find our rough edges rubbed off and our desire for influence or status in the group challenged by the still, small voice of the divine. Those who identify as followers of Jesus must heed the teaching of Jesus that we are not to seek leadership or status. When we begin to think that our contribution is important and maybe even earning us a place in history, Jesus cautions that "the first will be last." When we are too impressed with our own contribution, we are warned that and we need the humility of "a little child". When others around us, whom we had hoped to influence, are unimpressed with our efforts or our spiritual vision, we will remember that Jesus was also rejected by the world of his time, particularly by those in power.

Then, at the end of this extraordinary story, the disciples were heartbroken by Jesus' execution, not only by the horrific loss of their friend and mentor, but by the dashing of all their hopes and dreams. Had they given up everything for nothing? There are no guarantees of success in this conflicted and dangerous world. Our fan base during the times of our popularity can swiftly evaporate when we face criticism. And sometimes, *we* are the ones who fail our friends during their times of need. The disciples failed to stand by Jesus when their lives were threatened. They could not stay awake during his time of anguish before the arrest, and afterwards, fled and denied him. Facing his own lack of courage and his inability to stand faithfully with the one he loved, Peter wept bitterly. Sometimes it may seem like we have failed most dreadfully.

In the end, we cannot prove the worth of our values or our convictions about the world. We can only take heart from knowing that some others along the way are encouraged and enriched by our journey. We may never see the rich outcome of our efforts. So often pioneers in various fields do not live to see the final development of their vision. It must be enough to know that we have done what we could. The rest is out of our hands. The promise is simply that the presence of the divine will be with us on the faith journey, no more and no less.

Like all adventure stories, first comes the sense of calling, the vision of something new, the desire to create something good. Along the way mistakes, opposition and loss cause the adventurer to lose heart. There are never guarantees of success and anything worthwhile will require sacrifice and perseverance. At those times we need to hold the vision and 'push through' to the next phase of our calling. We will grow in understanding and self-awareness as we face our 'demons' and the harshness of the world. Finally, we will be grateful for those unexpected encounters, for companions and for the rewards of being fully alive.

CHAPTER NINE

Hopes and Dreams of a Better Future

> *Whatever we do counts;*
> *if we do not serve what coheres and endures,*
> *we serve what disintegrates and destroys.*
>
> Wendell Berry

While globally, there is much cause for anxiety and grief, hopes and dreams will not leave us alone. The divine impulse that meets us at every turn lures us towards goodness and beauty and inspires a vision of a different and better future. Within our beautiful, messy lives we keep the vision alive and seek ways of making it real.

What is it that we strive towards? If the mission statements of big business do not inspire, if the self-preservation of the institutional churches disappoint, if inward-looking New Age spiritualities leave us cold, and self-promoting politicians abandon us, what is left that is worthy of our hearts and minds? What Story can we tell as an alternative to the harsh, unforgiving, destructive forces of our time? What hope will sustain us when the world appears to be moving in the opposite direction?

Religion taught us to trust that we will be given a place in an otherworldly, perfect heaven, the residence of God. The path to heaven was through death by which our spirits would be taken out of this material, flawed existence. Although the new spirituality does not deny the possibility of an everlasting spiritual life, it does not focus upon it. Our spiritual existence beyond physical death can only ever be a subject for wonder and musing — never one upon which we can speak with knowledge. Perhaps all we can do is express the hope that if God is the one who comes to us at every moment of our existence, inviting us towards the good, beautiful and loving, we can trust that we will experience that same divine invitation at the moment of our death.

Bruce Epperly expresses a similar faith in his "prayer for this moment and eternity."

> *Amid the passing of time, of life's perpetual perishing, and Earth's precarious future, give us hope for today and tomorrow. Let us trust that our lives matter and that our acts make a difference in the future of our planet. Let us lean toward God's everlasting vision and the hope of life everlasting. Let us find eternity in perpetual perishing and hope in finitude, for you are the*

Holy Adventure that dries every tear and embraces every creature now and forevermore. Amen. [135]

Jesus' Comprehensive Vision for His Time

In what is now referred to as the Sermon on the Mount, the author of Matthew's Gospel has collected sayings around Jesus' spiritual ethic.[136] Here we read that Jesus valued humility, peacemaking, care of the grieving, mercy, compassion, forgiveness, and purity of heart. His vision is contrary to those scriptural passages that presume a warrior God who spares no-one in battle, not even women and children, and takes revenge on the enemies of Israel. In contrast, Jesus imagines God as the one who urges us to understand, even love our enemies as fellow human beings.

Although trained in the breadth of the Hebrew scriptures, Jesus stressed love of God in association with love of neighbour (Matthew 22: 34-40). His spirituality focussed on the heart rather than outward religious observance. For instance, Jesus taught that not only was sexual abuse unacceptable, but out of deep respect for all, society should not regard women simply as sex objects.[137] Rather than demand what is ours, he urged us to give even

---

[135] Bruce Epperly, *Praying with Process Theology: Spiritual Practices for Personal and Planetary Healing*, River Lane Press 2017, pp. 136-137.
[136] Matthew 5
[137] Matthew 5: 27-28

more generously to those who ask for material things. Rather than resist violence with greater violence, Jesus famously told his followers to "turn the other cheek" when they were assaulted. He was totally committed to a non-violent strategy of resisting injustice. He taught his followers that this way of living was better than the religious traditions in which they'd been raised. Adhering to instructions and regulations was merely superficial. Spirituality, for Jesus, was about being transformed in the depths of our being.

Clearly, Jesus' own spiritual vision was not determined by the first-century practices of his own Judaism. He rejected those parts of scripture that assumed very different images of God and selected only the image of the divine presence that was worthy of his prayer and meditation. During his homeland's occupation by a foreign power, instead of reinforcing Jewish national identity by preaching the traditions of his religion, Jesus taught an alternative spiritual ethic. The values he espoused were supported by select quotations from the scriptures, which he used very judiciously. In other words, Jesus himself prioritised values over beliefs and tradition. We need to do the same. For us, it is not the traditions of Judaism alone that we must use with discernment, but also of Christianity. As progressives who are willing to re-examine our inherited belief system, and only very selectively refer to our scriptures, we are following Jesus more closely than many have realised.

Hopes and Dreams of a Better Future

Jesus' idea of the Kingdom of God was based on values that he associated with the divine life. He invited his friends and community to choose what really mattered in the big scheme of things and in the eyes of God. Some sacrifice would be essential if they were going to make a difference. At times, making the world a better place means that we must choose between two or more 'good' things. Amongst the many intriguing parables Jesus told were these, urging us to prioritise wholeheartedly.

> *The kingdom of heaven is like treasure hidden in a field, which someone found and hid; then in his joy he goes and sells all that he has and buys that field.*
>
> *Again, the kingdom of heaven is like a merchant in search of fine pearls; on finding one pearl of great value, he went and sold all that he had and bought it.*[138]

The stories Jesus told about God's realm can still inspire us. But the world has moved on a long way since the first century. Social, psychological, scientific and technological developments have presented religious and ethical dilemmas unimaginable to Jesus. It's not that the ethic of Jesus as outlined above is not relevant today. It is. However, with the scientific insights available to us, we need to expand the application of his values for our own time. This means further developing his radical ideas of

---

[138] Matthew 13: 44-46

inclusion and equality, while including the perspective of our interconnectedness with the natural world.

A More Beautiful World

The new spiritual vision affirms that we participate in the divine life in this world of earth and flesh with all its impermanence, fragility and imperfection. The vision that inspires our hopes and dreams is not one of being taken out of this world, but of loving it and healing it. Our dreams are to create a richer, more joyful future for our land, oceans, forests and every living thing that creeps upon the earth, including human community.

The thinkers and authors who have inspired many of the ideas in my previous chapters have different ways of articulating their future vision. Two thousand years ago, Jesus described the ideal, earth-based human community as the 'Kingdom of God'. Martin Luther King Jr preferred the phrase the 'Beloved Community'. In 1963, his "I have a dream" speech from the steps of the Lincoln Memorial is perhaps the most beloved vision of community in the Western world. Others have had similar visions and dreams. Some, who hold the same values as Jesus, have modernised his phrase to the 'kin-dom of God' or the 'Commonwealth of God' so as to avoid the authoritarian and masculine connotations of 'kingdom'. Lorraine Parkinson refers to Jesus' 'blueprint for the best possible world'. Ched Myers and Wendell Berry speak about 'the

Great Economy'. Charles Eisenstein simply calls it, 'the more beautiful world we know is possible.' I doubt anyone can give themselves to the task of 'making a difference' without a similar vision.

Utopia will never exist because each person born, each generation must necessarily learn the same spiritual lessons and develop the same psychological maturity through their own experience of the world. We cannot inherit wisdom and maturity at birth. We can only learn from earlier generations at the pace of human development. We are taught values by our family and community, but we each need to make them our own through the choices we make every day. That is not to say that humanity doesn't and cannot make progress towards a better world. As a woman, for instance, I am glad not to have been born in ancient or medieval times. We may still have a way to go, and yet the possibility of gender equality is closer now than it was even fifty years ago.

However, life has no guarantees and the fragility of the human condition means that there will always be disappointments and times to choose either bitterness or forgiveness. Individuals who choose to force their own agenda onto others for selfish ends still influence the conversation in public life. Even in the twenty-first century, it is possible for us to lose sight of the values of racial, gender and cultural equality. Those basic human rights, for which social activists fought so hard in previous decades, can be at risk if we do not reaffirm them with the next generation in every sector of society.

We see this struggle in our own community. Although our laws and cultural institutions officially give priority to fairness, honesty, respect and equal opportunities for everyone, the incidence of workplace bullying, domestic violence, discrimination and dishonesty is alarmingly high. In an age of broad-based education, we might wonder how these behaviours could become so prevalent. This social reality firstly highlights that values will only shape a society when we have a strategy to instil them in the thinking and habits of each generation. Secondly, it warns us not to be complacent — we can never take for granted the gains we have made towards gracious, respectful community life. It is possible to go 'backwards', even in a liberal democracy.

Across the board, the challenges of spiritual and psychological development, however we describe it, must not be ignored or taken for granted. We need to name our values and ideals in education, politics, sport, business, environmental management, the voluntary sector and religion. And then we need to be serious about strategies to promote and demonstrate these values. It is not sufficient to have a politically correct mission statement if we turn a blind eye to theft, bullying, discrimination or corruption. We need to encourage and protect those who speak the truth to power without fostering hatred or violence. Corporations, civil service, political and community groups will need to be serious about the promotion of their values of fairness and respect and provide protection for whistleblowers when they fail in this task. And for those who feel such strategic thinking is beyond them, take heart, remember the story of how every little thing matters. There is always something I can do, if I acknowledge that *the needs of the world are also my* needs. Charles Eisenstein addressed the issue of motivation like this,

> *To do the things that are really necessary requires real courage, so for me the question becomes where does that courage come from, the commitment to do whatever it takes? It comes from love and from a direct feedback loop that what you love is in danger.*[139]

The challenge facing us today is little changed from that which Jesus accepted. He walked that fine line between refusing to adopt the values of the Romans and the Jewish aristocracy who exploited the vulnerable poor, while also refusing to take up arms. His vision that 'the first shall be last and the last become first' could have been heard as a rallying call to violent revolution. Instead, he painted it as an image of the greatness of humility and patience. By grounding his revolutionary dreams of a better world in the spiritual values of God, Jesus did not allow the fight against injustice to become a shallow conflict between two classes of people. Instead, he understood that every person from every social background needs an inner transformation.

---

[139] Charles Eisenstein, *Love as an Ecological Act*, podcast with Amisha Ghadiali, 2017 on www.thefutureisbeautiful.co

A Spiritual Tapestry

There are not two classes of people. We all participate in the human condition and all carry the possibilities of glory and shame. All of us need the creative transformation of raw honesty, self-awareness, facing our own darkness and openness to the 'other'. Just as the 'God' in the 'Noah and the Flood' story learned that it is not possible to divide humanity into 'the good' and 'the evil', we also need to mature in our understanding of human nature, including our own individual natures. When we demonise our opponents, we pretend we are somehow different. But when we listen deeply to those who are angry and hurt, we open up the possibility of understanding and healing. Reconciliation in human communities requires the hard work of listening, sharing and listening even more until understanding becomes real. We need to love our enemies.

By way of summarising the spiritual values presented in this book, the following is a description of what the world would look like if we could click our fingers and simply make it happen. Understanding the idealism of such a picture, it is nevertheless a useful exercise for people of faith to articulate what vision of life inspires them. Doing so reveals which values we have prioritised. What is your dream for this global village?

Imagine — human communities in balance with the rest of the natural order; food production and power supplies based on respect for the health of soil, waterways, diverse plant life, animals and the seasonal rhythm of nature; fair distribution of resources; adequate inclusion of the marginal and care of the vulnerable; communal barriers that might foster hatred all dismantled; no thought of violence as the default way to address conflict; ideologies that exclude others totally forgotten; religions cleansed of all violence and exclusion; every child educated by respectful adults; integrity in business and all levels of leadership; those who give generous support to the rest of the community held in highest esteem; stories that upset pretentions of power told and retold; the joy of community and interconnection celebrated.

Realising how much needs to change can be daunting. Seeing some aspects of this vision slip further away before our eyes can lead to despair and a withdrawal from engagement. We might wonder what reason there is to hope. John Cobb reflected on this very question.

> *My expectations are now deeply pessimistic. I do not believe that we can avoid the consequences of our present actions. Many, many species of living things have already disappeared forever... The rising ocean level will flood whole islands and low-lying coastal lands, deltas will become too salty to produce crops, the exhaustion of aquifers will lead to the abandonment of farming in large areas, and many of the world's rivers will run dry much of the year because glaciers will be gone. The human population of the planet will be greatly reduced not by thoughtful planning but by starvation and war and disease.*
>
> *With such a prospect, one response is to eat, drink, and be merry. If catastrophe is inevitable,*

> *forget activism... Another response is theological hope. We are called to hope as we are called to faith and love. We are not thereby called to ignore the realities of our world or to expect supernatural intervention to save us from the consequences of our collective actions... Hope is not confidence or assurance. One knows that what one hopes for may not happen... I have been shaped by the prophetic tradition. Almost alone among the great traditions of human kind, it is deeply historical. It views God as a participant in human history. God's participation is the one source of hope and calls for our response of hope. I try to be responsive.*[140]

The Kingdom of God is Among You

We are in danger of repeating the mistake of traditional Christianity. That religious error was to diminish the significance of our everyday lives and the earth on which we live, by turning our attention to a heavenly future. We assumed that the 'eternal' was naturally much more important than the transitory existence we have now. And yet, Jesus was very much focussed on issues of justice for his suffering homeland. There is no indication that the historical Jesus spoke much at all about heaven. The community he longed to create and

---

[140] John Cobb, *Reasons to Hope*, March 2014, *Process and Faith*, https://processandfaith.org

the visionary convictions for which he died required a social transformation in the real world. Because of this very distinct gap between Jesus' focus and that of the church, Christians have always puzzled over his sayings, "The time is fulfilled, and the Kingdom of God has come near"[141] and "The Kingdom of God is among you."[142]

To say, "the Kingdom of God is among you" was radical on two levels. Firstly, Jesus was talking to the peasants, the ordinary people whose existence was impoverished by overlords and who were treated as of no account. He dignified their lives with the message that in their vulnerability, their humility and their hard work to survive and care for their loved ones, God was very much present. Evidence of the realm or 'Kingdom of God' was not to be found in the trappings of wealth or the corruption of the powerful, but in the little acts of love and generosity that could be found in simple village life.

If we want to see the kingdom of God, we need look no further than the faithful, compassionate lives of ordinary people who welcome outsiders and practice generosity. It is not that ordinary people are perfect. Their lives are as messy and challenging as those of the powerful. All of us need personal transformation — away from the demands of the self towards the priority of community; away from illusions of separation towards the realisation of interconnection. However, without the affectations of

---

[141] Mark 1: 15
[142] Luke 17: 21

importance and privilege, the spirits of ordinary people are more readily open to honest self-reflection and the needs of others.

On the other, second level of meaning, the presence of God's Kingdom *among* us is perhaps more radical for us now than it was in the first century. Not everyone in ancient times believed in an after-life. It was not remarkable for his time, that Jesus' spiritual vision concerned real community in real time. But after two thousand years of Christian focus on salvation for the life hereafter, it feels unnatural for us to focus our spiritual hopes on the present. The insights of many inspiring thinkers, already quoted in this book, converge on this very central issue.

We listen to the conviction of Martin Luther King Jr that injustice anywhere is a threat to justice everywhere and that hate cannot drive out hate — only love can. We are touched by Wendell Berry's love of land, of its rhythms and living creatures. From Ched Myers, we heed the conviction that love for the planet must be grounded in a real-time commitment to a specific place. We take in the reflection of Charles Eisenstein that when others thrive we all thrive, and that love is 'an ecological act'. We absorb the profound wisdom of John Cobb and other process theologians that every responsive move we make towards the divine call is forever held and treasured in God's own self. We remember the remarkable statement in the New Testament that identifies God with Love itself. "[L]et us love one another, because love is from God … for God is love."[143] These profound insights all come together as they bring into focus the divine presence in Love embodied, right here, right now.

None of us need convincing that both the first-century world of Jesus and that of our own twenty-first century are far from what we might imagine as the Kingdom of God. So how is it *among us*? We make the mistake of separating the little things we do that help grow the Kingdom, from its fulfillment. We describe acts of love or kindness as previews of a future that one day will be ushered in by God. We suspect, and hope, that there is a connection between these two, between what we do now and what is to come. However, we so often assume that our very flawed, imperfect actions and experiences here and now are distinct from a future creation of the 'Kingdom'. As in the old tradition, the value of our earthly, messy, beautiful lives is diminished by the division we imagine exists between the present and the future.

Jesus said, "The Kingdom of God is among you." Although Jesus would not have thought in modern philosophical terms, it seems he intuitively sensed the significance of the present moment. A way to make sense of his radical saying is to collapse the distinction between the final achievement of the just, interconnected community of love and the 'way of God' that makes it a reality. Present experiences of love, healing, goodness and beauty are forever absorbed into the eternal being of God.

---

[143] 1 John 4: 7-8

A Spiritual Tapestry

Even experiences of loss and suffering become part of the divine life. In our spirit's imagination, God's love heals what is wounded, completes what is incomplete and restores what is lost. It is a vision of the inexpressible love of God that incorporates, transforms, heals and treasures all things within God's own being.

The interconnected community of love that we are co-creating with God amidst the imperfection of the world and the messiness of our earthly lives has eternal value. Nothing of worth is ever lost. Whether large or small in our eyes, every experience of deep connection, from all times and all lives, constitutes the eternal reality that is the Kingdom of God. We do not need to separate our own responses to the call of God now from the magnificent consummation of all things in God. The Kingdom of God is among us.

Recommended Reading

Andrews, Dave	*Not Religion but Love: Practising a radical spirituality of compassion* (Tafina Press 1999)
Berry, Thomas	*The Great Work: Our Way Into the Future* (Bell Tower 1999)
Berry, Wendell	*The Selected Poems of Wendell Berry* (Counterpoint 1999)
Bodycomb, John	*No Fixed Address: Faith as Journey* (Spectrum 2010)
Bodycomb, John	*Aware and Attentive: 'Worship' in Evolving Christianity* (Spectrum 2012)
Borg, Marcus & Crossan, John Dominic	*The Last Week: What the Gospels Really Teach About Jesus' Final Days in Jerusalem* (HarperCollins 2006)
Borg, Marcus & Crossan, John Dominic	*The First Christmas: What the Gospels Really Teach About Jesus' Birth* (HarperCollins 2007)
Borg, Marcus & Crossan, John Dominic	*The First Paul: Reclaiming the Radical Visionary Behind the Church's Conservative Icon* (HarperCollins 2009)

Brown, Brene	*The Gifts of Imperfection: Let Go of Who You Think You're Supposed to Be and Embrace Who You Are* (Hazelden 2010)
Brueggemann, Walter	*Mandate to Difference: An Invitation to the Contemporary Church* (Westminster John Knox Press 2007)
Campbell, Joseph	*Myths to Live By* (Penguin Compass 1972)
Claremont School Of Theology	*Real Spirituality for Real Life* https://processandfaith.org
Crossan, John Dominic	*Jesus and the Violence of Scripture: How to Read the Bible and Still Be a Christian* (SPCK 2015)
Eisenstein, Charles	*The More Beautiful World Our Hearts Know is Possible* (North Atlantic Books 2013)
Eisenstein, Charles	*Sacred Economics: Money, Gift and Society in the Age of Transition* (North Atlantic Books 2011)
Epperly, Bruce	*Praying with Process Theology: Spiritual Practices for Personal and Planetary Healing* (River Lane Press 2017)
Harpur, Tom	*Born Again: My journey From Fundamentalism to Freedom* (Dundurn Press 2011)

Hunt, Rex, Smith, John ed.	*Why Weren't We Told? A Handbook on Progressive Christianity* (Polebridge Press 2013)
Moore, Thomas	*Care of the Soul: A Guide for Cultivating Depth and Sacredness in Everyday Life*, (Harper Collins 1992)
Myers, Ched	*Binding the Strong Man: A Political Reading of Mark's Story of Jesus* (Orbis Books 1988)
Myers, Ched	*Who Will Roll Away the Stone? Discipleship Queries for First World Christians* (Orbis Books 1994)
Parkinson, Lorraine	*The World According to Jesus: his blueprint for the best possible world* (Spectrum 2011)
Parkinson, Lorraine	*Made on Earth: How gospel writers created the Christ* (Spectrum 2015)
Schwartzentruber, Michael ed.	*The Emerging Christian Way: Thoughts, Stories and Wisdom for a Faith of Transformation* (Copper House 2006)
Suchocki, Marjorie Hewitt,	*In God's Presence: Theological Reflections on Prayer* (Chalice Press 1996)
Webb, Val	*Stepping Out with the Sacred: Human Attempts to Engage the Divine* (Continuum 2010)

Notes

Notes

Notes

www.ingramcontent.com/pod-product-compliance
Lightning Source LLC
Chambersburg PA
CBHW070530010526
44118CB00012B/1091